Japan in Postwar Asia

Japan in Postwar Asia

LAWRENCE OLSON

PUBLISHED FOR THE
COUNCIL ON FOREIGN RELATIONS
BY

PRAEGER PUBLISHERS
New York · Washington · London

PRAEGER PUBLISHERS
111 Fourth Avenue, New York, N.Y. 10003, U.S.A.
5, Cromwell Place, London S.W.7, England

Published in the United States of America in 1970
by Praeger Publishers, Inc.

Library of Congress Catalog Card Number: 79–101674

For a partial list of Council publications, see pages 290–92.

Printed in the United States of America

To Jeane

"In its most general sense, the commerce of mankind involves every species of interchange which proceeds by way of mutual persuasion."
—ALFRED NORTH WHITEHEAD, in *Adventures of Ideas*

Contents

Part Two / Japan and Asia, 1964–69

Acknowledgments

I am grateful to Wesleyan University for giving me a leave of absence during the 1968–69 academic year and to the Council on Foreign Relations for a Visiting Fellowship to pursue work on this book in Asia and in this country. While drafting the book, I was fortunate to have the advice and counsel of a study group which included the following members: William P. Bundy, Chairman, James C. Abegglen, William J. Barnds, Robert W. Barnett, William Brannigan, Wesley R. Fishel, George S. Franklin, Jr., Teg C. Grondahl, Marius Jansen, Louis Kraar, John M. H. Lindbeck, William Lockwood, David W. MacEachron, John G. McLean, August Maffry, George Packard, Herbert Passin, Gerard Piel, Richard Sneider, Arthur R. Taylor, Col. Sam S. Walker, USA, Capt. Robert O. Welander, USN, Clifton R. Wharton, Jr., W. Howard Wriggins, and Kenneth T. Young, Jr. My thanks for much stimulating criticism go to each member of this group, even as I must stress my sole responsibility for all statements of fact and opinion in the book.

I owe a debt of gratitude to many Japanese and others in Asia who gave time from their busy lives to talk with me or help in other ways. Their names are too numerous to list here, but they will know who they are and receive my thanks. I am grateful to the Asia Society for permission to use in slightly altered form a few paragraphs which originally appeared in my article, "Japan and Asia: An American Viewpoint," in *Asia*, No. 8, 1967. Appreciation also goes to George Denney and Anthony Dicks for the right to cite their newsletters written for the Institute of Current World Affairs, and to the American Universities Field Staff for permission to quote from reports of Willard A. Hanna and myself. Edwin O. Reischauer and Henry Rosovsky read the entire manuscript and made many valuable suggestions. Finally, I wish to thank my wife, to whom the book is dedicated, for her insight and criticism, which so often and so swiftly reached to the heart of the matter.

L. O.

Jerusalem Road
Canaan, New Hampshire
January, 1970

Japan in Postwar Asia

I. Introduction

My interest in the subject of this book began in the summer of 1952, when I was a passenger on a Norwegian freighter between Manila and San Francisco. As we entered Kobe harbor, then already rebuilt and its factories and shipyards booming with orders generated in large part by the Korean War, a Filipino student standing beside me at the ship's rail turned and said in a bitter voice, "All this ought to be ours." This remark set me to thinking about Asian claims on Japan for World War II and military occupation, which were then beginning to be negotiated at governmental level. I had just spent a year in the United States Information Service in the Philippines and had some sense of the hatred of the Japanese that was felt at that time by Filipinos.

When I went to Japan to live and work for the American Universities Field Staff in 1955, I read the writings of Japanese intellectuals who felt compelled to condemn their own government's attempts to make amends for the past and restore normal relationships with South and Southeast Asia. Many of these intellectuals demanded immediate recognition of Communist China instead. I learned that they seldom knew much about actual conditions of life and society in the rest of Asia, including China, but looked down on other Asians while building theories or repeating stereotyped opinions about them. I saw that intellectuals as well as most other Japanese were better informed about the West than about Asia, that they were separated from Asians by a cultural distance which varied from country to country but which had been created by differences of language and values, by discrepancies in the rate of material development, and by political differences and the record of the past. The reality that Asia was not "one" bore in more sharply upon me the longer I stayed there, and I was fascinated by the phenomenon of Japan as an intermediate nation, condescending to those nations and peoples below it on the ladder of secular progress and feeling by turns insecure and prideful toward those more technically advanced. At that stage, I had not gone much beyond an examination of attitudes of Japanese toward Asians and vice versa, and, therefore, I wrote articles about Filipino views of Japan or about Japanese professors who criticized their colleagues for indulging in abstract fantasies concerning the rest of Asia without ever going there or wanting to go.

In 1957 and again in 1961, I traveled extensively in Southeast Asia and India and soon discovered that what Japanese intellectuals thought and wrote did not mean very much in terms of the country's relations. Instead, as I met and talked with businessmen, government officials, journalists, and other professional people I was deeply struck, like most other observers, by Japanese commercial energy and aggressiveness, by what seemed a nearly total absorption with profit. The search for markets and raw materials, especially the latter, was the most obvious propellant of the Japanese abroad, whether to mainland China or non-Communist regions. Believing that economic interest would provide powerful clues to the direction in which Japan was to go politically, I plunged into the study of a welter of commercial activities—with no prior training in economics or business—and sought there for a better understanding of Japan's role. The strictures of Tokyo intellectuals about Japanese neocolonialism and the return of what they called the "ugly Japanese" * to Southeast Asia remained in the back of my mind but were less important the more I studied the total picture of Japan's overseas actions and policies.

From these travels, I wrote several articles on Japan's economic and cultural activities in South and Southeast Asia and an article about its difficult relationship with Communist China; most of these were published in an earlier book. By about 1963, I had become convinced that a separate book could and should be written describing Japan's return to Asia. At the very least, the Japanese technological role in the Asian future seemed to me inevitably immense, just as their problems of communication with other Asians were very profound. I accordingly began to gather materials for a book on cultural and economic aspects of the Japan-Asia relationship but was not able to devote concentrated time to this until 1968.

By then, however, there was more evidence than before to show that Japan's government and private organizations were groping more or less consciously toward new policies that would promote Asian political stability and enhance Japan's own role in the area. Such gropings had been intermittently visible ever since the early 1950s, but Japan's Asian relations in that decade were overwhelmingly commercial in character. They were still so in more recent times, and there was much justification for the description of Japan as an "economic animal"; but, by the late 1960s, one could begin to see more clearly the return of Japan as an independent force in world politics, and the country's search for prestige as well as profits was more obvious. This trend was first evident in Premier Ikeda's journeys to Asia in the early 1960s and the nationalistic statements made afterward. It could be seen in Japan's admission to the Organization for Economic Cooperation and

* Taken from the term "ugly American," from the novel of the same name by William J. Lederer and Eugene Burdick. Originally used in a laudatory sense—the "ugly American" was a good American in Southeast Asia—the term came often to be used erroneously in a pejorative sense by Americans and Japanese alike.

Development in 1963, the Tokyo Olympics of the following year, and, above all, in the new confidence that came with very high economic growth rates and the redoubled search for markets and raw materials as the decade of the 1960s passed. The Japanese reaction to still other events, such as the Chinese nuclear explosions in October 1964 and thereafter and the Indonesian coup attempt in September 1965, also indicated rising feelings of nationalism and a growing consciousness of the Japanese interest in preserving stability in Asia. Thus, the division of the book into the two periods 1952–64 and 1964–69 is not an arbitrary one. From the signing of the San Francisco Peace Treaty to the end of the Ikeda period, Japan took a "low posture" in Asia; after 1964, the silhouette of its presence in the region became steadily more visible.

The logic of the book, therefore, lies in its attempt to trace the slow, often only half-grasped searchings of the Japanese between 1952 and the present, as seen through the complex of their attitudes, actions, and policies vis-à-vis other Asian countries, for a national role expressive of Japan's true interests in the whole region. Chapter II reviews in detail Japanese efforts between 1952 and 1964 to make amends for war and occupation, pay reparations obligations, and re-establish trust and a new network of economic relationships in South and Southeast Asia. In the first part of the period covered by this chapter, Japanese economic interest in Asia was intense. There was much anxiety about the market for Japanese goods in the United States; and Asia, including Communist China, was touted by many as a natural trading partner. Chapter III records attempts by Japanese to do business with the Chinese mainland during the same period, when Chinese "cultural diplomacy" seemed bent upon offering inducements to divert Japan from its basic alignment with the United States. This chapter also discusses Japan's relations with South Korea in the years immediately after the San Francisco Peace Treaty. Later in the 1950s, hopes for trade with Southeast Asia waned as the Japanese became better aware of the immense problems of underdevelopment. Their expectations of trade with the region had to be reduced even as the American market for Japanese goods was expanding beyond all predictions. At the same time, Communist China's policy toward Japan was reversed, and the wish of many Japanese businessmen and politicians for closer ties with the mainland went unrealized.

However, by about 1964, a second wave of interest in Asia was discernible in Tokyo. There, economic considerations were still all-important; but political themes now began to surface more frequently in the policy discussions that were conducted not only in government offices but in the press and the journals of opinion. No abrupt changes occurred or were likely to occur in those basic foreign policy positions. It was natural for a country that had prospered under American protection and avoided direct involvement in Asia's wars since 1945 not to want such a condition to end. Domestic opinion in Japan and elsewhere in Asia was still strongly opposed to expansion of any military role for the Japanese overseas, although some Japanese and others saw such a role as likely one day, perhaps sooner than later.

Meanwhile, foreign aid programs gradually became better accepted in Tokyo as necessary for maintenance of political stability as well as for Japan's prestige and status in the larger world beyond Asia. Aid had few lobbyists in Japan, but to most people it was more palatable than military pacts with other Asians. Many Japanese who feared that American escalation of the Vietnam war would involve their country in a disastrous conflict talked more loudly of the importance of economic development to prevent the spread of communism. By 1965, Japan's foreign aid had begun to increase slowly as a proportion of national income; and the government, without committing itself to unpopular political alliances, showed clearer signs of trying to steer Japan into a role of leadership in what many Japanese regarded as a contest with the Chinese to demonstrate to Asians the best way of building a modern industrial state. In short, while the data for a study of Japan's relations with Asia remained largely commercial in nature, political objectives lay, as always, behind commercial activities; new links were expressed between economic and political goals; and the latter began to take on some meaning and form.

Chapter IV uses Japanese sources to present the main positions in the two key debates that developed in Tokyo in the mid-1960s and that are still going on today. One debate was over Japan's security and how it may be affected by events in mainland China; the other was over the "North-South problem"—whether and how much economic aid should be given to the less developed countries of Asia and how Japan might best ensure success for its aid programs. There is, moreover, a growing linkage in Japanese minds between the two debates.

In Chapter V the focus of the book shifts to Japanese economic and other activities in a number of non-Communist Asian countries, as observed on the scene during the late summer and autumn of 1968. In this chapter I have tried to describe the general level of Japanese business involvement, technical assistance, loans and credits for plant export or other construction projects, consortia aid, Youth Volunteer Corps activities, and the like. I have also attempted to suggest recent and current Japanese attitudes toward Asians and vice versa as accurately as possible, and I have mentioned cultural activities where they were observed and seemed significant. Out of all this it is hoped that the reader will gain a comprehensive view of the slow return of Japan to the status of a major power in Asia.

The scope of the book includes South Korea, mainland China, India, and most but not all of Southeast Asia. Burma is treated for the years up to 1961 but not thereafter, when problems of access ruled out much useful work. Pakistan, Ceylon, and Hong Kong are omitted for lack of time and opportunity to cover them. Vietnam, Laos, and Cambodia are mentioned from time to time, especially with reference to the Mekong River basin project, but no separate section is devoted to their relations with Japan. The same is true for Australia. For the rest, I have written in more or less detail on Japan's postwar relations with South Korea, mainland

China, Taiwan, the Philippines, Indonesia, Singapore, Malaysia, Thailand, and India.

The most important written sources are in Japanese. Oral sources include Japanese in Japan and abroad, other Asians, and Westerners in Asia and the West. Interviews were conducted during periods of prolonged foreign residence as well as periods of travel between 1955 and 1968. I must specifically disclaim any special expertise on China, although I have written periodically on Japan's relations with the mainland. The approach of the book is chronological and descriptive, but I have tried to clarify and comment upon the meaning of the events in each chapter as I went along and in Chapter VI to suggest something of their possible future significance for Japan and for the United States as well. My method has been as far as possible to allow the material to produce its own meanings. This runs the usual risk that the facts in their intransigence and disorder may yield illuminations so rare or slight as to be imperceptible to the reader. In this he has my sympathy; but he is little worse off than the Japanese, whose government and private representatives have for the most part been groping in their *ad hoc* way, most of them seeking only to make profits, a few of the more thoughtful to find some way of expressing a new Japaneseness (itself less capable of definition than before) in an ominous Asia.

Finally, in Chapter VI, I have tried to indicate that with American interest in Asia showing signs of waning after the end of the Vietnam war (whenever that time comes), we may make the mistake of assuming that the Japanese are ready and willing to do our errands or that other Asians desire this. But we cannot use the Japanese in such a way. Japan is a great nation; it will act in support of its own interests, which since 1945 have coincided broadly with our own but will not necessarily do so in the future. It is my hope that Americans will work to enlarge areas of common interest with the Japanese, economically and politically, by cooperating with them to help raise levels of living elsewhere in Asia through all possible bilateral and especially multilateral means.

Asian stability is a world problem, which neither we nor the Japanese can solve alone. Our common economic ingenuity and pragmatism suggest that Americans and Japanese could work together to help others and that this would be in our self-interest as well as theirs. We have made some beginnings in this direction, but we will need to apply much more imagination to our future policies toward China and Southeast Asia and how Japan fits into them if we expect to influence Japanese energies in ways consonant with our own interests and avoid serious frictions in the future. A return to isolationism in this country could only breed trouble in Asia as elsewhere.

PART ONE

Japan's Return to Asia, 1952–64

II. The First Steps: Relations with Southeast Asia and India

The San Francisco Peace Treaty, signed in September 1951 by Japan and the Western allies but not by the Communist states, restored Japan's political autonomy and control over its foreign affairs. At the same time, in order to obtain the end of the American Occupation, the Japanese government agreed to security arrangements with the United States that, in effect, aligned it with the West. In April 1952 a separate treaty with the Chinese Nationalist government in Taiwan further confirmed that alignment and shut Japan off from normal diplomatic ties with mainland China for an indefinite future.

These decisions, from which the opposition parties and many vocal members of the intellectual community bitterly dissented, were taken by Japan's conservative leaders as the necessary if somewhat disagreeable price of their country's security in a time of national weakness, when Japan was unarmed and Asia torn by war and revolution. After seven years of almost total isolation Japan returned to an environment that was unpromising, to say the least. In China, communism had won out after a century of unsuccessful efforts by the Chinese to unify their country; resistance to Japanese aggression had been a crucial cause of that victory. In Korea, negotiations had begun to end that conflict, but the fighting continued. Six million Japanese had been repatriated from all over Asia at war's end and dumped into Yokohama and other ports at a time of economic paralysis, but many thousands of others were still overseas in 1952, in Chinese or Russian hands. Many were to die there; for the rest, repatriation had to be negotiated.

Japan had been almost completely out of contact with Southeast Asia [1] since 1945. Except for a few hundred stragglers who remained behind and married local wives, Southeast Asia was stripped of Japanese, and Japan's interest in the region was understandably low after the war. The mood of the Japanese people was one of numbed withdrawal from all but their most immediate concerns; the focus of their nationalism was narrowed down to an examination of the self and its needs. The public wanted peace at nearly any price; its fear of the ugly past's returning made it shudder at involvement in the disputes of others, for which most Japanese fancied they had little responsibility. A substantial political opposition played on these fears, but the Socialists themselves lacked much knowledge of conditions in Southeast Asia. Their platforms called for closer relations with neutralist regimes, but they had little contact with other Asian Socialists.

For their part, Premier Yoshida and his conservative associates in the early 1950s clearly believed that Japan must cleave to the United States if it hoped to regain the wealth and influence that had been forfeited by a failed militarism. Only with American goods, technology, money, and protection might radicalism at home be modulated and a "sound" polity and citizenry, one which would make it possible to exorcise the worst excesses of the American Occupation, be assured. During the Occupation the Japanese economy had been sharply redirected away from the lost Asian empire and toward America and the West. In 1934–36, exports to mainland China, Korea, and Taiwan totaled 41 per cent of Japan's exports; in 1951–53 they were 9 per cent. Most of the energy of Japan's leaders in the post-Occupation years was to go into restoring and cultivating close relations with the West, and especially with its principal power. At the time of the Peace Treaty Japan still faced severe problems of economic rebuilding; the changes that were to come in the next twenty years could hardly have been imagined by the leaders in Tokyo. The Korean War helped put the economy back on its feet and made it viable again, but per capita income in 1952 was less than $200 a year; only American special procurements for the Korean fighting prevented enormous balance-of-payments deficits. Exports in 1953 were only one-third of the 1934–36 level, and less than two-thirds of imports. With the birth rate high, though falling, and food imports a heavy burden on foreign exchange, the situation was far from reassuring. Grim diagnoses of the future were common at this time and for a long while after. In such circumstances every argument that could be devised for Japan's own weakness would be advanced to avoid commitments to others.

With their attention focused on the West, Japan's leaders in 1952 had little disposition to think of Asia. But the Peace Treaty left unresolved a host of problems with countries that had been overrun by Japan during the war, and that now confronted their former occupiers with demands for restitution. Until agreements were completed settling their claims, the Japanese could have no normal relations with the rest of Asia even after the Peace Treaty had been signed.

1. Reparations Negotiations and Trade, 1952–58

Article 14 of the San Francisco Peace Treaty stated in part:

> It is recognized that Japan should pay reparations to the Allied Powers for the damage and suffering caused by it during the war. Nevertheless it is also recognized that the resources of Japan are not presently sufficient, if it is to maintain a viable economy, to make complete reparation for all such damage and suffering and at the same time meet its other obligations. Therefore Japan will promptly enter into negotiations with Allied Powers so desiring,

whose present territories were occupied by Japanese forces and damaged by Japan, with a view to assisting to compensate those countries for the cost of repairing the damage done, by making available the services of the Japanese people in production, salvaging and other work for the Allied Powers in question. Such arrangements shall avoid the imposition of additional liabilities on other Allied Powers, and, where the manufacturing of raw materials is called for, they shall be supplied by the Allied Powers in question, so as not to throw any foreign exchange burden upon Japan. . . .

The requirement that Japan pay war damage reparations was inserted in the Peace Treaty at the insistence of the Southeast Asian nations that had been occupied by the Japanese. Early in the Allied Occupation of Japan, industrial equipment worth some $160 million had been dismantled and shipped to China, the Philippines, and Indonesia, as well as to the United Kingdom (for its Asian areas). However, shipments were stopped in 1949 when Allied policy shifted from punishment and reform to economic stabilization and rebuilding; and in framing the Peace Treaty the American drafters had hoped to avoid mention of reparations entirely.[2] This was not, however, to prove possible if a Peace Treaty was to be signed at all. As it was, the Philippines and Indonesia initialed the treaty but refused to ratify it until reparations agreements satisfying their claims were reached. Negotiation of these agreements was to require years.

The first negotiating team from any Southeast Asian country arrived in Tokyo from Indonesia in December 1951, before the Peace Treaty had been ratified by the Western allies. The Indonesians presented claims for the equivalent of $18 billion in consumer goods and services, based on their estimates of total loss of life and real property. The Japanese replied that they could not pay such claims and still survive economically. In this interchange Japan had the language of the Peace Treaty in its favor; Article 14 clearly ruled out blanket restitution of war losses. Little resulted from this first meeting except a so-called interim agreement, which merely repeated that reparations would be paid in services and would not destroy the Japanese economy. This was denounced in

Djakarta, and there the matter rested. The Indonesian government was wary of Japan's pro-Western orientation in any case, and a final agreement was not to be reached between the two countries for six more years.

A month later, in January 1952, negotiations with the Philippines commenced in Manila. The Philippine delegation demanded the equivalent of $8 billion in cash, to be paid over a ten- to fifteen-year period; its claim, like the Indonesian one, was based on life and property losses and was made as an opening gambit more than anything else. The Filipinos further suggested a "token" payment of $800 million be made in advance as an earnest of Japanese intentions. The Japanese responded that cash payment was ruled out by the treaty, which specified services, and only in an amount within Japan's capacity to pay. Clearly $8 billion was no less impossible than $18 billion even if paid over a long period of years. Eight billion dollars was approximately three times the Japanese government's budget in fiscal 1954. The negotiations ended without agreement; for the rest of 1952 no progress was made, and in November of that year the American Ambassador in Tokyo remarked in an address that Japan was being dilatory in confronting the problem.[3] The Philippine side later admitted that its first claims were ridiculously high; yet up to the end of 1952 Japan made no specific offers of reparations to anyone, but merely waited for proposals from the other side.

In December 1952 the Japanese Foreign Ministry, reacting to American prodding, proposed to the Philippines a long list of services which might answer the definition of reparations; these included salvage of sunken ships littering Philippine harbors and provision of new ships, rolling stock, farm and mining machinery, and other capital goods and equipment, but no cash. A few days later the *Asahi Shimbun* reported that the Japanese government was prepared to pay reparations worth the yen equivalent of $200 million to the Philippines. This was the first definite figure mentioned by the Japanese side, and it left plenty of room for maneuver.

In 1953 more active exploration of the problem began on both sides. The Japanese had begun to feel the need for markets now that the Korean War boom seemed finally over. Their eagerness to do business with Southeast Asia was not concealed, and it was well matched by the desire of the leaders of those countries to wring the last ounce of benefit from their claims on the past. In March 1953 an interim agreement was signed for salvage by Japanese engineers of about 200,000 tons of sunken Japanese and American shipping in Manila, Cebu, Cavite, and other Philippine harbors; these hulks had been a peril to navigation since 1944 and represented valuable scrap metal to the Filipinos. Hopes seemed bright for a settlement of over-all claims, but implementation of the salvage agreement was to be delayed for more than two years by haggling over the price of scrap and Philippine accusations of overpricing by the Japanese. This was the first of innumerable charges of dishonesty connected with reparations programs. In the end the Japanese reduced their price per ton for the scrap after the most tenacious and pedantic bargaining. Salvage operations finally got under way in August 1955.[4]

In September 1953, again after having been prodded by the United States, the Japanese sent a mission to Southeast Asia to "lay the groundwork for reparations agreements,"[5] an exercise one would have supposed had been going on ever since the Peace Treaty. Foreign Minister Okazaki observed in Manila that Japan would pay, although he did not say how much, over a period of five to ten years, and that payments would include equipment as well as personal services. He acknowledged the demands of the claimants for help in their new industrialization programs, then only beginning to take form. However, with a Philippine election forthcoming, nothing specific came of the Okazaki mission, except that the Philippine side abandoned its $8 billion claim and asked Japan to name a figure. Some kind of formula for negotiation seemed to be slowly emerging. Okazaki moved on to Djakarta, where he negotiated another "interim" agreement for ship salvage, which was destined to remain unratified by the Indonesian parliament.

By 1954 Philippine demands were down to $2 billion, Japan's public offers up to $250 million. Some Japanese economists expressed concern over the long-range effect of reparations payments on their country's normal exports, fearing that large shipments of textile plants and other industrial machinery to Southeast Asia would create competition for Japan's own industries. In the context of those times there was some basis for such fears: in 1955 textiles were more than 40 per cent of Japanese exports to that area. But other manufacturers facing a decline in American military spending in Japan were convinced that reparations must open the door to rich raw materials and new markets for equipment, spare parts and after-services, and they therefore pressed for Japan's commercial return to Southeast Asia. In 1954 and 1955 Japanese business was gearing up for sustained and dynamic growth. Economic opportunities in the Philippines and elsewhere were beginning to be pursued, despite hatreds left over from the past, and Japanese businessmen were trying to form new relationships or to renew old ones with those families of the Philippine elite who controlled mining, timber, and certain other industries.

By April 1954 negotiators had produced the first preliminary agreement on over-all reparations between Japan and the Philippines. This called for Japanese "investment" of the equivalent of $400 million over ten years in the development of Philippine resources, notably abaca around Davao in the island of Mindanao, where many Japanese had lived before the war and had a thriving enclave of their own, and mineral resources in the northern part of Luzon. Land was to be reclaimed on a large scale in Mindanao and used to grow rice, which would help produce self-sufficiency for the Philippines and create a surplus for export to Japan, where it would earn foreign exchange for import of more Japanese goods into the country. The agreement would, it was asserted, eventually net the islands a return of $1 billion.[6] There would be a small cash payment in addition to these services. Japanese could not acquire property rights, but the extent of their real participation in the proposed investments was left unclear. The day after the so-called Ōno-Garcia agreement was initialed, the Japanese Foreign Ministry dispatched to Manila Shōzō Murata, wartime Ambassador to the Japan-sponsored Philippine Republic, with instructions to sign a more formal reparations pact.

It was not signed, and the supposition by the Japanese that it could have been signed revealed a certain naïveté in their grasp of the postwar Philippines and their own position there. Most Filipinos viewed Japanese with intense repugnance; their attitude toward them was far less ambivalent than that of Indonesians or Burmese. Already promised independence before the war started, Filipinos validated their nationalism in fighting against the Japanese, not in fighting the return of Western colonialism after the war ended. The heart of the Filipino struggle was in the guerrilla movement in the hills, which in the ferocity of its resistance had no real counterpart in the rest of Southeast Asia.[7] Nationalism was the essential raw material of Philippine political rhetoric, and the Ōno-Garcia agreement, whatever the intentions behind it, sounded altogether too much like a replay of Japan's prewar role in the Philippines. The politicians in Manila were eager to make capital out of the Japanese. The acerbic Claro Recto, who had himself been a prominent collaborator during the war, rejected the agreement as a step toward another Greater East Asia Co-prosperity Sphere and demanded an absolute minimum of $1 billion in reparations. Within a day or two other politicians denounced the agreement; only 5 of the 24 members of the Philippine Senate were reported to be definitely in favor of it. President Magsaysay was forced to inform Murata that the agreement was nothing more than a starting point for negotiations, to which Murata blandly replied that his government regarded it as binding; but his mission ended in failure, and he soon returned to Tokyo, where Premier Yoshida announced that he would adopt a "wait and see" policy on Philippine reparations.

The Philippines continued its demands, and reparations became the chief bait or prize in a game for influence played with unceasing calculation and much callousness on both sides. Businessmen in both countries were as eager as ever to do business; and Recto himself was the first to point out that the Philippines had much to learn from Japan's experience of industrialization. Filipinos yearned for some kind of Asian identity after their political independence from the United States, as many had before, and believed that closer ties with Japan would eventually be inevitable, and indeed more or less desirable. The notion of Japan as a model of modernization had flourished in much of Asia ever since the Russo-Japanese War, though largely in abstract terms that had never received very minute examination.

By 1955, Japan, though still faced with economic problems, had passed through the shallows that followed the Korean War. A Philippine government mission sent to Tokyo to study Japan's capacity to pay reparations reported, not surprisingly, that the economy could sustain payment of $400 million in goods and services. (A separate group sent by rival political forces in Manila reported the same conclusion.) The country's progress in the previous year had been remarkable. In August 1954 the London *Times* spoke of "saving Japan from the collapse now threatened by her trade debt." [8] A year later, the mood of the whole country was changing. In December 1955 I wrote from Kyoto, summing up the situation at the year-end:

The clamor of Japan's New Year celebration has already begun. Shoppers, many of them carrying *furoshiki* full of purchases, crowd the retail districts, jam the department stores, and elbow one another on the packed, swaying streetcars. No one pays much attention to the government's Confucian-patterned "new life" movement designed to reduce elaborate parties and eliminate gift-exchanging and other extravagances. The elegant, expensive teahouses and restaurants of Kyoto's Gion and Pontochō districts report heavy bookings for New Year parties of businessmen and government officials. Students and lower-salaried men will crowd into *pachinko* (pinball) parlors, coffee shops and beer halls, while the lowest wage earners will fill the *ippaiya* where cheap *sake* may be had for a few yen a drink and food stalls where conversation will grow raucous over bowls of *soba* and *udon*. Although most people have little to spend, nearly everybody will spend a little, and some will spend a lot.[9]

These were impressions of Kyoto city people. But I further pointed out that Japanese industrial production stood at twice the level of 1950; that the largest rice crop in history had just been harvested; and that while trade totals were still below prewar levels, there was a $500 million balance-of-payments surplus in 1955, and iron and steel exports were expected to grow more than a quarter larger than in the previous year.

Such facts indicated the beginning of very rapid economic growth that was to be sustained for more than a decade. With growth came a slow return of morale and a feeling that the country should get on with the settlement of old scores for the sake of commerce, if for no other reason. By the mid-1950s, also, the reparations issue had become entangled in Japan's domestic politics; rivals of Premier Yoshida in the conservative camp were conspiring to bring his long regime to an end and were using the failure to reach reparations agreements as a weapon against his government.

In such a changing atmosphere, a Burmese delegation arrived in Tokyo in the summer of 1954 and within three months signed a reparations agreement that was ratified by both countries in the spring of 1955. Burmese negotiators were reported by the Japanese to be "very rational."[10] Burma's initial claims had been in the billions, the Japanese offer less than $100 million. Compromise was reached at $200 million in goods and services over ten years in actual reparations, plus $50 million in private loans, to be "facilitated" by the Japanese government but negotiated later on a case-by-case basis; thus the Japanese effectively retained control over such loans. Japan also agreed to an escalator clause by which it would re-examine the agreement in the event other countries later received more than the Burmese had. By this time, it was being reported in Tokyo that the Philippines, Indonesia, and Burma would be paid off according to a 4:2:1 formula.[11] It was clear that reparations would be scaled well within Japan's capacity to pay. What would be their effect in recipient countries was much less clear.

In December 1954, Yoshida resigned and was succeeded by Ichirō Hatoyama, who had pledged among other things to settle reparations, if need be on a more generous basis. In early 1955, Foreign Minister Shigemitsu called for Japan's long-term "economic cooperation" with Southeast Asia to "stabilize" the region —language that would be used repeatedly in the following years. Japan was now beginning its return to the region economically. In December 1954, it joined the Colombo Plan; in March 1955 the U.N.'s Economic Commission for Asia and the Far East (ECAFE) held its regular meeting in Tokyo, underlining Japan's "potential role in Asian economic affairs." [12] In April, Japan agreed to settle claims arising from yen issued in Thailand during the war that subsequently became worthless.

In April 1955, too, Japan sent to the Afro-Asian Conference at Bandung a delegation of more than thirty persons, including Diet members and important representatives of business. In Tokyo there were differences of opinion over Japan's proper role in the Bandung Conference. Some conservative politicians and bureaucrats favored clear-cut cooperation with Western programs of economic development and political association in Southeast Asia; others preferred a more adventurist, "pro-Asian" policy. The leading Japanese delegate, Tatsunosuke Takasaki, took an apologetic stance, publicly announcing repentance for Japanese wartime expansion and pledging economic cooperation [13] with everybody in the Afro-Asian world, but carefully avoiding any political commitments that might cause Japan trouble in Peking, Washington, or anywhere else. Extreme caution in any but the commercial sense was already apparent. At home the press criticized the delegation for its alleged supineness; some papers thought Japan should seize the opportunity for leadership of the "Asian bloc."

Press reports anticipated later accusations, inside and outside Japan, that the government would not stand up and be counted on political issues in Asia.

Takasaki himself, writing in a Japanese magazine three years later, gave a somewhat fuller explanation of his feelings during the conference. Memory of the war in Southeast Asia was still extremely vivid. Other Asians were suspicious of Japanese intentions and feared their economic penetration or even their territorial ambitions. It would be many years before good will and trust could be rebuilt. Beyond these elementary perceptions, Takasaki warned of the consequences of too close an association with American policy in Asia, which, he thought, could easily identify Japan with white neocolonialism or could make the Japanese appear, as another of them put it, "yellow Americans." Takasaki reported that he had told Chou En-lai at Bandung that "Japan cannot do other than follow American policy at present," but that following America made him uneasy. He referred to Japan's loneliness, its loss of prominence in the Asian hierarchy of nations, its alliance with a basically uncongenial America in an ideological conflict in which it was not wise for Japan to become embroiled, because it might lead to confrontations and unpleasantness with the Chinese and others.[14]

The visceral desire of some Japanese, at least, to leave room for an independent policy in Asia at some future time was evident in Takasaki's account. The government in 1955 was very far from being pushed into taking any overt political lead in the region. However, it was definitely beginning to clean up the mess left by the war. Philippine and Indonesian reparations were the last and most difficult obstacles remaining. Negotiations with the Philippines reopened during the winter of 1954–55; President Magsaysay cabled Premier Hatoyama in March 1955, asking him to break the deadlocked talks; Hatoyama replied that the issue must be settled or Japan "will never develop friendly relations with Southeast Asia." In April, private Japanese companies revealed their eagerness to make profits from reparations by offering to supervise construction of $150 million worth of public buildings, including the proposed new capitol building in Quezon City. This was turned down by Philippine negotiators, who strongly denied charges of bribery and secret deals with the Japanese. As usual the atmosphere was heavy with suspicion and distaste on both sides.

In May 1955 the Philippine side presented new demands for $800 million; the Japanese offered $600 million. In early June the Japanese were reported to be "earnestly studying payment of $800 million," but later in the month this was denied; the strain on Japan's economy, it was maintained, would be too great. A more important reason for not wanting to pay so much was strong opposition within the rival Liberal party. Hatoyama and the Democrats had come to power on a promise of generosity, but $800 million was too generous; it would raise Indonesian demands and stir the Burmese to make further claims. In early September Hatoyama asked Yoshida for his support for the $800 million formula, but Yoshida refused. Hatoyama then offered the Philippines a compromise: $500 million over twenty years in reparations goods, $30 million in technical services, including ship salvage, and $20 million in cash for Filipino war widows and orphans. In addition, the Japanese government agreed to facilitate $250 million worth of private, long-term, low-interest "commercial" loans on terms to be negotiated later. The contradictory language in the agreement concerning these loans was to produce difficulties later.

Another nine months of negotiations were required before Japan and the Philippines initialed a reparations agreement along the above lines on April 27, 1956. The agreement was ratified by the Diet on June 4, by the Philippine Senate on July 10. It went into effect on July 23, and diplomatic relations were restored. The Philippines thus had settled for about 10 per cent of its original claim. But this was not to be the end of Japan's problems: the resumption of normal trade and other economic ties was carefully separated from reparations by the Philippine side, which insisted that such relations could not be legally renewed until the two countries had signed a Treaty of Friendship, Commerce and Navigation.

Reparations for Indonesia were not settled until 1958, when the amount was set at $223 million over twelve years, plus $400 million in private loans and investments. In addition, a trade debt to Japan of $177 million, which had been left deliberately unpaid for years, was canceled. Finally, in May 1959, a small reparations agreement was signed with South Vietnam, to be used almost entirely for construction of a hydroelectric project on the Da Ninh River. Other agreements in lieu of reparations were later made with Laos and Cambodia. By this time Burma was already calling for renegotiation of its claim under the escalator clause.

One of the greatest fears expressed by the Japanese when the Peace Treaty was signed was that reparations would be so huge the economy would not be able to sustain the burden. This was quite unfounded. In 1956, when payments to Burma alone had begun, reparations amounted to 0.6 per cent of the general account budget. The next year, when the Philippines were added, the reparations total was 1.1 per cent; in 1958, 1.1 per cent; in 1959, 2.1 per cent.[15] Between 1962 and 1965, the period of heaviest payments, they averaged only 2 per cent of the annual budget. In 1961 reparations were slightly more than half the amount appropriated for unemployment compensation, half that for social security, and about equal to sums for promotion of science and technology and for tuberculosis prevention. However, appropriations for reparations were nearly twice as large as for new government housing and six times as large as for support of small industries,[16] thus indicating something about the government's social policies.

Reparations were not a serious burden upon Japan at any time. They were indeed scaled to Japan's capacity to pay, and in the last analysis the Japanese called the tune in the negotiations. In the process, the vocabulary of the whole exercise was altered to lay stress upon the economic needs of the recipient countries; but by the late 1950s, certain economic realities were clear to everyone concerned. Japan had entered a period of very high-level economic growth. In the first postwar economic plan, adopted by the Hatoyama government in December 1955, the annual growth rate of the GNP was set at 5 per cent, with emphasis placed on the expansion of heavy and chemical industries. The actual growth rate turned out to be 10 per cent a year, however, and the plan's targets were reached in about two years instead of five. A new five-year plan was accordingly adopted in 1957. The gap was already widening between Japan's growth and that of Southeast Asia, and Japan's principal economic interests were increasingly seen to be in the West, which could buy its finished goods for cash.

The fear that payment of reparations would seriously injure Japan's ordinary exports was also unfounded. In 1957 reparations equaled 1.7 per cent of exports on a customs clearance basis [17] but subsequently declined to about 1.1 per cent during the peak payment period in 1962–65. Authorized payments amounted to about $70 million annually in that period, when all four countries were being paid simultaneously. Actual payments, however, were somewhat smaller, since there was some unevenness in the utilization of reparations goods by the recipients. This had less to do with their innate capacity to absorb reparations than their ability to plan, coordinate, and effectively use the goods when they reached their destination. (The implementation of the reparations program will be discussed below.) However, while reparations payments soon reached their ceiling, Japan's commodity exports had no ceiling and grew more rapidly than anyone had thought possible a few years earlier, doubling between 1956 and 1962 and almost doubling again by 1965.

Except for Burma, ordinary exports to the countries receiving reparations rose fairly steadily. In the Burmese case there were special problems. Japanese exports to Burma in 1955, the year before reparations began, totaled 13.7 billion yen. In 1962, at the peak of reparations, they were 19.2 billion yen, but the increase

equaled reparations payments almost to the yen. Thus, in 1962
reparations to Burma were 29 per cent of Japan's total exports to
that country, and in some years the percentage was even higher.
However, stagnation of normal exports to Burma was not due
solely to their replacement by reparations (some consumer goods
were sent as reparations) but also to the sharp fall in Japanese
purchases of Burmese rice and the Burmese government's consequent import controls.[18]

Exports to the Philippines more than doubled between 1955
and 1962. In this case there were fewer restrictions on normal
trade, and reparations amounted to a smaller percentage of total
exports; the figure fell from 23 per cent in 1957 to 13 per cent in
1960, 8 per cent in 1961, and 6 per cent in 1962. Imports from
the Philippines were consistently larger than exports, due to heavy
Japanese purchases of Philippine logs, iron ore, and other raw
materials. What is especially notable from about 1957 is the decline in the export of Japanese textiles and other light manufactures to the whole area, and the rise in export of metal products,
machinery, and chemicals. Undoubtedly, reparations shipments
of cement plants, ships, rolling stock, and other heavy goods fig-
ured in this trend, but they were not solely responsible for it.
Structural changes in the Japanese economy in the direction of
more capital-intensive exports would have occurred without
reparations.

Exports to Indonesia likewise increased, though less rapidly
than to the Philippines, and reparations formed a larger share of
the increase. On the whole, however, payments of reparations
opened the way to wider trade, not only in capital goods but in
consumer goods as well.[19]

Nevertheless, Southeast Asia did not measure up to commercial
expectations held for it by Japan in the early 1950s. In 1952 some
economists had described the area as an inevitable, natural trading
partner. But such statements were made before the intractable
problems of economic growth in Southeast Asia and the chronic

political disorders there had fully revealed themselves to the Japanese and before the immense expansion of the American market. For a variety of reasons, by now well-known, world trade in primary products did not keep pace with trade in manufactured goods, and foreign-exchange shortages forced many Asian countries to rely on aid rather than normal trade to finance imports. As a result, South and Southeast Asia were neither the great market nor the unlimited source of raw materials they had been professed to be by some people in Tokyo; and as Japan's total exports nearly quadrupled in the decade 1956–66, the share of Asia fell in the total.[20]

The reparations negotiations have been described in detail because they reveal something of the style as well as the substance of Japan's relations with Southeast Asia after 1952. The Japanese accepted the obligation to pay that was imposed upon them by the peace settlement. Once agreements were reached, they paid in a straightforward manner, as was their custom in such international dealings. Unevennesses in the time schedules of payment and other irregularities were caused primarily by inadequacies of planning and implementation of programs to use reparations goods in the recipient countries and by corruption, rather than by any fiscal delinquency of the Japanese. However, reparations, like all transactions involving the transfer of resources, were regarded by the Japanese as an occasion for the most dogged bargaining, unclouded by the influence of any sentimental regard for the recipients in whatever country. Many Japanese felt ambivalence toward the whole matter, if not outright distaste. By its humiliation of the white powers during the Second World War, Japan had helped to make a European return afterward impossible. At the same time, Japanese attempts to stave off defeat by rallying local peoples to a factitious pan-Asian cause under Japanese leadership had ended in dismal failure. By the mid-1950s a few Japanese at least still professed to interpret the war primarily as an enterprise to rid Asia of the hated white man; but even among those who did not, a tone of self-justification was often discernible where discussions of tropical Asia were concerned.[21]

"Poor Japan" was a stock phrase of that period—and indeed until very recently. It is not much heard nowadays: Japan now sometimes calls itself the "poorest member of the rich men's club." Such self-deprecation has its usefulness in the negotiation of international settlements; it also shows that the consciousness of occupying an intermediate position between the developed "north" and the underdeveloped "south" is very acute. But there were older, deeper reasons for Japanese caution vis-à-vis South and Southeast Asia in the early 1950s. For their national comparisons, responsible leaders like Yoshida looked primarily to the West, and had ever since the nineteenth century. In 1952 they began again on the ruins of a bankrupt Asian policy. Although they realized the necessity of building a new policy based on peaceful cooperation with the whole region, they viewed it coolly, without much affection or illusion. Yoshida himself once asserted that the leaders there were "not even aware of what their position in the world really is." [22] His eyes were upon the West, from whence, among other things, came his country's help. In 1952 the solution of Japan's national rehabilitation lay in America, not in India or Indonesia or the Philippines; or so Yoshida and his peers believed.

Catching up with the West before the war had implied leading Japan against other Asians, not toward them. It had meant exploitation, not cooperation. Some Japanese had of course cast their careers in Asia; some were genuinely fond of other Asians; others still cherished romantic or sentimental slogans for Asian unity. But long before the war most Japanese had lived at a cultural distance from other Asians, and pan-Asian slogans could not mask the fact that others had often been put to the service of Japanese national or personal goals or a complex mixture of the two. Tutelage of others economically and culturally less fortunate was a characteristic impulse, while the concept of equality or partnership in international as in personal relations was very weakly grasped by the Japanese people as a whole. As one Japanese scholar wrote, they moved into the modern world "in wedge formation." [23]

For all these reasons, Japan's first steps toward South and Southeast Asia after the Occupation were tentative and slow. Before reparations agreements were signed, few Japanese traveled to the area at all, and those who did came back with cautionary reports. Taketora Ōgata, an important conservative political leader who visited several Asian countries as Yoshida's special envoy in the spring of 1952, reported that Japan should watch and wait, that it was questionable how free the newly independent countries really were, and that Japanese diplomats should try to get closer to the local people and develop new contacts, somewhat after the manner of American Ambassador Chester Bowles in India, whose tactics Ōgata compared with earlier American missionaries. Such advice was to be repeated from time to time; yet very early in the reparations negotiations the continuity with prewar or wartime personnel on both sides became very noticeable. Ōgata also thought trade relations might be pushed better by setting up large Japanese trading companies in the region—a prophetic recommendation—but his main message was for Japan to keep quiet, to take a low posture, and to learn to reach the people and their needs.[24]

A little later another commentator wrote that the Japanese should not suppose that their former enemies had forgotten the war simply because of peace treaties or reparations agreements. Memory of what had happened to them was still fresh, and all Japanese should realize this fact. He urged that the "right kind" of people be sent to Southeast Asia—carefully selected men who would give useful technical advice. He also gave vent to the deep sense of loneliness in the postwar world that was felt by many sensitive Japanese of whatever calling. The Occupation, he wrote, had prevented this loneliness from being fully felt, because it had masked Japan's real problems; but with independence everyone had to accept the fact that Japan was cared for by nobody; it had to look after itself, accept its plight, and work toward true independence and autonomy; only in this way could it rid others of the fear of its aggressive resurgence.[25]

Reparations were not a foreign policy but merely the first step toward a new relationship, taken with a look back toward the ugly past. From the beginning of the negotiations the recipient countries were determined to draw every ounce of blood possible from Japan. The public attitude of the Japanese toward reparations was essentially negative. The subject was seldom discussed in the press once the talks had been concluded; today the issue is a dead one in Tokyo. Payments to Indonesia end in 1970, to the Philippines in 1976; but in Japan they will go unnoticed for the most part and naturally so. In a time of immensely rapid technological progress, of unprecedented economic "miracles," the era of "my car" and "my home," when per capita income approaches European levels and aggregate output exceeds that of all countries but the United States and the Soviet Union, few Japanese today wish to be reminded of obligations that might turn their thoughts to a past that they would prefer to forget and that many cannot remember because they were not yet born. Little wonder that the Foreign Ministry official who supplied a copy of the most definitive government study of reparations admitted blandly he had not read it and had no intention of doing so. "We still have plenty of undistributed copies," he remarked, as he handed me mine.

2. NEW MOVES IN ECONOMIC DIPLOMACY, 1957–61

Even before the last of the reparations agreements had been signed, other Japanese approaches to Southeast Asia were beginning to be made. In January 1956 a conference of Foreign Ministry officials concerned with Asia made recommendations for a more forward policy than had previously been expressed. Remaining reparations problems should be settled immediately, and economic cooperation with underdeveloped nations (later to be called developing nations in Japanese as in English) should be pushed. To promote this the operations of the Export-Import Bank of Japan, a government institution founded in 1950, should be expanded to permit more credit for Japanese enterprises wishing to do business abroad as well as for foreign applicants for industrial financing. The diplomats also urged that new courses on Southeast Asia be offered in Japanese universities and that more leaders from those countries be invited to visit Japan. Japanese diplomats should take part in more international conferences; and, last but not least, housing and living conditions abroad for them and their families should be greatly improved.

These recommendations were made against the background of the unification of conservative political forces in the Liberal Democratic party, accomplished in November 1955. Behind them also lay the desire of business interests to expand markets in Southeast Asia, where Communist China was beginning to compete in sales of light manufactures, and to find raw materials to feed Japan's industrial growth. A statement by the Vice-Minister of Foreign Affairs demonstrated the rising interest in Asia, even as it revealed a certain lack of prescience where trade with the West was concerned:

> It goes without saying that Japan should place emphasis on machinery and chemical products in its future export drive. It is also evident that Japan cannot hope to sell these items to the United States and other advanced nations. Outlets for these exports are located in Asia in the broad sense, which includes the Middle East and Southeast Asia. This means Japan must seek its own prosperity through that of Asia as a whole. Leadership in international diplomacy as well as in other fields belongs to any nation that is quick to grab an embryonic opportunity for the future in the eternal current of history.[26]

The recommendations of the diplomatic conference of January 1956 represented the views of some of the Foreign Ministry's most senior officials. For these men there was never much doubt of their mission to build a new position of influence and prestige for their country in Asia. Taking open political positions was another matter. Because of the harsh divisions within Japan and the distrustful attitude of other Asians, it was natural for Japanese diplomacy in this period to emphasize economic objectives. Such tactics were in complete accord with domestic priorities. Japan had been burned before in seeking "greatness" in Asia; it knew it was still disliked. Criticism from America and elsewhere that it was not doing its part then and later to help less-developed nations was troubling to Japanese leaders, and the government sought to act generally in accord with "free world" interests in Asia; but Japan did so with a certain consciousness of its isolation in that area, which dictated that it move slowly, keep the future as open as possible, take a "low posture," and stress economic diplomacy, which was no less diplomacy for being economic.

The diplomats' recommendation for new university courses on Southeast Asia reflected a desire to begin training a new generation of Southeast Asian specialists. A certain number of people were left over from wartime civil administration bureaucracies; some of these now served on the staffs of private or government research bureaus. New organizations were also created to help fill the need for information of the type most sought by the Japanese in that period.

One of the first of these was the Asia Association, a quasi-governmental agency founded in 1954 with the blessing of the Foreign Ministry. Receiving a small subsidy from the government, its directors and research staff included retired Foreign Ministry officials, academic economists in and out of government, and a sprinkling of engineers and other professionals from the old South Manchurian Railroad Research Department. Continuity with the past was noticeable; the President of the Association was a financier important in Empire days and after the war President of the Japan Development Bank; the executive director was a long-time professor of economics at Tokyo University. The Asia Association was set up partly to promote export of Japanese equipment and technical know-how, partly to oversee Japan's participation in the foreign trainee program of the Colombo Plan. The Association did not survive for long but was superseded by other organizations in the bureaucratic warfare for control of economic programs overseas. During its brief existence it put out a quarterly in English, which carried some fairly weighty articles on economic growth by professors or government officials on active service. It also published a monthly magazine in Japanese containing articles by businessmen and others on the possibilities of overseas investment, technical licensing agreements, and trade prospects in Southeast Asia and elsewhere. In short, the Association was one of a number of research bodies—public, private or in-between—that undertook the collection and dissemination of information about the "new Asia." During these years, too, as trade increased with Asian countries, a number of "friendship" societies were formed, whose focus was on profit however much they might be tricked out with cultural finery. To them gravitated businessmen with prewar or wartime connections in some Asian area or other, as well as an assortment of people, academic or otherwise, with an interest in foreign countries.

As far as Japanese universities were concerned, a few scholars of ancient history, religion, or linguistics of South or Southeast Asia thrived, but scholarly work in more recent history or in the social sciences was meager. In those fields the Japanese were to learn primarily from what Americans and Europeans had written, a debt that continues to the present day. The poverty of serious research on Southeast Asia was due primarily to the almost total absence of prestige attaching to such work in Japan. Southeast Asian studies were suspect on at least three grounds: to most professors anything contemporary was useless by definition; Southeast Asian cultures were minor and uninteresting; and Asia for scholarly purposes traditionally meant China. It followed that anyone undertaking to specialize on Southeast Asia must be either a dolt or a reactionary in the service of the Japanese government's allegedly nefarious goals in that part of the world.[27] A few scholars were courageous and far-sighted enough to criticize this situation. For example, in late 1958 a young anthropologist at

Tokyo University, Miss Chie Nakane, published an article attacking Japanese intellectuals' ignorance of actual conditions of life in Asia and their tendency to build elaborate theories about the area rather than to study it empirically. She had spent several years in field work in India and was struck by her colleagues' preference for European culture, which she felt had left Japan a kind of Asian orphan.[28]

Other intellectuals were less concerned with Japanese ignorance of Southeast Asia than with what they conceived to be the reappearance of the "ugly Japanese" in the area during the mid-1950s:

In the late autumn of 1956 a Japanese novelist enroute to a writers conference in New Delhi, made certain private observations about the other Japanese passengers in the airplane as it flew westward over the Indian Ocean. Most of the passengers were Westerners, but five of them were his fellow countrymen. His seat companion was a Japanese trading company employee, at most 26 or 27, who was going to India to make contracts for orders. The novelist approved of the young merchant, and felt that such ventures were "reassuring." He was delighted, too, by the mission of another passenger, a technician of the Japan National Railway Corporation, who was on his way to provide "aftercare" for locomotives purchased by the Indian government. The third Japanese was a foreign correspondent of a Tokyo newspaper who had just been assigned to Egypt, and who amused the novelist by complaining that "although he knew nothing about the situation, he would have to file his first dispatch on the day he arrived in Cairo." The fourth passenger, a bank employee, was a member of the party of a Japanese bank director, who was on a business trip to Europe. While the director traveled first class, his assistant had been relegated to tourist along with the novelist and the others.

The fifth and last Japanese was on his way to a remote district of Pakistan, "said to be extremely barbaric but not dangerous," to buy jute. This man was physically rather overbearing, with thick eyebrows, large eyes and nose; and around his already fat waist he had strapped a money belt stuffed, as the novelist remarked, "with more bills than I had ever seen before." After the plane took off from Bangkok he produced a bottle of rye whiskey "of unknown ingredients," which he passed to the neighboring passengers. The novelist found it too raw for his throat, but "the 'jute-buying general' soon felt livelier and began to make a speech in a loud voice. The plane was filled with white people; but he tore off his necktie, stripped off his shirt, kicked off his shoes, and I thought would give the impression that here was the Japanese male." Soon he began upbraiding the bank clerk "because his bank was not helping the expansion of Japanese trade. I tried to think of some way to stop him, but he got so excited that I was afraid he would start singing the 'Warship March' next, and I was torn completely to pieces by the experience." Instead of singing, however, the businessman soon was snoring loudly in his seat. When the plane touched down at Calcutta the novelist woke him with mild warnings about his overindulgence; but he merely slapped his money-belt with his hand and replied: "They don't drink in Pakistan."

The novelist was left with mixed feelings about his fellow passengers. On the one hand he was glad to see them setting out with some magnanimity, as he thought, to help understand and solve the problems of the poverty of Asia. "When I came back to Japan two years after the war," he wrote, "I liked to see freight trains. Wherever they were going they were helping to relieve the miseries of life during that period. Now I felt much the same way toward my fellow countrymen, who were going out to all parts of Asia. Because Asia's basic problem is poverty and oppression; and thus the patriotism of a Japanese abroad was born in me." Yet at the same time he was disturbed by the behavior of the drunken businessman. When the plane doors opened at Calcutta and the other Japanese passengers made noisily for the exit, the novelist decided that the rough behavior of one of them had affected them all and created a poor impression on the other passengers: "It reminded me of China during the war, when a group of Japanese military would come down the stairs of a restaurant and make for the door. And I wondered, unhappily, whether that same 'jute-buying general' had not behaved in the same way during the war in Burma or thereabouts. He was very generous with his harsh whiskey, but I was not very happy about the whole affair." [29]

This passage from a sensitive novelist's travel record revealed how pervasive the memory of the war still was more than a decade after it had ended and how behavior patterns even slightly reminiscent of the military period could produce sharp anxiety in the

Japanese spirit. The passage also clearly indicated something of the breadth and diversity of the Japanese outreach by 1957 or thereabouts, when reparations payments were getting underway. It was hardly surprising that a certain number of "jute-buying generals" headed for Southeast Asia with their money belts full. So did their Western, not to mention their Russian and Chinese, counterparts. But such crude types were already outnumbered and lost in the generality of bank clerks, businessmen, technical consultants, scientists, economists, journalists, politicians, and other Japanese, young and old, who were returning to Asia or going there for the first time, and who reflected the diversity of contemporary Japanese society and its interests, as well as the interests of other Asians in allowing them to come.

The flow of travelers released by reparations became a wave after government decisions in the mid-1950s to promote economic diplomacy. As official tours by Japanese leaders grew more frequent, their tenor changed. In 1954 Premier Yoshida had returned from an official visit to Southeast Asia with the observation that "you have to trade with rich men; you can't trade with beggars." But in 1957 the new Premier, Nobusuke Kishi, made two tours of his own, visiting twelve countries in a far more determined attempt to improve relations than Yoshida had ever made.

Behind these new initiatives lay the need to balance the trade account, which had been in deficit with the United States ever since the Occupation. Trade balances with Southeast Asia also were unfavorable in 1955 and 1956. Kishi and the men around him were determined to take advantage of their new-found political unity to move the economy vigorously forward and to enhance Japanese influence wherever possible. The steel industry required large quantities of iron ore if production targets set in the economic plans were to be achieved. Eighty per cent of Japan's iron had to be imported, but only a portion of it could be had from the West. Communist China was an uncertain source, and Chinese exports were of unpredictable quality. The Philippines and Malaya were still good sources of iron, but reserves in both countries were limited. Japan's steel manufacturers began to look beyond Southeast Asia to India, where, in Goa, and more importantly, in eastern India, were located large reserves of high quality iron ore.

The exploitation of Indian iron was linked with a broader concern that Japan not be shut out of the Indian market in the future. Tokyo businessmen and government officials already had their eyes on India's economic plans. They saw widening European and American participation in assisting India, and they recognized the paramount importance of the Western role in Indian development. They also were not unaware of the formidable cultural and linguistic barriers that stood between Japanese and Indians. No two people could have been more unlike or more mutually impenetrable. Few underestimated the difficulties of operating in India, and all who wrote of the Japanese there were driven to stress the frustrations and bafflements on both sides. But by 1957 Japanese textiles were being shut out of the Indian market, and some saw the day not far off when other of their exports would be excluded. Partly at Indian urging, committees were established to study long-range problems of Indo-Japanese economic cooperation and promote exchange of information. Japanese businessmen urged the government to push plant exports to India and to help them to establish factories behind Indian tariff walls.

Kishi took up these matters with Prime Minister Nehru in New Delhi, and in October 1957 Nehru visited Tokyo to work out terms for a credit that would make them possible. Because Japan had concluded no general trade agreement with India since the war, the negotiations led, in February 1958, to the signing of a comprehensive agreement, providing for most-favored-nation treatment; and a second agreement was signed extending a yen credit worth $50 million to India, repayable in ten years at prevalent World Bank interest rates. A few weeks later a government-sponsored mission reached agreement with the Indian government for Japanese participation in a scheme to develop iron mines in the Rourkela district of Orissa, near India's east coast. Of an estimated $33 million required for the project, Japan would lend India about $8 million in rolling stock, mining machinery, and harbor facilities; the Indian government was supposed to ask the remainder from the United States. Once production was underway, Japan would have an assured supply of at least two million tons of ore annually for ten years.[30]

The yen credit to India was the first such credit to be extended by Japan in the postwar period and the first concrete result of Japan's new economic diplomacy.[31] The credit was to be used within three years for the import of Japanese equipment for both the public and private sectors. About 90 per cent of the funds had been so used by August 1961, for electrical machinery, coal washeries, vehicles and road building machines, communications equipment, and an assortment of small industrial plants. To install this machinery and help Indians operate it, Japanese technicians went to India for the first time since 1945.

The yen credit and the iron ore agreement were opposed by the Finance Ministry in Tokyo on the grounds that Japan had its own balance-of-payments difficulties and that a credit to India would surely lead to demands from other countries for the same treatment, which would then be more difficult to refuse. Throughout the period under review Finance Ministry officials were at odds with Japanese diplomats over the issue of such credits and other forms of aid. As an American official said, one could "tell it from the difference in their eyes" at international conferences. But the prevailing view in favor of the credit was expressed by an official of the Ministry of International Trade and Industry, who wrote:

It is high time that Japan made big strides in her economic cooperation with these nations in spite of whatever investment risks might be involved. Otherwise, it would almost be a certainty that the advanced Western countries would sweep the whole Asian region with their stronger competitive power. An agreement with each of the Asian countries should be concluded at the earliest possible date. Extension of loans would result in an increased inflow of our capital goods and techniques to the country and contribute toward the expansion of the Japanese economic sphere in this part of the world.[32]

This well expressed the hopeful mood that prevailed in Tokyo toward Asia at that time. The Indian credit was regarded by Export-Import Bank of Japan officials as a purely political move, a model engineered at the highest level by Kishi and Nehru and indicative of Japan's wish not to be left at the post by the Western nations in the competition for prestige and profit in India. The Foreign Ministry had its usual reasons for supporting the development of Indian iron ore resources and asking for American collaboration in the project. As one Ministry official remarked, "If the United States doesn't help with Rourkela, the other side will, and this we must prevent." And the *Asahi Shimbun*, in a lead editorial, put its own characteristically proud interpretation on the transaction: "The development of iron ore resources in India will demonstrate to other Southeast Asian countries one way in which Japan's industrial power and technique can cooperate in the exploitation of resources. The smooth operation of the current project will undoubtedly have a widespread and beneficial effect on international relations as a whole." [33]

The Japanese competitive advantage in plant and machinery exports seemed substantial, if high quality could be maintained and old prejudices against Japanese merchandise finally overcome. What was less clear was the capacity of the importing countries to pay for the goods with the kind and quantity of primary materials Japan wanted. The Japanese market for such materials was huge and was becoming global in dimensions. India alone could never supply all, or even the principal part, of the iron ore Japan needed. In fact, imports of iron resulting from Japanese investment in developing overseas iron ore resources amounted to only about 20 per cent of Japan's total iron ore imports in the late 1950s, and the percentage later fell as total imports of ore rose to more than 30 million tons in 1964.[34] These and other statistics illuminated a fundamental fact: Japan was a developed country trading primarily with other developed countries. This fact was later to cause discouragement to those "Asia firsters" who exaggerated the prospects of trade and economic diplomacy in Asia in the latter part of the 1950s. Japan's trade with Asia of course grew, but its trade with the United States grew more. In 1967 imports from America were $3.2 billion; from all of Southeast Asia, $1.8 billion.[35] Likewise, direct Japanese investment in all of Southeast Asia was only two-thirds of that in North America and less than that in Latin America.

In 1957 and 1958, however, there was clearly a rising interest in new economic relationships with non-Communist Asia. Economic diplomacy became the third slogan of the government's foreign policy, along with support of the U. S. alliance and the United Nations. Kishi himself called for creation of an Asian Development Fund that would combine American capital, Japanese goods and skills, and Southeast Asian labor and resources in a sort of triangular arrangement for the development of the area.[36] New friendship societies and "Asian associations" as well as government bureaus and other agencies concerned with economic cooperation proliferated. The Finance Ministry, which passed on foreign investments, the Economic Planning Board, which wrote national plans, the Ministry of International Trade and Industry (MITI) and the Foreign Ministry all laid claim to their share of control over the flow of Japanese money, people, or machinery overseas. From the mid-1950s on there was talk of a central aid agency patterned after the American model, but most of those in favor of the agency came from outside the government or from the weaker sections of the bureaucracy, such as those concerned with technical assistance. The key bureaucrats themselves appeared content to struggle, as was their custom, to maintain and enlarge their separate budgets and defend their separate ministerial kingdoms. The Premier's office, responding to demands for some kind of coordination, in 1958 set up an advisory council on overseas aid programs; but, like other such councils, this one was mainly honorific and proved moribund almost from the moment of its creation.

The first yen credit was followed by six others to India, worth a total of slightly over $400 million. The last of these, given within the framework of the aid-India consortium in September 1967, was for fertilizers, synthetic textiles, spare parts, and raw materials. Earlier credits were mostly for capital goods; all were tied to purchases in Japan. Interest rates averaged 5.75 per cent, with 10 to 15 years to repay. Between 1958 and 1967 Japanese credit terms improved slightly: by the seventh credit the interest was down to 5.5 per cent, the term up to 18 years. All such credits were administered through the Export-Import Bank of Japan.[37] By April 1967 yen credits had also been extended to Pakistan, Iran, Taiwan, Korea, Ceylon, Malaysia, and elsewhere.

The credits were a major stimulus to Japanese plant exports. Some idea of the extent of the activity they generated is indicated by the great proliferation of private and semi-private organizations set up to promote trade. Nine such organizations were busy in India in 1958: the Japan Plant Export Association (which promoted Japanese assistance in a Bombay subway project), the Indo-Japanese Industrial Cooperation Council, Asia Association, Japan Machinery Export Guild, International Construction Technology Association, International Technical Cooperation Development Company, Overseas Machinery Export Promotion Committee, Japan Export Trade Recovery Organization, and Japan Overseas Industrial Technology Association. Some of these were single-industry bodies, others multi-industry groups; some, like JETRO, were official government organs. Criticizing the confusion produced by so many overlapping and often competing bodies, some Japanese called for a central organization overseas that would consolidate the functions of all of them, supported by the government and dedicated to implementing a unified national policy.[38] However, like the administration of economic cooperation programs at home, Japanese activities abroad remained without centralized organization.

3. PRIVATE BUSINESS ACTIVITIES

Reparations, yen credits, and new trade agreements naturally stimulated private business ventures. Before 1958 there was little Japanese private investment of any kind in Southeast Asia: the total was estimated at about $19 million between 1951 and 1957.[39] Compared with Japanese foreign investment elsewhere, most ventures in Southeast Asia were small-scale, averaging less than $400,000 per investment, of which something more than half represented equity.[40] Included were investments in manufacturing enterprises, in which equity was perhaps three-fourths of the total; natural resource development, in which loans greatly exceeded equity; and a smaller amount of purely commercial investment in warehousing and other service facilities.

All these flows of capital and goods brought Japanese into the area again in substantial numbers, not only in the capital cities but also in the provincial towns. The Japanese language once again was heard in nearly every hotel elevator, tourists bought the local products of renown, and businessmen clustered in hotel lobbies. Japanese advertising again became a part of the urban landscape and was seen in the countryside as well; everything from patent medicines to tractors was advertised in local newspapers, and one began to hear that the Japanese were getting by trade and business what they had failed to get by arms: a new kind of co-prosperity sphere was in the making. At the same time complaints were often heard of Japanese clannishness, inability to communicate, parsimony, and fondness for short-term loans and quick profits. Such comments compounded the dilemma felt by many thoughtful Japanese. For it was difficult enough for Japan, a society at a much more advanced stage of national development than the rest of Asia, to relate intelligently and usefully to the former colonial societies to the south without having to be constantly reminded of past failures or accused of "banker's attitudes" and intrigues reminiscent of the past. If those in Southeast Asia who spoke glibly of a "new co-prosperity sphere" had stopped to consider Japan's most pressing problems in the 1950s and 1960s—the desire for stability during a time of very rapid economic growth; the need for a new consensus on the meaning of representative institutions in an era of very rapid urbanization; political and social tumult; and alienation—they might have realized that the country's greatest need was not for new spheres or blocs but for an open world that would permit it to trade and associate freely with all. Southeast Asians, preoccupied with achieving a degree of basic national unity, might be excused for distrusting Japan for its past record. They might naturally fear Japan's growing economic power or deplore the activities of individual "jute-buying generals." But if they truly believed that Japanese business in the 1950s represented the advance guard of a self-conscious national design to put the area under Japanese guardianship or exploit it for Japan's purposes alone in the old manner, they lacked insight into the nature of Japanese modernity and the extent to which countervailing forces operated within Japanese society. The Japanese were searching for a new national role in Asia; they may have been overcautious and niggardly, but nobody other than a few antiquarians wished to repeat the past.

The kinds of problems faced by Japanese businessmen operating in Southeast Asia revealed the gap in the time-scale of development between the two areas. One analysis of joint ventures in nine countries in the area began with a list of do's and don'ts for those contemplating opening businesses overseas, which may be paraphrased as follows:

1. Make careful preliminary investigations and save grief later.
2. Don't be deceived by a crooked partner. Overseas Chinese may often be the most likely partners, but should be judged with care.
3. Respect the wishes of local people for management control. Japanese may have to take majority control at first, but should relinquish it if so desired by local partners once the business is established.

4. Don't rush the local people in negotiations. Delays must be borne patiently when dealing with local authorities.

5. Send the right people abroad. Those stationed overseas for long periods should learn the local language. Furthermore, when they return from overseas posts, they should be reintegrated into the home organization, not discover that they have lost out in seniority and the competition for responsibility. Japanese businessmen remain at foreign posts for much shorter periods than their American or European counterparts. This often impairs foreign operations, but one of the reasons for this is the fear of losing out at home.

6. Overseas labor relations must be understood. This often means studying religious and social problems. Respect the spirit of the labor laws even though they may not be well enforced by local authorities. Among other things, this involves getting a good local job interviewer for personnel work.

7. Improve training facilities for foreigners in Japan, so that they may return home able to raise the level of the local enterprise from top to bottom. Many foreign employees sent to Japan go back home with less usefulness than they went with.

8. Make sure that techniques suitable to local conditions are introduced into the business. Technological sophistication in Japan does not necessarily mean that any technique can be automatically transferred abroad.

9. Make a careful study of future product demand.

10. To succeed, the business must make a long-range contribution to the economic goals of the host nation. This implies reinvestment of profits.[41]

To help ensure better business results, the report urged that the Japanese government assist in various ways to prepare business surveys, improve the investment guarantee system, look to the education of Japanese children in the Asian tropics, support joint research operations by private Japanese and Southeast Asian economic research bureaus, and encourage more coordination of Japanese research with that of Americans in the area.

This report, in two immensely detailed volumes, was the product of the research staff of the Federation of Economic Organizations (*Keidanren*). Based on questionnaires sent to member firms, it represented the viewpoint of some of the most influential busi-

nessmen in Japan. What was most striking was the similarity between the problems faced by Japanese and those faced by
Americans or Europeans in Southeast Asia. Describing in detail
the investment environment from Pakistan to the Philippines,
the report concluded that private investment prospects were
brightest in Thailand, Malaysia, Singapore, Ceylon, India, and
Pakistan, and most dubious in Burma, South Vietnam, Laos,
Cambodia, the Philippines, and Indonesia. The two latter, it
noted, might improve in the near future (Japanese reports had
been saying that for many years). Much detail on the political
and economic life of the region was included, but problems were
stressed, such as the perils of not making exhaustive preinvestment
inquiries and the difficulties of making them in places where data
were scarce or unreliable or where there were language and other
barriers. The high cost of leasable land for factory construction
was lamented; the need for patience urged in regard to time in
"the southern countries," where Japanese speed could often become a liability, and slow-but-steady was the best policy.

Other problems concerned the lack of entrepreneurial spirit
abroad and the limitations of a local partner, who knew how to
get licenses and deal with the local bureaucracy, but who might
also have a tendency to put his relatives on the payroll. Local
partners could use their influence to borrow from local banks,
which were often preferable to branches of Japanese banks that
might require 100 per cent guarantees from the home company
in Tokyo. The effects of caste on work efficiency were noted, as
well as the tendency of local employees who were trained in
Japan to sell their new skills to other employers upon their return. Language problems recurred; they run like a leitmotif through
every study of the Japanese abroad. The report analyzed wage
and labor problems, as well as problems connected with the import of raw materials for plants located abroad, excessive competition among Japanese companies in a limited market in some
countries, the absence of a market in others, the torpor of the
Tokyo bureaucracy, and so on.

In manufacturing ventures, difficulties were found in market surveys and product distribution; raw material supply, production and fabricating processes, funding, and labor problems also needed constant attention. In mining and raw material exploitation, labor conditions were often the main problem. In remote areas, workers were scarce, illiterate, turbulent, or, in some cases, primitive peoples like the Manobos of Mindanao, who were known to have killed timber operatives encroaching upon their traditional territories.[42]

Cases illustrating the problems of setting up a Japanese enterprise abroad in the 1950s were not difficult to find. In 1958 I reported the following:

One of the most interesting Japanese ventures in India is the Asahi Glass Company's investment in an Indian glass-making concern. The experience of this company may throw some light on the practical problems the Japanese face in operating in Southeast Asia today.

Asahi Glass is one of the largest plate glass makers in Japan. In 1954 Asahi Glass participated in international bidding for management and sales of an Indian glass firm in Bihar, which had gone bankrupt and had been taken over by the Indian Finance Corporation. Asahi won the bidding and acquired the plant in July 1955 for 486 million yen, repayable in 17 years at 3.5 per cent interest per annum. Asahi's investment was made not in cash but in the form of equipment and knowhow. The India-Asahi Glass Company began operations under a Japanese president in May 1957 as a wholly-owned Japanese subsidiary. Its monthly production now is 20,000 cases of sheet glass, the largest single operation of the type in India. The parent company in Japan believes that demand for glass products will rise steadily as the Five Year Plan progresses. They also plan to market their glass products in the Middle East, with India as a base. However, talks with management in Tokyo reveal some peculiar difficulties. [These were later confirmed by conversations with management in Calcutta.]

In the first place, they say, it is quite impossible for a Japanese accustomed to the small scale of distances at home to grasp the physical vastness of India. "India is not a country but a continent." Great distances mean long hauls for certain raw materials, but there are seldom enough freight cars, and the railroads have a disconcerting habit of changing gauges from area to area. Loading and unloading facilities are inadequate, and work of this type goes on only sporadically. Full freight cars may stand idle on sidings for weeks, instead of being unloaded when they are needed. Sources and quality of sand, coal and feldspar, as well as other raw materials, are uncertain; many other ingredients must be imported now or in the near future.

Apart from such physical inconveniences there are numerous human problems. Asahi sent 40 engineers to Bihar in 1956, and today 20 remain. Before leaving Japan they attended indoctrination lectures on Indian customs, religion, and so on. However, caste divisions still baffle the Japanese engineers. Orders in the factory may involve relays through various levels, in the course of which original instructions may be garbled beyond recognition. On this point Japanese management believes that Japan is a far freer society than India, much less bound by social discrimination. Above all, there is an obvious shortage of technically trained personnel on the spot. The Bihar plant of India-Asahi employs 700 people in its shops and offices. Of these, management estimates that 90 per cent are illiterate. Those Indian engineers who are trained are, from the Japanese point of view, "migratory," that is, they are in such demand that they move from job to job wherever they can make the most money. To Japanese, who are accustomed to work all their lives for one company, and who put loyalty to the company above most other values, such behavior is incomprehensible, and makes it difficult for the Japanese to want to train the Indian personnel further. As the Asahi official who was in charge of setting up the Indian plant said to me, "Why should we pay for bringing Indian engineers to Japan and training them, when they will go back and immediately leave our company? If they are not loyal to the company they are a bad investment."

On a broader scale the difficulties of the India-Asahi Company reflect some of the basic problems of Indian industrialization. In Japan light industries developed first, along with the transportation network, the power grid, and a national program of education for the new industrial labor force. All of this process, which went on over a long period of years, came at a time when world trade was still relatively free and raw materials relatively abundant and accessible. Today many of these conditions have changed. Unindustrialized countries have farther to catch up, and they believe that they have less time. The Japanese say that Indians "want to have heavy industry overnight" and feel when they say it that Japan, for all its relative poverty vis-à-vis the industrial West, is far advanced when compared with the still agricultural East.[43]

4. REPARATIONS PAYMENTS BEGIN

Burma. Payments to Burma began in 1955, and consisted primarily of transport equipment (buses, small cars, and rolling stock), "raw materials" (including many consumer goods), and the Balu Chaung hydroelectric power plant. This project, located in Shan territory in the Kayah State about midway between Rangoon and Mandalay, was designed to supply electricity to both cities. It has been called the single most important industrial achievement in postwar Burma, and it introduced, or reintroduced, into that country an interesting Japanese type, the construction engineer.

The idea for the project was conceived in 1953, when Yutaka Kubota, a consulting engineer who had been involved in building hydroelectric plants on the Yalu River between Korea and Manchuria before the war, visited Burma to seek opportunities for his reorganized company, Nippon Kōei. Kubota had collected engineers with prewar experience in this firm, which was about to move into South Vietnam, Indonesia, and elsewhere on the heels of reparations. Technicians like Kubota, whose careers had been spent abroad, could be put to the service of diverse political ends. At one time they had served the Empire; now their skills were to be used to build productive monuments in less-developed countries and spread Japanese machinery and contracts throughout Southeast Asia.[44] Kubota was retained by the Burma Electricity Supply Board. He contracted with the Kajima Construction Company, one of the largest Tokyo building concerns, which, in turn, made further contracts with Japanese suppliers of equipment, establishing a pattern that was to became familiar in many reparations-financed projects throughout the area. The first stage of the plant, inaugurated in March 1960, was proof that Japanese engineers and equipment could hold their own in heavy construction projects under difficult climatic, logistic, and political conditions.[45]

Apart from Balu Chaung, Japanese reparations were used by different Burmese regimes to further the objectives of the moment or to meet their most pressing economic needs. Until early 1962, consumer goods were imported to help stabilize prices at a time when domestic production had not returned to prewar levels and the collapse of the rice price had caused a foreign-exchange crisis in Rangoon. Thus, imports of rayon cloth, galvanized iron sheets for roofing, canned fish, and a few luxury items such as pool tables and hi-fi sets were charged against reparations by the U Nu government. When General Ne Win took over for the second time, in March 1962, his regime nationalized virtually all businesses, foreign-connected or not, including the import trade. He and his army associates proclaimed "military socialism" and rigid neutralism for Burma, and reparations priorities were shifted to truck-assembly plants and plants for making electrical and other machinery under government operation and control.

Japanese reparations amounted to a major share of total foreign aid to Burma: in 1956–57 they were 39.8 per cent; in 1957–58, 53.6 per cent; in 1960–61, 75.2 per cent; and in 1961–62, 65.8 per cent.[46] These figures reflected the shrinkage of other sources of aid. Reparations were important for achieving price stability, but, aside from Balu Chaung, it was hard to see that any enduring monument to Japan's atonement for the war would remain when they had all been paid. Even before Ne Win's accession to power, Burma had been an exasperation and an enigma to the Japanese. Imports of rice from Burma fell sharply in the late 1950s as Japanese harvests set records and eating habits also began to change. Exports to Burma rose slightly but were insignificant in Japan's total trade; in Burma's trade, however, Japan rivaled England as the principal source of imports. No particular animosity remained between the two peoples because of the war, nor was there any particular closeness. Some educated Burmese liked to describe the Japanese as Westernized heretics who had betrayed their Asian heritage; but, to the Japanese, Burma was simply inaccessible and hence tended to be overlooked among their more pressing concerns. Burmese reparations were extended and supplemented by $140 million in 1965. Japanese importers continued to be interested in Burmese iron and antimony, but contact with the country was slight.

The Philippines. No productive monument comparable to Balu Chaung was built with reparations in the Philippines. As in Burma, the goods poured in, to be used by successive administrations in differing ways, but with the same general result of dispersal. The Japanese government might privately deplore this state of affairs, but it had no control over the goods once they were authorized and arrived on the scene and had no intention of taking the blame for their misuse.

The Reparations Agreement with the Philippines became effective in July 1956. In the following nine years the yen equivalent of about $180 million was disbursed and charged against reparations for goods ordered by the Philippines in Japan. Such goods included fourteen merchant vessels; a quantity of rolling stock, automobiles, and trucks; a Presidential yacht; two floating canneries; thirty-four fishing vessels, some of them expensively equipped; four dredges; eight tugboats; sawmills and plants for making cement, paper, ceramic ware, and textiles; glass-bottle and food-processing plants; auto repair shops; refrigeration equipment; plywood-making equipment; and other production goods, as well as a small amount of consumer goods, mainly canned food for the National Marketing Corporation.

About a third of all reparations goods went to the public sector, the rest into private hands. Policy on sector use fluctuated: in the first year everything went to the government, but private interests soon rallied to take advantage of reparations. The terms on which goods were provided to Filipino end-users were generous: nonprofit government agencies got them free; others in government or in the private sector were able to obtain goods with down payments as low as 5 per cent plus a 2 per cent service fee, with the balance to be paid over 10 years for machinery or 20 years for ocean-going vessels, at 3 per cent interest.

The Reparations Law passed by the Philippine Congress to regulate the program required that all goods fit into over-all economic development plans as decided by the National Economic Council, which was supposed to set priorities and report them to a Reparations Mission in Tokyo, which would authorize the goods to be secured from the Japanese side. Pesos received by the Philippine government in payment for reparations goods were to go into an economic development fund. From the beginning, the program was beset by corruption and rumors of corruption and was treated in both Manila and Tokyo as a scandal and a joke. Acquisition of the goods by Filipinos afforded numerous opportunities for private gain. For example, no provision was made in either the agreement or the Reparations Law for public bidding on goods to be supplied to private users. Such users were allowed to deal directly with Japanese manufacturers, reach mutually agreeable terms, and present these for approval to the Philippine Reparations Mission in Tokyo. The Mission was empowered to alter such arrangements only in cases where Philippine citizens said their interests had been abused or thwarted. Far from complaining to their own Mission, however, Filipinos who had arranged private terms with Japanese manufacturers were accused by the Manila press of receiving kickbacks and conspiring with Japanese deliberately to overprice reparations goods. Since no foreign exchange was earned by reparations, the Japanese government tended to look leniently on its own merchants in dealings of this sort. This situation meant that a profit could often be made on reparations contracts even before the goods had been shipped. Once they had reached Manila they might go undelivered for months or might never be delivered but left on the government's hands to rust on the docks or be reassigned from one "end-user" to another in the search for someone who had the funds and the desire to assemble the machinery and put it to use.[47]

The administration of reparations brought out some of the worst qualities in Philippine public life, and the whole program was scarcely designed to inspire probity in the Japanese. Some reparations projects remained unfulfilled for many years. A good example was the extension of the Manila Railroad from San José in Tarlac province to Tuguegarao in the Cagayan Valley of northern Luzon. Originally supposed to have been financed with Japanese loans secured by reparations, this project was pushed by some Philippine presidents, dropped by others. Some politicians favored a "Friendship Highway" to the north that would generate local contracts for a large share of total costs, whereas the railroad would be built primarily with imported materials. The Japanese regarded the idea of building a railroad into the backward north of Luzon, where there was little power or other resources, as ill-judged in the first place. The Manila Railroad Company was in notoriously poor financial shape: it was estimated that not more than 40 per cent of its passengers paid fares. More than $5 million loaned by Japan to the Philippines for preliminary work on the project was by agreement partially diverted to other sections of the railroad. But whatever the project's future, like the long-discussed but never built Marikina Dam, it illustrated a basic fact about the Philippines; namely, that politicians intervened continually and often balefully in economic decisions.

Nevertheless, the contribution of reparations to the Philippine economy, even in the early years of payment, was not entirely negligible, even if scattered. Reparations were estimated to average 20 to 25 per cent of annual Philippine expenditure on infrastructure. The $85 million worth of ships re-created a small merchant navy and made possible shipment of increasing quantities of other reparations goods in Philippine bottoms. While some private end-users had no real entrepreneurial purpose but merely sought quick profits from reparations contracts, others put their goods to use to manufacture cement, glass, textiles, and other products. Reparations failed in the sense that they were not used to further an over-all plan of economic development, any more than they were in Burma. Given the nature of Philippine politics and the country's stage of national development, it was naïve to suppose that they might have been used systematically. But this is not the same thing as saying that they were without positive effect.

One definite effect was an increase in the number of Japanese businessmen going to the Philippines or desiring to go there. This, in turn, led to negotiations for a Treaty of Friendship, Commerce and Navigation that would allow for more normal commercial and other interchange. Such a treaty was signed on December 19, 1960, and was ratified by the Japanese Diet soon afterward, but it had not been acted on by the Philippine Senate at the time of this writing. Signing of the treaty stirred strong fears of Japanese economic penetration. Many Filipinos felt it might lead to an invasion of Japanese capital, whereas a Filipino counterinvasion of Japan was obviously out of the question. Guarantees of most-favored-nation treatment with respect to travel and residence of Japanese were also considered too generous, even though the question of permanent residence was specifically excluded from the treaty.

The chief Philippine delegate in the treaty negotiations, José P. Laurel, Jr., whose father had been President of the puppet Philippine Republic during the war, replied to critics that since this was the first such treaty signed by the Philippines, and since Japan was likely to receive the smallest concessions of any country with whom the Philippines might conceivably deal, the treaty would reduce to a minimum subsequent problems of most-favored-nation treatment for other nationals. He also stressed that the treaty should be one of "amity," not "friendship," since the Philippines could not bring itself to use the latter word with reference to Japan. But Laurel's disingenuous arguments had little effect; they may even have raised suspicions higher, and the treaty was very soon another political issue inflaming nationalistic feelings in Manila. Various laws were introduced in the Philippine Senate to remedy its weaknesses, and some were passed. Japanese businessmen resumed quasi-normal relationships in the absence of specific legal prohibitions, but they lacked the legal sanctions that a treaty would allow them to invoke, and their activities in the Philippines rested on an uncertain base.

Unable to open branch offices, and lacking legal incentives to invest, they nevertheless went about exploiting raw materials and selling goods with their usual vigor. Philippine dependence on Japan as a market steadily increased as America's importance declined, and Japanese loans began to flow into the country. Japan's share of Philippine exports, 10 per cent in 1952, rose to 25 per cent in 1961; and Filipinos who realized that their country's preferential position in the American market was scheduled to disappear in 1974 began to admit that closer ties with Japan were inevitable. Imports of logs from the Philippines in 1959 were more than half of Japan's total log imports, and they were at least 80 per cent of Philippine log exports. In 1960 Japan's imports of metal ores (principally iron and chrome) were a quarter of Japan's total imports of such commodities, but Japan took nearly all of Philippine ore shipments. The United States remained the largest Philippine market, and the Philippine preference for American goods continued strong, while Japanese brand names were relatively unknown. But Philippine entrepreneurs were buying cheap Japanese tools and machinery, and the Japanese were focusing on such competitive lines as vehicles, agricultural machinery, textiles, and electrical goods. Shrewd Japanese could make much money in this growing market; and it was interesting to watch the return of familiar names to the area, where they often had to operate on short-term visas behind unmarked doors or in the offices of their Filipino associates or dummies. The big trading companies, Mitsui, Mitsubishi, and the rest, were soon very active. Marubeni-Iida, a postwar mutation of the old Daidō

Trading Company, which had abaca plantations in Mindanao before the war, by 1961 handled about 15 per cent of the Japan-Philippine trade. At the same time the Philippines was only one country in Japan's global network of suppliers and a small country at that; and Japanese trading company executives expressed concern over the long-range future of the Philippine trade. Iron ore reserves were being exhausted; and logs, too, the largest export item, would not last forever in view of the low state of reforestation. By the early 1960s Japanese log buyers were looking beyond Mindanao to Sabah, Indonesian Borneo, and elsewhere. Philippine resources were rich, but they were not inexhaustible.

Indonesia. Before reparations payments began in 1958, Japan had not been extensively involved in Indonesia since World War II, in spite of much commercial interest. The country was regarded as the largest potential market and richest source of raw materials in Southeast Asia; but, like the Philippines, Indonesia severely restricted Japanese residence and granted visas capriciously. The memory of the wartime occupation was vivid, attitudes toward the Japanese ambivalent, the political situation confused and turbulent. Trade debts with Japan accumulated steadily after 1952. The Japanese, however ambivalent their own feelings toward their country's wartime role, were allergic to reappearing in the guise of exploiters. At the Bandung Conference in 1955 Tatsunosuke Takasaki noted the presence of several hundred Japanese in Indonesia left over from the war. He thought Japan might expect good things from them in the future, but like other stragglers in the area few were people of significance in the total picture of the country's relations. By 1956 there were perhaps 80 Japanese business representatives in Djakarta on short-term visas. But up to 1958 only one Japanese company was reported to have extended any substantial commercial credits in Indonesia.[48]

Reparations payments were applied primarily to ships and other capital projects, not to consumer goods, although quantities of the latter were also requested and shipped. (The Japanese in principle disapproved of sending consumer goods, which would hurt normal exports at a time when mainland China was cutting into the market for Japanese light manufactured goods. However, sending textiles to Indonesia in 1958 had the effect of reducing stocks and holding up textile prices at home.) With the forced withdrawal of the Dutch merchant fleet, merchant ships were a prime Indonesian need, and ten vessels, five of them new and the others refurbished, were included in the first year's agreement.[49] More merchant vessels followed in subsequent years; twenty-four had been provided by 1963. In addition, between 1958 and 1963, Japan supplied Indonesia with five dredgers and six other vessels, three paper manufacturing plants (one in north Sumatra, one in Celebes, one in Borneo), a plywood and veneer plant (in Borneo), three cotton spinning plants (two in Java, one in Bali), a battery plant (Java), and a bamboo-pulp paper plant (Java). Other items included a fertilizer factory, a chemical plant, railroad and road equipment, earth movers, trucks, and smaller vehicles. Reparations goods and technical services also were supplied for a river development project in East Java, involving dams, diversion tunnels, and other hydraulic works.[50]

A provision not found in the agreements with Burma and the Philippines called for training of Indonesian students and factory apprentices to a combined total of some 2,250 people for long periods in Japan, and a center for these students was built in Tokyo. A whole panoply of problems arose from this provision. Differences in climate and life-style created formidable difficulties for Indonesians who went to Japan. The students complained that they were segregated at a university outside Tokyo. They had serious problems learning the Japanese language from teachers who were not always interested or sympathetic. There were disputes over curriculum and teaching methods, living allowances for students, and the like. Nothing brought out the difference between Japan and Southeast Asia better than this student program, which continues today and continues to be a problem. Like most such programs, the idea behind it was filled with merit. Through the program Indonesians could learn Japanese skills, Japanese could train cadres who would help Indonesian development and at the same time identify to some extent with Japan throughout life. But those who sometimes jumped to the conclusion that because Japan had modernized, Japan could be used as a model with little modification by other countries should ponder the difficulties experienced by the foreign student program in Tokyo. Perhaps these difficulties were summed up best in the remark of one Indonesian student: "The Japanese have worked hard. But who wants to work as hard as the Japanese?"

These programs were paid for by reparations *per se*. In addition, the Japanese government agreed to facilitate loans totaling $400 million by private Japanese citizens to either the Indonesian government or its private citizens. However, the Japanese had been burned before by experience with Indonesian trade debts and had no intention of risking any sizable loans as long as political and economic conditions were so unpredictable. Reparations payments coincided with the brief ascendancy of Sukarno and his "guided democracy," an era characterized by overblown development schemes, economic decay, and political feverishness. Foreign currency balances evaporated, large foreign loans were sought from East and West, and "neutralist" Indonesia became a hunting ground for competing ideologies. Japanese businessmen had a reputation for taking risks, but the government was more cautious where Indonesia was concerned: the Export-Import Bank granted a few medium-term credits on a selective basis, but there was no desire to risk investing in a deteriorating situation. In the late 1950s Sukarno constantly requested loans from Tokyo to be secured by reparations, but without success.

However, Japan wanted oil, logs, nickel, and other resources, which were beyond the ability of the Indonesians alone to exploit. Normal Indonesian exports to Japan were tiny and the trade was lopsided: in 1960 Japan imported $45 million worth of goods from Indonesia and exported $104 million worth. To help get out the resources with what appeared to be minimal financial risk and at the same time to satisfy the economic nationalism of the Indonesians, an arrangement for "production-sharing" was devised between the two governments in 1960–61, affecting the three commodities mentioned. The Japanese government agreed to lend Permina, the Indonesian government's oil corporation, a total of more than $50 million over 10 years. In June 1960 the Japanese government and a consortium of Japanese companies set up the North Sumatra Oil Development Company (NOSODECO) to exploit old Shell installations destroyed or damaged repeatedly during and after the war. NOSODECO supplied equipment and technical assistance; Permina agreed to discharge the loan with shipments of 40 per cent of production after reserving a basic amount annually with a total scheduled repayment of 5.8 million kiloliters. By the end of August 1968 the Japanese had furnished about 70 per cent of their pledges and had received about half of the total repayment in crude oil. Agreements for exploitation of nickel and timber followed a similar pattern; the nickel agreement envisaged the possibility of eventually building a smelter in Celebes to process the ore.

Reparations encouraged the same structural changes in Japanese exports to Indonesia that were seen in trade with the whole area: producer's goods rose, and light manufactures declined. The terms of residence for Japanese visitors also improved, and they accordingly grew in number. Reparations projects were very unevenly fulfilled, lagging far behind schedule, often to the frustration of Japanese engineers in remote billets. Corruption in Indonesia equaled or exceeded that in the Philippines. Japanese business interests, usually in close coordination with the Liberal Democratic party and the Tokyo central bureaucracy, pushed ahead with their personal connections in Indonesia. They cultivated Sukarno in appropriate ways, entertaining him and his entourage during his regular visits to Tokyo. He represented continuity with the wartime occupation, and Indonesia was full of rich plums if the orchard were ever put in order. Some Japanese recalled their country's role in stimulating the anti-Dutch liberation movement and stressed supposed cultural similarities between the two peoples. Indonesians, unlike Filipinos, were said to share Buddhist values and physically to resemble Japanese more than other Southeast Asians. Islam was called a "thin veneer."

There was a good deal of wishful thinking in these views. Reparations to all three countries, Burma, the Philippines, and Indonesia, were paid while those countries were being run by politicians more skilled at tearing down the past than at building the future. The virulent nationalism that was the trademark of Sukarno and his era of charismatic spellbinding exploited reparations even as it fed on anti-Japanese feelings among the people. Indonesia was still in the age of the monument builders. In the traffic circles of Djakarta the people were presented with Socialist-realist images of their own dreams of grandeur and freedom from servitude. Meanwhile, they and their problems multiplied, rice production could not keep pace, the plantations decayed further. Japan had much to give and much to gain from Indonesia. At one time the Japanese had been regarded as deliverers from the Dutch, and this was remembered by many: it was Japanese who had made Dutchmen sweep the streets of Djakarta. But these memories were mixed with others of the military occupation that were less pleasant to recall. The Japanese were distrusted, and Indonesian development was a world problem.

Some Japanese, of course, would try to do business even under the worst of circumstances. In 1955 the Daiwa Bank, a commercial concern, approached the Bank of Tokyo for funds to set up a joint enterprise with Chinese partners in Djakarta. The Bank of Tokyo refused, but Daiwa found funds elsewhere; and in February 1956, before the Sukarno regime had totally excluded foreign investment, formed the Perdania Bank, with resources of $1.25 million. Nominally, the Japanese side owned 49 per cent, the Indonesian side 51 per cent; but the latter represented a dollar loan from the Japanese, to be repaid from dividends. Behind this interesting little venture was a trading company, Ishihara

Sangyō, which had interests in Indonesia before the war. Ishihara, a client of the Daiwa Bank, was interested in exploiting copper resources in central Java. However, the venture failed to thrive for several reasons. The Indonesians had no intention of allowing Ishihara to invest in the exploitation of their copper mines. The only arrangement they would countenance was production-sharing, which involved no foreign equity. Overseas Chinese interests were being pushed to the wall at this time, and the Japanese found themselves with partners who were accused of being in league with the opposition Masjumi party. Other Japanese trading companies, rivals of Ishihara, fearing that they would give away commercial secrets if they banked at Perdania, refused to deposit there. Inflation grew more acute, while the Indonesian government tightened the noose around all foreign business operations. Instead of becoming a bridgehead for Japanese investment in resource development, Perdania became a small-time commercial bank for purely local operations and was regarded as a kind of orphan by the Japanese in Djakarta.

After the Indonesian confrontation with Malaysia in 1963–64, Western aid to the country virtually came to an end, and Soviet credits also dwindled. But the Japanese were reluctant to give up their stake altogether. The government, especially the Foreign Ministry, believed that if all credits were cut off, the drift to the left would be accelerated. Suppliers' credits continued to be given in small amounts for consumer goods and motor vehicles until the attempted coup of September 1965. In December of that year Japan cut off export insurance on shipments to Indonesia. No further bank loans were possible, and Japanese companies were left stranded. Business on a cash basis alone continued.

5. New Moves Toward Economic Cooperation

In the first half of the 1960s most Japanese continued to show little interest in giving aid to underdeveloped countries in quantities larger than was required to satisfy Western, meaning principally American, pressure for such aid. Responsible circles perceived that their fate was linked with the dollar, which must be defended, if necessary, by enlarging Japan's aid share to some extent. But there was a lack of faith in the efficacy of aid, which was only confirmed by the wastage in American aid programs and by failures of economic planning in India, Burma, Indonesia, and elsewhere as the "decade of development" passed. Osaka and Tokyo merchants, economists, and others pointed to warnings that they had given their counterparts in Southeast Asia but that had gone unheeded. Food production had been neglected for ill-conceived steel mills, and one Japanese economist annoyed the Calcutta Chamber of Commerce by insisting that the progress they expected in thirty years might take a hundred. "They all got excited and waved their arms around, but anyway I urged cottage industries on them." [51]

Caution and profit continued to be the watchwords of Japan's Asian policy. The initiatives represented by Kishi's tours of 1957 had not come to much in a political sense. The desire to remain unentangled in the Asian revolution, to sit out the storm if at all possible, continued to motivate most conservative policy-makers. "Once burned twice shy" was still their motto. Their wish to remain politically inconspicuous while doing a brisk business did not have to be inferred; it was stated plainly enough: "If Japan adopts a forward policy in Asia, disasters may lie ahead should we move unskillfully. We should avoid as far as possible being ensnared in the confrontations and struggles in the area, which will only exacerbate political differences within Japan." [52] This expressed the overriding conservative fear of domestic instability, especially after 1960. Nevertheless, statements linking Japan's fate with the rest of non-Communist Asia slowly began to appear from about 1961. To some extent these were a response to foreign criticism of Japan's passivity, but they also revealed more clearly not only the desire for commercial gain but also other goals that had long been present: membership in the club of rich nations, a position of security vis-à-vis Communist China, and prestige and influence in the world. Economism was producing brilliant results, and there was little desire to alter the formula of prosperity through peaceful trade and American protection. Yet the suggestion of an awareness of new policy imperatives, even a hint of new responsibilities, was seen at least as early as February 1961 in the following excerpt from the report of a mission sent to Southeast Asia by the Japan Committee for Economic Development (*Keizai Dōyūkai*):

> It is obvious to everyone that economic development of Southeast Asia is essential to improve the welfare of the people of those areas and to raise their living standard. On our trip we received the strong impression that the development of the region is also an essential condition for the maturing of Japan's own economy. Industrialization in these countries is inevitable, if economic levels are to rise. Much must be done in agriculture, but industry is the only way to give jobs to these rapidly growing populations. The advanced countries must not be frightened at the thought of creating competitors or try to prevent the industrial advance of these backward lands. If one industrial country fails to help, the process will go ahead anyway with the help of others, and the country that hesitates will have lost its position entirely. Japan must still import capital, but we must also become an exporter of capital to less developed areas. There may be limits to what we can do, because our national income is low compared with the other industrial societies; but we must do what we can do.[53]

Although such statements had occasionally been made before, this one had to be seen in the context of the new economic plans of Premier Hayato Ikeda, which called for doubling the national income in ten years. Such plans implied ever more aggressive Japanese trade drives in the West and elsewhere. But economists also noted the beginnings of labor scarcity in Japan, with rapidly rising wages. Competition was increasing from Hong Kong, Taiwan, South Korea, and India, as well as mainland China, all of which were underselling Japanese toys, textiles, sewing machines, and other sundry goods in Southeast Asia and in Western markets.[54] A few economists foresaw the day when such

goods would have to be allowed into Japan itself. Japanese travelers returning from Indonesia reported that Chinese-made bicycles
with their heavy frames and produce baskets were better suited
to that market than the slimmer sports-type cycles now turned
out in Japanese factories. Conversely, with reparations, yen credits,
and expanding commercial loans, Japanese exports of plant and
equipment to Asia had greatly increased, and the future was seen
to lie in more and bigger capital goods exports.

To facilitate more foreign credits with which to buy these
things, the Japanese government in March 1961 created a new
lending agency, the Overseas Economic Cooperation Fund
(OECF). The Export-Import Bank of Japan, which depended
for part of its resources on government trust funds, charged from
5.5 to 7 per cent; the OECF, whose funds were appropriated, was
to charge 3.5 per cent, and its loans could be repaid over longer
periods of time. The OECF was very small-scale. Starting with
capital of $15.1 million left over from an earlier loan fund for
Southeast Asia, it grew to only $70 million by the end of fiscal
1966. Moreover, especially in its first years, it was narrowly restricted to specific development projects that would promote
Japanese equipment exports. The emphasis of Tokyo's officials
was still on selling Japanese goods overseas, rather than on
how those goods fit the requirements of economic planning in
other countries. Administration of the OECF was disputed by
various ministries, and it was finally placed in the relatively "neutral" Economic Planning Agency. As of March 1967, nearly half
of its loans had been extended to Asia, about 40 per cent to Latin
America. The terms of reference of the OECF were gradually
widened, but its focus remained on selling Japanese goods, and
its activities were very limited when compared to the economic
power that was being generated in Japan in the middle and
late 1960s.[55]

Other events of 1961 and immediately thereafter indicated a
slowly changing relationship with Southeast Asia. In November
of that year Premier Ikeda toured the region, settling Thailand's

claims left over from the war and negotiating Burma's claim for more reparations. Ikeda asserted on his return that "Asia thinks of Japan as an advanced elder brother." [56] He might have added that criticism of the elder brother's failure to give more of his substance to his younger brothers was being heard more often.

Those who had talked of Japan as a model for national development were startled by the gap in growth rate between Japan and the rest of Asia and the large absolute gap in productivity and general affluence that was now painfully evident. GNP in Ikeda's time grew at 10 per cent or more a year. The birth rate was at its lowest point in Japanese history, lower than the American rate; life expectancy in Japan was much higher than in most of Asia; causes of death were Western: heart disease, cancer, and automobile accidents, in that order. Agriculture accounted for less than 15 per cent of national income, but food production mounted to new records; and steel makers set a target of 48 million tons for 1970 (1968 production was nearly 70 million tons). In an interesting essay, one Japanese economist noted that Indian per capita income in 1965 was about equal to Japan's in 1905; India's steel and electricity production per capita in 1965 about matched Japan's in 1919. While the percentage of population in the younger brackets in South and Southeast Asia was higher now than it had been in Japan when the Japanese reached a similar stage of development, only about half of Indian children in 1965 were in primary school, compared with 81 per cent of Japanese children in 1900, and 98 per cent in 1910.[57] Informed persons in Southeast Asia also noted these discrepancies. Their response was to demand more Japanese aid: Japan should share more of the burden of helping the underdeveloped to grow and become rich. The Japanese response was to lend money carefully and to hope without much expectation of success that it would stimulate self-help and orderly, planned development. In this period one began to hear the argument repeated over and over again in Tokyo that Japanese per capita income was very low by Western standards and that Japan could not be expected to give as much as the West.

After Ikeda's Asian trip, some important businessmen called for more "economic cooperation." The head of the Japan Development Bank declared Japan should "make a fresh start" in cooperation with free Asia. The Vice-President of the Fuji Bank said Japan should not make vague promises but should undertake concrete projects. He did not yet suggest that Japanese aid be geared to the programs of recipients rather than projects designed to sell Japanese equipment. But in 1961 an Asia Productivity Organization was established in Tokyo, with American blessing and support, to provide for technical training of Asians in Japan in marketing and other fields. Because the Foreign Ministry saw China as the chief rival for influence in Southeast Asia, the diplomats pressed the politicians for more exchange of persons and other cultural programs and more technical assistance.

Out of these and other pressures in 1962 came still another bureaucratic organ, the Overseas Technical Cooperation Agency (OTCA), to superintend Japan's small technical assistance program, including a Youth Volunteer Corps modeled to some extent on the American Peace Corps. The OTCA was a Ministry of Foreign Affairs candidate for a role in overseas aid programs. (In 1968 its director was a former Ambassador to Thailand.) Its activities were not limited to exchange of technical expertise, but included research in a wide variety of fields, such as Mekong River development, tropical agriculture and medicine, and highway construction. Some of OTCA's studies on Indonesian corn and other subjects were made with an eye to Japanese trade expansion. It also set up overseas technical assistance training centers in several areas.

Another government organ created in this period was the Asia Economic Research Institute, or "Ajiken," established in 1958 as a "foundation" and reorganized in 1960 and put under the jurisdiction of the Ministry of International Trade and Industry.

Ajiken soon became the principal government training center for new specialists on postwar Asia, having grown out of a petition from three noted academic economists for better research facilities. Business interests also lay behind this organization, although most of its operating budget came from the government. The Foreign Ministry contested with MITI for control over it, but the latter won out. Ajiken thrived; its staff grew to some 250 by 1968, with about 25 representatives stationed abroad for short-term research or long-term training.

Although Ajiken conducted research on many subjects, most of its work was concerned with Asian economic conditions and in one way or another was directed toward Japan's commercial interests in the area if it was not determined by them. In its first years it engaged principally in collecting what might be called basic intelligence, assembling a library of data, and training young specialists from the universities, some of whom later moved back to teach. Its subsidies to scholars and opportunities for travel and study abroad for up to two years were attractive to the small number of Japanese university graduates who were interested in Asia and were not bothered by the official coloration Ajiken gave them and their work. (Some said there was a reverse influence on Ajiken from university intellectuals who carried into it their anti-government views; but it was hard to tell how much academics assumed poses to protect their reputations from attack by their peers.)

The earliest directors of Ajiken, like the directors of most Japanese organizations, were mostly men whose careers had been shaped before the war. (The director in 1968 was a famous agricultural economist and professor emeritus at Tokyo University. Some of the senior officials were younger and grew up during and after the war.) Ajiken published profusely. Its output included bibliographic compilations on Asia, country studies, technical works on economic development in its manifold aspects, books on the politics of Asian countries, and special studies commissioned by government agencies on such subjects as tropical agriculture, the demand for petroleum products, or problems of the price of primary goods. It published a magazine in Japanese on Asian developmental problems and a magazine in English, *Developing Economies*, featuring articles on growth theory. A special section was set up to produce data on foreign investment in Asia. In 1963 Ajiken undertook to build up its China section, which in the early years had been somewhat neglected for South and Southeast Asia. One well-known China specialist in 1968 called Ajiken's research on Communist China the best being done in Japan at that time.

6. Summary

Japan's leaders after 1952 were preoccupied with restoring their country's economic strength. Interested above all in themselves and their internal problems, their first goal was stability at a high rate of growth. For this, trade with America was the first essential. Two Premiers, Kishi and Ikeda, spoke of new initiatives in Asia and returned from tours of the area with slogans about Japan's leadership role. Asia's economic performance in the 1950s, however, was discouraging to all but the most sanguine Asia-firsters. Japanese politicians were primarily concerned not to disturb the alliance with the United States, where Japan's economic and military salvation was seen to lie. Some American officials urged a stronger Asian role on the Japanese, but the latter were unsure of their image and not ready to undertake new departures in foreign policy. No Japanese government after 1952 made any serious effort to educate public opinion at home concerning South and Southeast Asia. Not until Ikeda's time, in the early 1960s, was Japan's well-being linked, even in a few minds, with the economic betterment of the Asian south. This link came to be made slowly. But aid to others that would not bring measurable and rapid economic return was not regarded with much favor. Although in the period under review a few enlightened people spoke of Japan's obligation to assist others less fortunate, an official public opinion poll in mid-1968 showed that over 60 per cent of Japanese associated economic aid with export markets rather than any more altruistic objectives.[58]

The obligation to pay reparations was accepted. They were paid regularly and were seen as an economic stepping stone back into Southeast Asia. Their exact effect on the Japanese economy was difficult to measure, but they clearly stimulated machinery exports and sent businessmen and technicians back into the area in substantial numbers. For the recipient countries reparations had some beneficial effects, but these were lessened by dispersal of goods received and by corruption and mismanagement in the administration of reparations programs. In any case, reparations were only a palliative; the needs of those countries were far more comprehensive than could be filled by reparations alone.

Trade increased between Japan and Southeast Asia, but less significantly than Japan's trade with the United States and less rapidly than its over-all trade. Asian trade was merely a portion of Japan's global commerce, and it was full of stubborn problems. The terms of trade of Southeast Asia with the world steadily deteriorated throughout the period after 1952, and the trade of the region as a whole with Japan was in deficit after 1956. There were some exceptions: Malaysia and the Philippines ran surpluses with Japan; in both countries, Communist-led insurgencies were met and controlled, governments were relatively stable, raw material resources were rich and exploitable in a fairly orderly fashion. Both countries still relied mainly on their exports of primary goods. Although the prices of such exports fell, the problem of what to sell to Japan instead of such goods had not yet seriously arisen.

Elsewhere in the area the trade imbalance became more or less chronic. Rice imports from Burma fell, and nothing replaced them. In Thailand the search for substitute exports turned farmers to yellow corn for Japanese chickens and cows, especially after the U.S.-built Friendship Highway opened up the Thai hinterland. Japanese trade with Laos, Vietnam, and Cambodia was increasingly affected by the warfare in that region. India, Hong Kong, and Taiwan put pressure on Japan to buy more light industrial products and semi-finished goods; but the small-industry sector in Japan was still heavily protected, as was agriculture. Liberalization of these sectors was overdue, but since they were strongholds of conservative voting strength, the Liberal Democratic party was not likely to adopt new policies toward them very abruptly. How long Japanese apple growers could block lower tariffs on tropical fruits was a difficult question.

In the broadest sense Japan's post-Occupation leaders conceived of their goals in terms of pulling up to the West—hardly ever in terms of going ahead of the rest of Asia, which seems to have been taken for granted as part of the historical record. It was not, at any rate, often formulated as a goal of any special worth. However, this really left unanswered the question of how to relate to Asia on any but commercial terms. Prewar leaders had rationalized Japanese national interest in terms of Confucian big-brother guidance, sometimes expressed by the notion that Japan knew China best, had a special interest in Manchuria, and so on. Such slogans were appropriate to an era of blocs and spheres of influence; and the American disinclination seriously to challenge such ideas in the 1930s, stemming as it did from a general lack of interest in Asia, contributed to their growth and spread. After 1952, in a period when Japanese interest in any overt political role in Southeast Asia was slight, and America was deeply embroiled in the area, echoes of such clichés could still be heard in statements such as Premier Ikeda's that other Asians thought of Japan as an "elder brother." It was fairer to say that most Asians thought of Japan as a rich but distant relative who was to be dunned and divested of as much of his largesse as possible. Conversely, most Japanese thought of Asians to the south as poor relations with dubious credit.

Those who went to that area often encountered language and other problems. They were accused of intense clannishness, of merely wanting to mine resources or sell goods. If they stayed long, they often lost out in the power struggles of the office at home. Living conditions were difficult and education of children a trial. These were, many of them, the same problems faced by Americans or Europeans overseas. The Japanese were merely the latest to have them because they were the latest to modernize, but, being Asians, "cultural distance" was in many ways a greater problem for them than for most Westerners, although some Japanese could adapt well to local Asian conditions. But South and Southeast Asia created few vibrations except economic ones in most Japanese minds, which had little interest in the art, music, history, or culture of the area.

For their part, South and Southeast Asians gradually stopped fearing the Japanese for their past record but began to worry about their possible penetration and exploitation in the future. A few Japanese made inspiring contributions to development of small industry, fishing, or agriculture abroad. Some perceived that more of the "right" people should be sent where they could contribute skills of relevance to local needs. Like others of whatever nationality, some Japanese were devoted to the relief of human poverty through teaching how to achieve greater productivity and efficiency. Some were personally stirred by the needs confronting them; their capacity for compassion was as great as for self-pity; and their contributions were often more impressive than all the talk of Japan as a model for economic development.

By the early 1960s, when the first stirrings of reawakened self-confidence in Japan could be perceived, a few Japanese became aware of a link between their country's well-being and the economic and political fate of underdeveloped Asia. This theme would grow in importance as the decade passed and would receive stimulus from a series of events inside and outside Japan. But it could not be forced. More Japanese than not continued to feel condescension toward other Asians for their "soft" cultures and weak economic performance; or they felt pure distaste for life in Southeast Asia. None of the countries from Pakistan to the Philippines interested any large segment of the Japanese public. Few, if any, Japanese felt guilt for Japan's record in that area, as a good number did for the record in China. There was a gradually accelerating response to Western criticism and pressure to give more aid, but without any special conviction that doing so would have any decisive effect. Seeking influence abroad, the Japanese government was nevertheless reluctant to accept any obligation for greater aid to the underdeveloped portions of the world.

III. The Long Wait: Relations with China and Korea

The slow but steady return of Japan to South and Southeast Asia after 1952 contrasted with its protracted isolation from mainland China. Japanese of many persuasions perceived the irony of such an impasse in relations with the Asian country most closely bound up with Japan in history and culture. Many called for closer relations immediately, and nearly all thought they would some day come. However, stereotypes of past closeness were not as serviceable for future relationships as many Japanese believed. The "China problem" was coated over with a deceptive patina of sentiment, but the two countries seemed likely to remain in essential isolation for the foreseeable future.

1. Japan's Basic Position on China

On April 28, 1952, the day the San Francisco Peace Treaty went into effect, Japan and Nationalist China signed a separate peace treaty of their own. A protocol accompanying the treaty limited its applicability to territories which were then or would be in the future under Nationalist control; moreover, Premier Yoshida in a letter to Secretary of State Dulles insisted that Japan wished ultimately to recognize Peking and to have normal relations with that regime. Yoshida meant to leave the future open; but the treaty had the effect of acknowledging the legitimacy of the Chinese Nationalist regime as the government of China and made a peace treaty with Peking impossible.

Yoshida and his successors had no illusion about the reality of Communist control over the mainland. They never gave the Nationalists a chance to return there. Anti-Soviet and anti-Marxist, Japanese conservative leaders yet doubted the wisdom of America's attempts to "contain" China; a policy of attraction would, they thought, serve to moderate Chinese intransigence sooner than efforts at quarantine. But in a period of national weakness, when Yoshida himself had refused to sponsor re-armament because he believed it would tear his country apart, the leaders chose to follow the American lead on China. Japan simply could not be assured of the stability it sought without American protection. The conservative leadership thus acquiesced definitively in America's China policy and had to live with the consequences of that policy.

In the years that followed, through all the changes in inter-national politics, the Japanese government persisted in its basic position, attempting to trade with the mainland without recog-nizing it or provoking Taipei or Washington and to maintain political ties and a not inconsiderable trade with Taiwan without severing commercial relations with Peking. These policies involved the government in chronic strain within its own ranks and con-stant contention with the political opposition. No consensus on China policy was available in Japan. The Communist party main-tained close ties with Peking throughout the period, expelling influential dissidents who sided with the Soviet Union in the split with China or who supported the partial test-ban treaty signed by the United States and the Soviet Union. The Socialist party deplored Japan's close association with America in the world; it wanted immediate recognition of Peking and closer ties with the mainland. The Socialists regarded the status of Taiwan as a domestic Chinese problem for Peking and Taipei to solve; and they called for a Locarno-type nonaggression pact signed by the United States, the U.S.S.R., China, and Japan.

No other issue exposed the Japanese government so continually to the charge that it was a mere client of the United States. No other foreign policy issue had such psychological ramifications for the Japanese people. But the China policy of the conservatives did not cause them to be voted out of office, or even to falter seriously. As the years passed, a node of disagreement over how to handle the China question remained embedded within the party and segments of the business community. Isolation from China also affected Japanese intellectuals, many of whom were under Marxist influence and wished to take part in the Chinese revolution. Yet isolation from China, while it seemed unnatural to many, did not result in any particular damage to the Japanese national interest as conceived by those in power in Tokyo, at least up to the mid-1960s. On the contrary, by remaining aligned with the United States, Japan's leaders furthered their goal of stability at home and their commitment to the status quo in Asia and prospered beyond anyone's imagining, in spite of prolonged periods of hostility and threat from Peking or Taipei, episodes of American pressure, and constant accusations of supineness from the opposition at home.

2. CULTURAL DIPLOMACY AND TRADE

Tokyo and Peking had no diplomatic relations at any time after 1945; the war between them was not ended by a peace treaty. Their informal relations were dominated by Peking's attempt to draw Japan away from its pro-American orientation and to bring its great economic strength within the sphere of Chinese Communist influence. Peking also wanted official recognition. On its side, the Tokyo government wished to trade without recognizing the mainland regime. When the San Francisco Peace Treaty was signed, Chou En-lai called it a "flagrant act of provocation." [1]

Soon, however, following Moscow's lead, the Chinese tone changed, and for the next six years China sought to pursue its ends by offering a degree of accommodation to Japan. In this brief interlude of cultural diplomacy a few of the problems left over from the war were cleared away.

The first evidence of China's "lovable" policy came in the repatriation of Japanese. Even after large-scale repatriation in the 1940s, an indeterminate number of Japanese were left in Chinese hands. Early in 1953 a Japanese Red Cross mission visited Peking to arrange for their return. Although it was not the first Japanese postwar mission to go to China, it was a very early one. Included in it were two representatives each from two of the Communist front groups that dotted the political landscape in Japan: the Japan-China Friendship Association and the Japan Peace Liaison Committee. The delegates of these organizations soon received permission for the repatriation of about 30,000 persons, most of them Japanese civilians, many of them long-time residents of mainland China with Chinese wives.[2]

Repatriation began in March 1953, when the first shiploads of about 4,000 returnees arrived on Japanese freighters at Maizuru, a port on the Japan Sea. The whole operation was enveloped in the shrillest of propaganda; the repatriates were used as counters in a game of influence-mongering by Peking and by Communist organizations in Japan. Front groups friendly to Peking protested the questioning of returnees by officials at the port of entry and extracted every possible advantage from their return. Foreign observers reported that the repatriates were a mixed lot; some said Communist China was a paradise, others that they had been forced to work in arms factories at "pistol point."[3] Many were clearly handpicked to work with the Japan Communist party after their return.[4]

Repatriation continued until nearly all of the 30,000 people had been landed. Other Chinese moves followed. A "Radio Free Japan" was established on the mainland to broadcast propaganda in Japanese. A few Chinese ports were opened to Japanese fishing operations. Seizures of small fishing vessels and imprisonment of their crews, which had been going on for years, began to subside. In 1951, 55 vessels with 671 fishermen were taken; in 1953, 24 ships with 311 men; in 1954, 28 ships with 329 men. But with Yoshida's departure from power at the end of 1954, the number abruptly fell: in 1955 the Chinese seized only one ship with 10 men; in 1956, two with 24; and in 1957, none at all.[5]

Yoshida's successor, Ichirō Hatoyama, until mid-1955 headed a weak government that had come to power with Socialist help, and conservatives of Hatoyama's faction held a minority of Diet seats. He put emphasis upon restoring diplomatic relations with the Soviet Union, and to satisfy his supporters he was obliged frequently to speak out of both sides of his mouth about China. During this period there was sporadic talk in Tokyo about drawing closer to Peking, but in fact there were no new departures in Japan's China policy.

China's "invitational diplomacy" also characterized this period. From 1952 to the end of 1954 only five Japanese missions visited Peking, but in 1955 there were nine, including not only trade groups but also a mission of Diet members, and other groups of doctors, labor unionists, and members of the People's League to Protect the Constitution, headed by former Premier Katayama, a Christian Socialist. The following year fifteen missions visited China and in 1957 the number was twenty.[6] Manufacturers of metal goods and machinery, publishers, young people's and women's organizations, coal miners, sports teams, families of soldiers killed in the China fighting, *kabuki* actors, other entertainers and artists of various sorts made the pilgrimage in those years, visiting the prescribed cities, model farms and factories, talking with their Chinese counterparts around tables set with bowls of fruit or flowers, apologizing often for Japan's past sins of omission or commission, pledging friendship for the Peking regime. Others have noted the tributary quality of some of these voyages. Most visitors were favorably impressed. (A few hardeyed newspapermen were not. One called China a land of 700 million nuns.) Most had gone expecting to be impressed. On their return they issued statements or while still in China signed resolutions or declarations in concert with their Chinese hosts, usually members of some friendship society or other body set up to handle visitors from Japan as well as to promote trade. Many of the Chinese having such duties had been born in Japan or were educated there and spoke fluent Japanese.[7]

In this period, too, a small number of Chinese visited Japan: 10 in 1954; 112 in 1955; 142 in 1956.[8] Some distinguished Chinese came, including scholars like Kuo Mo-jo, later to be humiliated during the Cultural Revolution to the discomfiture of some Japanese intellectuals. In 1956 the famous female impersonator Mei Lan-fang and the Peking Opera gave thirty performances before audiences totaling 70,000 people in Japanese cities.

Books and magazines about China in Chinese and Japanese appeared in large numbers all over Japan and could be purchased in most bookstores. Outlets specializing in Communist literature flourished in Tokyo and Kyoto; the translated works of Lu Hsun were especially popular. Research organizations like the Communist-subsidized China Research Institute dominated the scholarly field and published a constant stream of Marxist-Leninist studies of the "new China."[9]

Along with cultural exchanges a small amount of trade got under way after 1952. Three agreements for barter transactions were signed by "unofficial" Japanese trade teams in 1952, 1953, and 1955. Each agreement set a limit of the equivalent of $84 million each way to be exchanged annually. Japanese interest in this trade was particularly keen among small manufacturers and traders in the western part of the country who had traded with China before the war and had fallen on slack times afterward. Such small operators had often been in the vanguard of those supporting a forward policy on the continent in the 1930s. Now they resented American tariffs on exports of such things as sewing machines, silk scarves, and other sundry goods and would support any moves to increase sales of traditional exports to their former markets on the mainland. To tell such small manufacturers that the prewar era was gone forever or that China could hardly find goods to export to Japan in return was useless.

Their grievances often were very specific and forcefully put. Typical was that of a small Osaka maker of talcum powder, who once organized a truck caravan and traveled to Tokyo to agitate for China trade. He put his problems in the following way in 1958:

> My best raw materials are now cut off in China, and the United States won't buy what I can manufacture from the talc stone I get in Hong Kong unless I can furnish a certificate of origin. So I am forced to use local Japanese stone of inferior quality and sell mostly in the domestic market. Southeast Asia is an unpredictable market; the people there have no ambition or entrepreneurship, and their purchasing power is low. The balance of U.S.-Japan trade is most unnatural, and the whole relationship between us must be readjusted. . . . I think our relations with China should be just as important as our relations with the United States.[10]

This man spoke of the inaccessibility of raw materials, but many others were more disturbed by restrictions on shipment of strategic materials to China. An embargo on such shipments had first been imposed by SCAP in 1950 after the outbreak of the Korean War. It continued in effect after the Occupation ended, and in September 1952 Japan joined the Consultative Group, an informal international organization with headquarters in Paris, which ever since 1948 had supervised through its Coordinating Committee the listing of commodities proscribed for shipment by the member nations of the group to the Soviet bloc. A China Committee of the Consultative Group was formed in 1952 and set even stricter lists than had been set for Russia. At about the same time the Battle Act passed by the U.S. Congress barred American aid to all countries not complying with the Cocom and Chincom lists. Japan's compliance with these measures made it impossible to fulfill the barter agreements reached with Peking. When the Chinese insisted on receiving embargoed machinery, plant, chemicals, or other strategic goods against their shipments of soy beans, salt, coal, iron, or other raw materials, the Japanese had little recourse but to refuse. The first agreement was only about 5 per cent fulfilled, the second 35 per cent. Resentment against the Tokyo government was widespread with some manufacturers lobbying busily for more trade, but they were not influential enough politically to be able to alter Japan's China policy in any significant respect.

The most important and powerful Japanese business interests were very wary of trade with China, considered its potential limited, and wanted to avoid doing anything that would offend the United States. Nevertheless, interest in the China trade continued high in certain export industries, including not only small and medium-sized concerns but also makers of chemical fertilizers, cotton textiles, and agricultural and other machinery. Importers of raw materials for the expanding steel industry wanted Chinese iron ore and coking coal, even though the principal sources of these materials were now scattered from the United States and Canada to South and Southeast Asia. Barring radical changes in the international order, Japan was not likely again to become dependent solely or even primarily upon China for any of its most important raw material needs; but neither could it put out of mind the potentially huge, nearby market on the mainland. Western sales to that market also disturbed many Japanese, who saw no reason why they should be outbid by British or European manufacturers. As early as October 1954 a 25-man mission of Diet members visiting China noted that Europeans were "riding the China trade bus" and resolved that Japan should not miss it. Japan's commercial aggressiveness was as evident here as elsewhere. In 1957, when Great Britain decided to abandon the stricter strategic list of exports to China and return to the Soviet list, Japan was not long in following suit.

Barter trade increased somewhat between 1955 and 1957, but exports never exceeded 3 per cent of total Japanese exports, and imports were in the 3 per cent range. Trade with China was more a hope than a reality, and the conditions surrounding it were abnormal. Most Japanese themselves realized this; as a report of the Ministry of International Trade and Industry stated, "When trade with Communist China declines, the overriding reasons are clearly political. An increase has economic causes: the expansion or recovery of the Chinese economy and the consequent growth of demand for imports." [11]

The Chinese coupled cultural diplomacy with constant pressure for political concessions. In October 1954 a joint Sino-Soviet declaration designed to draw Japan into closer political ties by holding out the prospect of more trade met with no response in Tokyo. The government still deeply distrusted the Soviet Union for attacking Japanese forces in Manchuria at the end of World War II in violation of its treaty with Japan; moreover, the Sino-Soviet Treaty of August 1945, a military pact aimed specifically at Japan, was still in effect. Chou En-lai called for normal relations on the basis of Peking's "five principles" of coexistence: mutual respect for territorial integrity and sovereignty, nonaggression, noninterference in internal affairs, mutual benefit and equality, and peaceful coexistence. These slogans were repeated in the "action programs" of the Japan Communist and left Socialist parties, but Chinese interference in Japan's domestic affairs through support of opposition parties and front groups and the many forms of Chinese propaganda were offensive to most of the Japanese people; and the government, in spite of its own weakness and its heavy trade deficits in the mid-1950s, would not recognize Peking. The decision to stick to the American alignment remained firm.

3. RELATIONS WITH TAIWAN

Another constraint felt by Japan vis-à-vis Peking was in its relations with Chiang Kai-shek's government in Taiwan. In return for recognition, Chiang treated Japan with some magnanimity. Japanese citizens in Taiwan were mostly repatriated, and reparations claims were abandoned, as they had not been by Peking. A sizable trade grew up, with Japan importing sugar, rice, bananas, and pineapple, and exporting chemical fertilizers, machinery and transportation equipment, metal products, and some canned food. In 1954 Japanese exports to Taiwan were $66 million, to mainland China $19 million; imports from Taiwan were $57 million, from the mainland $40 million.[12] Not until 1956 did the mainland trade exceed that with Taiwan.

The failure of the Japanese to sell large quantities of consumer goods to Taiwan was a reflection of Chinese efforts to manufacture for themselves and become self-sufficient. Nor did Japan profit as extensively as it had hoped from infusions of American aid into the island. Nevertheless, the trade with Taiwan by the middle 1950s had returned to roughly its prewar volume. Japanese businessmen experienced many of the same frustrations there that they faced farther south: short-term visas and laws discriminating against foreign business operations, which sometimes seemed to be directed against them in particular. Thus, just as the 1952 treaty was signed, new prohibitions against foreign business were put into effect in the island, forcing Japanese trading companies to work through Chinese associates or agents and forbidding the Bank of Tokyo or other Japanese commercial banks from opening branches.[13]

These difficulties reflected distrust of Japanese intentions on the part of the Nationalist government. Taiwan's politics were dominated by refugees who had fled from the mainland in 1949. Their hatred of the Chinese Communists made them allergic to the slightest moves toward Peking on the part of the Japanese, who were their recent enemies and never far from suspicion. Taipei's reaction to Tokyo's trade and cultural missions to Peking was thus predictable: any suggestion of rapprochement with the mainland produced a threat to break ties with Tokyo. The Nationalists were afraid, and saw Japan as the next target of Peking's aggression. However, Tokyo disagreed with this diagnosis; it would not give up its trade with the mainland so long as Peking allowed it, but neither did it want to lose its links with Taiwan, a valuable trading partner and a territory significantly near the Ryūkyū Islands, which Japan expected to reoccupy eventually. The result was a precarious, three-cornered relationship, by turns surly and conciliatory, and unremittingly calculating on all sides. Japanese visitors to Taiwan learned to make statements suitably anti-Communist for that environment, while their colleagues in Peking might even at the same moment sound very different, indeed.[14] The Japanese wanted the best of both worlds and American protection to boot; what could have been more natural?

The mainlanders in Taiwan quite naturally worried about what would happen if Japan "went Communist." Few Japanese thought about this, however; their insomnia derived from trade figures and interest rates, not Mao's legions. Taiwan to them was a small but reliable market; it was under American protection, and if it would steady itself economically, Japanese would like to invest there. They could get along without it; their exports to the island were only 5 per cent of total exports in 1955 and imports 2.5 per cent; on the other hand, Japan took more than 50 per cent of Taiwan's trade.

The Japanese had certain other advantages that were not so apparent. Their fifty-year rule had left a residue of Japanese-speaking Chinese on Taiwan. These people were hardly pro-Japanese; after 1945 they swiftly rid the island of most of the evidences of Japanese cultural influence; but their more recent and bloody experiences with Chinese carpetbaggers from the mainland, who plundered and ravaged the island in the late 1940s before Chiang's government arrived, had the effect of mitigating the memory of the exploitation they suffered earlier under Japanese colonialism. Japan's record, as one writer observed, seemed more "roseate" than it might have otherwise.[15] At any rate, a definite distinction had to be made between Chinese from the mainland and those native to Taiwan who were born and grew up under Japanese rule. After 1952 the Japanese had to deal with both, but it was with the Taiwan Chinese that their closest commercial and personal ties were formed. They far outnumbered the mainlanders and would, most Japanese thought, eventually inherit the positions of greatest power in the island. Among them were some who remembered the Japanese colonial era with something approaching nostalgia.

4. FURTHER ATTEMPTS AT TRADE

Efforts to trade with Peking increased as the decade of the 1950s wore on and Japan's trade deficits continued. In the words of the London *Economist*, there was "something artificial about a situation in which Japan, in 1954, took two-fifths of its imports from the United States and Canada alone, and could pay for much less than half of these by exports to those countries." Heavy spending in Japan for military purposes by the United States made up the difference. Here, of course, was the root of Japanese resentment at the Cocom embargo on trade with Peking. The later expansion of Japan's world trade was to reduce the importance of the mainland in the total, but as the Japanese in 1955 did not have the benefit of foresight, their dissatisfaction with the embargo was not unreasonable. With the unification of the conservative political forces in the Liberal Democratic party in the autumn of 1955, talk of political approaches to Peking declined, and Hatoyama at the end of his administration reaffirmed Japan's ties with the West. From time to time a certain restiveness was evident in the party, and the Tokyo press frequently criticized Japan's "passivity" vis-à-vis Peking; the *Asahi* wanted to know why the government should not talk with Peking at the consular level, at least, when Washington was having talks with the Chinese at the ambassadorial level in Europe. This was early in 1958. But nothing happened, except that Peking continued to issue threatening statements and attempted to intervene in Japanese affairs at election time.

By the fall of 1957 the tone of mainland propaganda was growing colder. Especially strong attacks came just after Tokyo decided to remove many of the remaining items from the strategic Cocom list. By this time a new Japanese Premier, Nobusuke Kishi, had taken office and given evidence of firm opposition to any rapprochement with Peking. The interlude of weak conservative government was over, and Kishi turned his attention to the problem of gaining more independence for Japanese policy within a framework of cooperation with the United States. His two Southeast Asian tours foreshadowed a larger Japanese concern with that area, and he cultivated Japan's ties with the Nationalist government in Taiwan. Peking's first efforts at cultural diplomacy had obviously failed.

Recognition of the failure was expressed on May 12, 1958, by the abrupt cancellation of a trade agreement, the fourth since 1952, which had just been concluded in Peking. This followed an earlier Japanese government refusal to endorse the agreement, reached by "unofficial" [16] delegations, on the grounds that it would have given Peking the right to fly its flag over the headquarters of its proposed trade mission in Tokyo, and the Japanese feared this might be interpreted as diplomatic recognition. Just at this moment the Chinese were given a pretext for cutting off trade negotiations when a young Japanese superpatriot tore down a small Chinese Communist flag at an exhibition of postage stamps in a Nagasaki department store.

China's cutoff of trade came as the Great Leap Forward was just beginning, and confidence in its own policies and in Soviet power was perhaps at its height. The move was clearly aimed at damaging the Kishi government; but Kishi's failures, which were considerable, did not come from Chinese causes. In September 1958, a prominent Socialist politician, visiting Peking to sound out the prospects of reopening trade, was given a set of demands: Japan must stop its hostile speeches and actions "immediately and for all time," it must refrain from "intrigue to create two Chinas," cease "sabotaging" efforts to "normalize" relations, hoist another Chinese flag on the spot where the first one was torn down, send an official delegation to Peking to offer a formal apology and then, and only then, send a trade delegation.[17] When these imperious demands were published in Tokyo, they produced a violent public reaction and sharply embarrassed the Socialists who had brought them back. If the Chinese wanted to insure that trade would not be resumed, they were quite successful; if that was not their intention, they badly misjudged the Japanese response. In any event, they gave offense, and not for the first time. As one Japanese journalist wrote, "Japan is not a small country that can be easily manipulated from abroad; it is a proud nation that does not scare easily." [18]

Trade between the two countries dropped to very low levels between 1958 and late 1960, when a new Premier, Hayato Ikeda, came to power. In the interim the Chinese never ceased to attack the Kishi regime and to give comfort to that regime's enemies through the principal means at its disposal, press and propaganda statements and invitations to Japanese sympathetic to its position. Prominent persons like former Premier Ishibashi were warned not to allow Japan to renew its "aggressive" treaty with the United States. The Chinese played on ancient cultural ties and spread their attacks against the treaty through the mainland press, where it was picked up and repeated by Japanese intellectual journals. The most famous of the Japanese visitors to Peking in that period, the Japanese Socialist leader, Inejirō Asanuma (called the "human locomotive" by Japanese because of his energy), obliged his hosts with a public statement to the effect that the United States was the "common enemy" of Japan and China. This remark, which caused the Socialists themselves some anguish, was widely used in China to promote anti-American feelings, and subsequent Socialist delegations were pressured into reaffirming the "Asanuma statement." [19]

In late 1960, with the evident failure of the Great Leap, the revision of the U.S.-Japan Security Treaty, and the growing estrangement between China and the Soviet Union, Peking began to show interest in the Japan trade again; or, perhaps more correctly, began to try again to use the trade as a means of altering Japan's pro-Western position. Commercial transactions between the two countries at that time were very small and were carried on by Japanese firms that had been designated as "friendly" by the Chinese. These included some small traders but also many dummies set up by larger Japanese companies solely or principally for the purpose of trading with China. The Daiichi Trading Company, for instance, was known to be a "friendly firm" subsidiary of the Mitsui group; Daiichi was reported to control nearly 20 per cent of the "friendly firm" trade with China at one point in the early 1960s.[20] Several leftist front associations in Tokyo competed for control over this trade.[21] "Friendly firms" kept a small number of more or less permanent representatives in Peking, where a community of perhaps a couple of hundred Japanese with Communist and/or Chinese interests was allowed to reside in the 1950s.

Trade with China in 1961 was much less than 1 per cent of Japan's total trade. From 1962, however, interest in the trade greatly increased in Tokyo. This was a period of immensely rapid economic expansion in Japan, with very heavy investment in new plants and equipment, large import surpluses, and overheating of the industrial economy. Many Japanese businessmen were as skeptical as they had ever been of China's ability to export raw materials in anything like the huge quantities necessary to pay for imports of the chemicals and machinery Japan wanted to sell. But "the old shimmering mirage of the illimitable Chinese market tantalized the minds of manufacturers in Tokyo and Osaka," [22] and the conservative government encouraged trade with the slogan, "separation of economics and politics." The old arguments that Japan might somehow mediate between East and West in China and reduce Chinese isolation were brought out and dusted off again, only to be countered by equally old warnings that Chinese promises were a snare and a delusion. Thus, while nearly all the leaders in power saw China as basically a rival and an adversary, the usual differences persisted about how to deal with that rival; some would draw closer, some keep their distance.

Premier Ikeda was ready to talk about certain new approaches as long as that did not upset Japan's relations with Taiwan or the United States too seriously. The mass media yearned for some break in the impasse that would give them new copy to write about China; they projected a generally favorable image of the mainland regime, although the failure of the Great Leap and the Sino-Soviet split baffled some intellectuals and journalists and produced more realism among China commentators, of whom Japan had more, perhaps, than any other country.

With its indefatigable sloganizing and numerology Peking called on the Ikeda government to abandon all thought of a "two-China" policy, and to accept "three principles" it laid down for trade and diplomatic relations. When Ikeda visited the United States in June 1961 and once again pronounced, as did each new Premier in ritual fashion, Japan's allegiance to the American alignment, he underwent the same vituperative attacks from Peking that Kishi had received. Nevertheless, the Chinese, suffering severe economic depression and needing technical assistance after the withdrawal of Russian technicians, were more willing than they had been for several years to accept negotiations for trade with Japan.[23]

The United States officially disapproved of expanded Japanese-Chinese trade and argued against its potential for growth. By this time, however, U.S. dealings with the Japanese government were becoming somewhat less heavy-handed than they had been in Dulles' day. Ikeda himself felt growing pressure from businessmen interested in the China trade, some of them important supporters of the Liberal Democratic party; and in late 1962 still another of the long series of "unofficial" missions visited Peking. The mission leader, Kenzō Matsumura, then aged 79 and long a member of the Diet, was known for his rather romantic views of China. He made much of cultural ties and liked to talk about going back to Japan's religious and esthetic home. A graduate of Waseda University, Matsumura dealt with Liao Cheng-chih,[24] a member of the central committee of the Chinese Communist party and chairman of the Japan-China Friendship Association, who had been born in Japan in 1908 and was also a graduate of Waseda. There were few accidents in Japanese-Chinese relations. Matsumura gave copies of Buddhist scriptures to Chinese libraries, visited famous monuments, and had a large store of quotations from the Chinese classics suitable for almost any occasion. His memoirs contain some long sentimental passages on Japanese-Chinese cultural ties, and there is no reason to doubt his sincerity; at the same time, such attitudes made him useful to conservative leaders of somewhat less romantic cast of mind, and he performed very capably the role of advance agent for the traders.

Chou En-lai instructed Matsumura in the Chinese conditions for a renewal of trade: the Japanese government must not be hostile to China, or comply with the United States in the "two-China" idea, or obstruct the gradual movement of Sino-Japanese relations toward "normalization." Trade must involve government agreements as well as privately negotiated contracts and meet other conditions. Chou insisted that, Ikeda notwithstanding, politics and economics could not be separated. Matsumura returned to Tokyo without having exactly refused these conditions, but neither had he bound anybody at home to accept them. All this personal diplomacy had profoundly traditional aspects; its vaguenesses were ramified by the imprecisions of the Japanese language; moreover, commitments made "unofficially" could always be repudiated later. In the absence of official relations such personal dealings were the only alternative if any business was to be done; but personal missions to China were always surrounded by a degree of secrecy that hardly characterized Japanese dealings with India or Southeast Asia, where English was the language of negotiation, feelings of cultural affinity rarely affected the conversations, and the foreign press operated at will.

Matsumura was followed to Peking in November 1962 by Tatsunosuke Takasaki, who had known Chou En-lai in Manchuria in the 1930s when Takasaki was head of Manchurian Heavy

Industries, and who had talked again to Chou at Bandung in 1955 during the era of Chinese "people's diplomacy." It was he who had told President Magsaysay at the signing of the Philippines reparations agreement that what worried him was not whether Japan would perform on its promises but whether the Philippines knew how to use reparations wisely when it got them. Takasaki was no "China romantic," but a shrewd economic bureaucrat with long experience in Japanese government-supported companies overseas. His trip to Peking, though "unofficial," was carefully coordinated beforehand with the Ikeda administration.

In the background of Takasaki's visit lay a great diversity of domestic opinion on China trade. The Japan-Communist China Export-Import Guild, which had the blessing of MITI, took a serious, even alarmist, view of the trade cutoff in May 1958. Representing Osaka interests, this organization in August 1958 issued an extensive "White Paper" detailing current and estimated losses from the stoppage of trade. The "White Paper" argued that imports of salt, rice, coking coal, and other raw materials had been growing during the previous several years and had already become a "tradition"; it would be very troublesome to switch to other sources. Salt, for instance, would have to come from the Red Sea and Mediterranean as well as Southeast Asia; coal would have to be imported from the United States, Australia, and elsewhere; rice from Italy, Egypt, and Spain. These arguments were little more than special pleading by small operators who missed the China trade. Imports of industrial raw materials from China had never been great since 1952, but Peking had cut off the trade at just the moment when long-term arrangements seemed about to be made. The "White Paper" correctly reported that chemical fertilizer exports would be hardest hit by the cutoff and that most of these could not be shifted to other markets. It also pointed out that goods China did not barter with Japan would be sold either as raw materials in Europe or as light finished products in Southeast Asia, thus competing with Japanese goods and increasing Chinese influence with that area. It predicted that Japan's exports to the mainland in 1962 could reach $260 million, or 5.6 per cent of total estimated exports. (Actually they were $38.4 million, or 0.8 per cent.) It viewed Southeast Asia with pessimism: shortages of foreign exchange there would inhibit economic exchanges with Japan. But when trade ties with China were resumed it would be easy to maintain stable business relations with a "planned economy"; Japan should therefore shift more of its imports of raw materials to the mainland. By doing so it could repair its dollar balance and produce more cheaply for the Southeast Asian market. In the words of the "White Paper," larger China trade would "fit the direction of maturity" of the Japanese economy.[25]

Such reports flew in the face of Japan's experience in trying to trade with Communist China, but they indicated that some sectors of Japanese business—sometimes vaguely estimated to equal "20 to 30 per cent of industry"—still dreamed of economic relationships in Asia rather like those of the 1930s but quite out of accord with political realities or the general drift of the Japanese economy in the late 1950s and early 1960s. These were, in a sense, the last of the backward-looking years and the beginning of Japan's true Great Leap into a global economy. Most sources inside and outside the government regarded the 1958 trade cutoff as less serious than the "White Paper" suggested and showed more interest than it did in trade with Southeast Asia. The Economic Planning Agency in its projections of the Japanese future stressed competition for Southeast Asian markets more than the potential of the mainland for Japan. Other vital centers of conservative power, such as the Federation of Economic Organizations (*Keidanren*), were primarily concerned with the possible ill effects more trade and contact with China might have on economic and financial relations with the United States.[26] Within the Liberal Democratic party itself there were "pro-China" and "pro-Southeast Asia" groups. Many different opinions were openly and constantly expressed. In view of the record, however, none but the most sanguine China enthusiasts had very great hopes for dealing with Peking. The same arguments that had been raised for years were renewed against the low quality of Chinese products and the undependability of that source. Most Japanese manufacturers were geared to other suppliers. Freight rates from the West competed with those from the China coast. Large Japanese freighters had difficulty entering small Chinese ports, and so on. No one would abandon the trade as long as economics could be separated from politics, but the Ikeda government wished to reduce Chinese political influence and propaganda exerted through the "friendly firms" by setting up a new mechanism for controlling the trade that would still be "unofficial" but could be overseen more easily.

These considerations lay behind the signing, in November 1962, of a five-year "unofficial" trade agreement calling for annual barter transactions of up to $100 million from 1963 to 1967. This was the so-called Liao-Takasaki, or "L-T," Agreement, after the initials of the two signers, Liao Cheng-chih and Tatsunosuke Takasaki. The agreement called for opening of trade missions in Peking and Tokyo.[27] Trade and other contacts rapidly increased. Japan held industrial fairs in Peking and elsewhere in China in 1963, and the Chinese followed with a trade exposition at the Harumi Pier in Tokyo in the summer of 1964. The role of the "friendly firms" in the trade declined somewhat, to the satisfaction of MITI; however, they still handled more than half of the trade.[28] More trade missions went to Peking. Ikeda reiterated that Tokyo would not recognize the mainland regime, but he tried to increase his leverage at home by insisting that Japan was an Asian country, knew China better than any Western nation possibly could, and was ready for more independent contact. In the Diet he answered Socialist interpellations by declaring, "It is obvious that Japan is not cooperating with America's policy to contain Communist China, judging from the fact that Japanese trade with the mainland is increasing by leaps and bounds." [29]

In Peking the smiles increased. In early 1964 the Chinese proposed an exchange of newspapermen, a move that shortly was to provide the Western world with its principal source of information on the unfolding of the Cultural Revolution in China. Peking also proposed airline connections between Fukuoka and Shanghai, something the Japanese in Kyūshū had long wanted and hoped for.[30] The Chinese were pushing hard for more actions that might lead to or be interpreted as diplomatic recognition. Chou En-lai chided Ikeda for his timidity toward political relations with Peking. The agreement for exchange of newsmen was signed in April 1964, but the air link was considered too dangerous; it would increase pressure on Tokyo to admit more Chinese, and the matter was not pursued by the Japanese.

As might have been expected, all this activity created a crisis in Taiwan. Chiang Kai-shek recalled his ambassador from Tokyo for indefinite consultations and prohibited further Nationalist government purchases from Japan—which meant perhaps 40 per cent of total Japanese exports to the island. The renewal of Peking-Tokyo barter trade was not the principal cause of the Generalissimo's anguish, however. What particularly alarmed the Nationalists was a new Japanese move to expand business with the mainland by extending long-term credits. In the summer of 1963 the Japanese government approved the export by the Kurashiki Rayon Company of a synthetic textile manufacturing plant, to cost the equivalent of $20 million. Repayment terms were 25 per cent down, the remainder in five years; the whole deal was guaranteed by the Export-Import Bank of Japan. A number of large machinery manufacturers received subcontracts for orders as a result of this agreement. According to rumors current in Tokyo at the time, the Kurashiki officials who dickered with the Chinese were ready to offer 4.5 per cent interest; when the Exim Bank ordered that the rate be set at 6 per cent, the company lowered its sale price enough to cancel the difference.

This transaction deeply disturbed Taipei and did not go unnoticed by American officials, who, while they may not have attempted openly to discourage such five-year credits to mainland China, often suggested to the Japanese that any credits contemplated beyond that limit might better be given to more friendly and cooperative recipients. Japanese fear that the Kurashiki deal might irritate Americans was obvious, for American impatience at the slow pace of Japan's economic cooperation programs was increasing. However, the plant export issue was a sensitive one inside Japan, where nationalistic feelings were beginning to come into the open. The *Asahi* newspaper loudly called for Japan to have its own China policy; and it would not do for Americans to put pressure too awkwardly on a conservative regime that was regarded as friendly, in a general sense, to the United States. Thus Japan found itself in its customary diplomatic dance with Peking, Taipei, and Washington. Reactions to its plant export deal forced it to send missions to Taipei to reassure the Nationalists and thus to open itself to opposition attacks at home. Former Premier Yoshida was brought out of retirement to fly to Taiwan to get Chiang Kai-shek's "understanding" of Japan's need for mainland trade. After returning home, Yoshida wrote Chiang a letter promising that Japan would not permit any further deferred-payment plant exports to Peking. This letter, in turn, led Peking to attack Ikeda as a lackey of the United States; and the "Yoshida letter" was to become an embarrassment to Ikeda's administration and that of his successor. Various politicians at various times asserted that such a letter had no binding power on the government, and after Yoshida's death in 1966 some of the crisper nationalists in the conservative party insisted that the letter was null and void. But the letter could be used by those who were genuinely grateful to Chiang Kai-shek for his magnanimity toward Japan at the war's end; more importantly, it had its usefulness to those who opposed or feared further extension of ties with Peking, especially in the ominous conditions on the mainland sometime later.

From the foregoing pages, it should be clear that neither the alleged logical necessity of trade nor the "natural complementarity" of the Chinese and Japanese economies in fact produced the close, sustained commercial relationship between them anticipated by partisans of the China trade. A small, politicized trade existed, but the two countries remained essentially at an impasse, the origins of which were to be found in the nature of the peace settlement of the early 1950s and the continued confrontation of the United States and China. Japan's leaders were not ready to act independently of the United States in China. With eyes still fixed on economic growth at home, they watched and waited, and tried to separate economics from politics, a tactic somewhat but not wholly disingenuous. They preferred to continue to lean on American protection abroad, meanwhile issuing periodic declarations of independence from American policy. Trade with the mainland rose rapidly in 1964 and 1965 and reached its highest postwar figure in 1966. In that year it was about 3 per cent of Japan's total trade; however, trade with America was nearly a third of the total, and that with all of Southeast Asia combined was about the same.

Human interchange continued but declined as the confusion in China increased. When France recognized Peking in early 1964, Japan did not follow suit. On the contrary, the Japanese government voted to make the entry of Communist China into the United Nations an "important question," requiring a two-thirds majority of General Assembly votes. Japan was not France, and the Liberal Democratic party produced no de Gaulle. Japan had no nuclear weapons; it had a "nuclear allergy." It was not around the world from China, but next door. When the new Premier, Eisaku Satō, the younger brother of former Premier Kishi, took over from Ikeda in late 1964, he faced a China where imponderable events made it less likely than before that Japan would alter the foreign policy laid down after the Occupation.

5. Japanese Attitudes Toward China

Most Japanese agreed that, quite apart from questions of policy, China evoked a more complex response than did any other country in Asia, although probably not as complex as that evoked by the United States. The image of China had greater historical resonance in more Japanese minds than the rest of Asia could possibly have.

The reasons for this had often been stated fairly clearly. On the most basic cultural level China was the only foreign country with which the Japanese claimed any particular kinship or affinity. Long ago, Japan had borrowed or adapted Chinese writing, philosophy, religion, art, and political institutions. The two peoples were ethnically akin, their writing systems were related, they shared the same ethic of performance and probity, and many hundreds of thousands of Japanese had made their lives and careers in parts of China for many years. China was the principal arena of Japan's external ambitions, the great incinerator of its imperialist hopes. Events there were bound to have a greater immediacy for the Japanese than those in more distant parts of Asia.

To be more specific, many of the older generation of Japanese, men like Kenzō Matsumura, who still sat at or near the power centers of their society, felt a quite natural and normal nostalgia for the old days, when Japan was paramount in large parts of the mainland. Few, if any, expected that Japan would ever be paramount again in the same way, but they had not entirely rid themselves of a manipulative mentality, though this was sometimes misted over with sentimental expressions of fondness for China's cultural achievements. These men were apt to repeat clichés about Japan's "special knowledge" of the Chinese people, which were true enough in a sense—Japanese scholarship on China before the war had been the most prodigious in the world—but which contained echoes of a past that was not very useful any longer when it came to conceiving a truly new role for Japan on the continent of Asia. These old men, whom I have called the "China romantics," though they were rapidly passing from the scene still could be used by their government as unofficial emissaries to scout out Chinese intentions. Matsumura was such a man, Tanzan Ishibashi another, men with a flair for praising Chinese painting or passing out Buddhist sutras with one hand while closing fertilizer deals with the other. Some other members of the older generation who through their experience in China could legitimately claim a special knowledge of the country took a rather mystical view of the Japan-China relationship; they often used the metaphor of Japan as a bridge between China and the West or spoke vaguely of a historical mission for Japan to fulfill vis-à-vis China.[31]

In these men's minds lay the conviction, which was shared by the late Premier Yoshida, that the Chinese were nationalists first and Communists second, that communism was merely a mode of modernization which the Chinese would in time throw off because they were essentially an "individualistic" people. As Yoshida once remarked to me, Japan's differences with China were "merely political" and must one day fade away. Doubtless this was true enough, though it might take a long time. But men with such convictions took long views about China, and they were prepared to wait. Such men also sometimes professed to be mystified at Western interest in India, which to them was running a poor third (behind Japan and China) in the race for modernization. These Japanese might be indicted for an unrealism sometimes bordering on euphoria about Chinese communism. But while emotionally some of them would have liked to abandon containment—a foolish policy to most of them—and "go it alone" with China, their political prudence caused them generally to adhere to the prevailing pro-American line, although certain dissenters grew increasingly restive with that line.

Old romantics like Matsumura were not the only conservative partisans of China trade, but they were somehow more ornamental than any of the others, some of whom acted as mere front men for business without putting on any cultural trimmings. Younger conservative politicians of the "new right" also actively supported a policy of attraction and diplomatic recognition of Peking apparently because they thought it was the best thing for their country to do. A wide variety of views could be and were entertained and openly expressed on nearly any subject under the sun, and China policy was no exception. Pressures for change in that policy existed, even though they were not strong enough to force a basic change.

Another category of Japanese with pronounced views about China and policy toward it were intellectuals, a self-consciously elitist group of people in universities and the more self-respecting areas of journalism, whose critical frame of reference tended to be heavily influenced by German historicism and Marxism. Some of the most illustrious of these men had collaborated with Japanese militarism; as someone has said, Japanese liberalism had few martyrs. After the war they were "liberated" by the American Occupation and flourished momentarily in an interval of reform and "democratization," only to become disillusioned by the Occupation's rapid turn against radical political activities in the late 1940s. Japanese intellectuals, Marxists or "liberals" alike, could not be expected to shift their ground as rapidly as Americans did at the onset of the Cold War. The Japanese had never fought for their freedom, and their experience of personal political oppression was unlike the Americans'. Ever since the war some of the most influential and vocal of the intellectuals had regarded the conservative party and bureaucracy much as American radicals regarded Nguyen Cao Ky. They feared a return of the rightist past far more than any supposed threat to Japan from China.

These intellectuals were a continuing challenge to the patience if not to the conscience of Americans. The presence of American bases and armed forces on Japanese soil was particularly galling to them. Underneath their protests against the bases lay deep feelings of nationalism and offended Japanese pride. They resented their country's long-continued dependence on Westerners and saw American "imperialism" or their own "neo-fascist" leaders, or a combination of both, as the main barrier preventing them from making contact with the "historical forces of the revolution" which were following out their inevitable course on the Chinese mainland, but which they, and Japan, were missing. Racial, personal, and ideological elements were thus mixed in their yearning for closer relationships with the Chinese who, most Japanese intellectuals believed, were unifying their country for the first time in the modern age, after having liberated it from its corrupt Kuomintang exploiters and lifted its foreign, including its Japanese, yoke. "Progressive" intellectuals were not inclined to feel much threat to themselves from this unification process. The Chinese were seen to be preoccupied with their domestic economic concerns and not given by nature to aggressiveness unless attacked; the West was to blame if they reacted aggressively to their own blockade and isolation. It may well be that the knowledge of the American military presence in the Western Pacific contributed to the lack of a sense of alarm toward China among Japanese intellectuals and made it possible for them to cherish such views with impunity.

Still another attitude often attributed to Japanese intellectuals was a sense of moral guilt for the years of cruelty and oppression perpetrated by the Japanese military. Moral guilt was probably not felt by a large number, although to a few the purgation of that guilt was a cardinal duty which the Japanese people had not yet even begun seriously to undertake.[32] But those who stressed Japan's guilt hardly ever suggested that the Chinese might therefore seek revenge; indeed, one sometimes wondered whether the articulation or ventilation of a sense of guilt may have helped to bolster the Japanese self-image vis-à-vis China. Be that as it may, the sense of guilt which was undoubtedly present in some sensitive, reflective minds did not prevent the same minds from having strong perceptions of Chinese backwardness in the material sphere. Here the superior achievements of the Japanese were taken for granted; and intellectuals felt a condescension toward China that was bred of cultural distance from the Chinese people at the same time that they felt guilt, or ideological fervor for the progress of the revolution. The life-style of the Japanese intellectual was Western bourgeois; he might talk and write about the "people," his own or the Chinese; but his knowledge of both was rather theoretical.

The technological gulf that opened between China and Japan in the late nineteenth and early twentieth centuries, and that widened steadily after World War II, had far more relevance to relations between the two countries in the 1950s and 1960s than all the talk about affinity or all the deep, supposedly unappeased moral guilt. Japan's isolation from China was not merely for political reasons but for economic and cultural reasons as well. This fact was not lost on many Japanese, who saw that just as Japan was a vastly more modern society than those societies to its south, so it was far more modern and advanced than China. Old politicians left over from the Empire might talk about cultural closeness in the past, but most young Japanese—those, say, under 40 or 45—were less preoccupied with China than with the West, when they thought at all about the outside world. For every student who studied Chinese, a thousand struggled with English; for every reader of Mao's thought, a thousand read magazines on business management or articles on the opportunities of investing in Alaska or elsewhere in the West, or in South or Southeast Asia. Both China and Japan continued to use old myths and old people when it suited their purposes; but it is at least arguable that Japan may have outgrown the period of its greatest need for China. As one Japanese scholar put it, the Japanese had been flung, half-civilized by the standards of traditional Chinese civilization, but at any rate flung, into the technical culture of the West a century ago. Since then they had concentrated almost exclusively on Western ideas and Western things. Most of them were cool toward Asia. They tended to look down on other Asians, who felt no unity among themselves and who had not yet made it into the modern world.

Finally, a majority of the Japanese people, if the polls had any significance, wished to establish official relations with the Peking regime but were at a loss to know what to do about solving the Taiwan problem, and they assented more or less willingly to their government's policy of wait-and-see and alignment with the United States, in spite of unremitting leftist propaganda against that alignment. The polls also showed that, despite all the talk about affinity, the Chinese people ranked low, along with Koreans and Russians, in the scale of Japanese esteem. Most people wanted to do business with both Chinas. They wanted the best of both worlds without the risk of commitment to either, trading with everybody, free to call for American protection if they needed it, although most did not feel it would ever be needed and wished to be rid of its outward evidences.

6. JAPANESE-KOREAN RELATIONS

Korea was not a separate, autonomous combatant in World War II and did not participate officially in the 1951 San Francisco peace settlement. In the treaty Japan formally renounced all claim to territory in the Korean peninsula. However, the treaty left many problems to be solved before normal diplomatic relations could be established with any government there. After the Republic of Korea was created in 1948, Japan treated it as the legal government of all Korea and had no official dealings with the North Korea government. But for most of the following seventeen years, until Japan and South Korea signed their own treaty settlement on June 22, 1965, relations between the two countries were marked by mutual recrimination, prejudice, and rancor. Memory of the past governed personal and official attitudes on both sides, and the legacy of colonialism got in the way of rapid settlement of difficulties. Japan's isolation from South Korea was practically as severe as its isolation from China, and there were fewer Japanese who felt any particular urgency about reducing it.

This situation had very deep causes, not to be quickly eradicated. No two people on earth liked each other less. The Japanese had, on the whole, a record of harsh oppression in Korea. Their policies aiming at assimilation of the Koreans had failed miserably; this might have been predicted, since Korean nationalism was built round a fiercely cantankerous independence of spirit. Japan did not give up its Empire more or less voluntarily or magnanimously, territory by territory; nor did it have time to reflect on the past wrongs of its colonial policies while fighting rearguard actions against guerrilla nationalists. Rather, the Japanese Empire was taken down and put away, as it were, overnight, before there could be time for any moderating of attitudes on the part of either rulers or ruled.

The South Koreans had in their first President, Syngman Rhee, the very incarnation of outraged nationalism. A Confucian, like Sun Yat-sen, onto whom a translucent layer of Christian ideas had been laminated (he wrote his thesis on international law at Princeton and was transiently influenced by Woodrow Wilson), Rhee helped organize guerrilla bands against the Japanese occupation and otherwise harassed the colonial administration for many years before its demise in 1945. In youthful exile he had seemed a liberal figure; but his social ideas were traditional, he had had a classical education before coming to the United States for graduate work, and the older he became and the longer he remained in power the more his conservative nature revealed itself. Throughout his life he detested the Japanese, and they reciprocated with energy.

Japanese negotiators of Korean matters included some hard-bitten, unregenerate types, especially in the early stages. They were unremorseful, to say the least, about their country's record in Korea. Decades of exploitation had built up a stereotype of Koreans as unruly children, to be punished or reasoned with according to one's temperament, but to be treated paternalistically in any event; most Japanese found it almost impossible to regard them as autonomous equals. The Japanese occupation had developed Korea, albeit for Japan's own benefit; it had built harbors, factories, railroads, had raised rice production, set up systems of education and public health, and enforced its own version of law and order on the people. This had involved much repression, but the Koreans ought to be grateful for what Japan had built, or so many Japanese thought. Never colonized themselves, the

Japanese had no experience of unchecked exploitation by aliens. Most of them, especially in the postwar period, knew very little about Korea and cared less. Cultural prejudice against Koreans was deep. Polls indicated that Korea was consistently on or near the bottom of the list of countries ranked in terms of esteem. Few Japanese felt much guilt for past treatment of Koreans in Japan; a few did, especially those who were old enough to recall how Koreans had been persecuted and killed following the Tokyo earthquake of 1923. The northern half of the Korean peninsula had minerals, now for all practical purposes unobtainable, but the south had almost nothing to export but labor. Trade with Korea was negligible. Few businessmen turned their attention from distant Chicago to nearby Pusan.

Thus in spite of reasons for restoring ties that might have been compelling in the abstract—such as the putative value of Japanese economic assistance to the war-devastated Korean economy or the dividends a more friendly relationship between the two countries might have paid for stability in the area—many years had to pass before a formal agreement settling the issues between them was signed, much less implemented. Progress of the negotiations was impeded at every step by the drag of the past as well as by Japan's reluctance to draw too near to its violently anti-Communist neighbor across the straits. Like leaders in some other countries, Rhee used his own and his countrymen's hatred of Japan as a tool to frighten them and strengthen his own position. The Japanese were portrayed as eager to reinfiltrate the Korean economy or as dangerously subversive, pro-Communist, and to be guarded against. Very few Japanese were allowed to enter Korea, and censorship of Japanese books and other materials was strictly enforced. (It was still being enforced under the Park regime in 1968. Certain textbooks, especially in the sciences and engineering, could be freely bought in Seoul, along with magazines like *The House-wife's Friend* [*Shufu no Tomo*] and other politically innocuous Japanese literature; but none of the principal vehicles of contemporary Japanese thought, such as the Tokyo press and intellectual magazines, could be obtained.) Rhee appeared to be obsessed with the danger of forgiving the Japanese or allowing them to restore relationships in Korea.

In this defensive frame of mind the Rhee government began negotiations with Japan in early 1952, before the San Francisco Peace Treaty had taken effect. There were half a dozen principal issues, but the question of the legal status and disposition of the Korean minority in Japan was particularly complicated. At war's end approximately 2.4 million Koreans were living in Japan. After initial repatriation programs had been completed just after the war, there were still perhaps 700,000 Koreans in the country. Some had been there since long before the war; others had been brought, or had come under varying degrees of pressure, as contract laborers in coal mines or factories during the war. Many of those who were repatriated in 1946–47 later re-entered Japan illegally. Large numbers were illiterate, many were unskilled. Communist-led and -supported Korean organizations in Japan gained semi-official control over the Korean minority in the early repatriation period. They set up Korean schools and gave indoctrination in Marxist-Leninist thought. *Chōsōren*, the most important of these organizations, was described as being little more than "an arm of North Korea's foreign office." [33]

During the American Occupation SCAP declared that the Koreans were to be treated as Japanese citizens, even though they had lost their citizenship as Japanese when Japan surrendered in 1945 and forfeited its Empire. The decision displeased many Koreans, who wanted the full status of foreigners in Japan that the nationals of other countries had. SCAP later required registration of Koreans as a law-and-order measure, and the Japanese government took steps to reduce leftist control over Korean schools. This further confused the minority about its rights. After the Peace Treaty in 1952 Koreans were no longer treated as Japanese citizens, but their residence and other status as foreigners was vague on account of their peculiar relationship with Japan. Culturally, they were also confused, with many adults unable to use

Japanese fluently while their children were losing touch with Korean. Pulled about by rival political groups, they lived for the most part in segregated communities and married only among themselves. A few Japanese saw that the Koreans were in Japan to stay; they would eventually go to Japanese public schools instead of Korean private ones (Korean public schools were prohibited). In the long run more of them would marry Japanese and might be genuinely assimilated into the Japanese generality. But to most Japanese they were a nuisance and an irritant, to be gotten rid of, if possible, the sooner the better. Indigent Koreans competed with Japanese for limited welfare funds, and all of them were considered outsiders with no prestige or power.

Unlike North Korea, the Seoul regime made only weak attempts to propagandize Korean expatriates. *Mindan,* the Korean organization in Japan supporting South Korea, was much weaker than *Chōsōren.* On the other hand, Rhee demanded that Koreans in Japan be compensated for unpaid wages and other services deriving from the war. He vehemently claimed them as citizens of South Korea, although such was the influence of *Chōsōren* that more than 75 per cent signed as North Korean citizens when they were required to register with the Japanese authorities. Rhee demanded for the Koreans special rights denied to other aliens in Japan; he appeared to want to use the Korean minority as a pawn in the negotiations, but he showed little interest in having them back.[34]

In addition to the minority problem, both sides presented property claims. The Koreans asked for hundreds of millions of dollars worth of unpaid pensions, postal savings deposits, insurance claims, payments to Koreans holding Japanese war bonds they had been forced to buy, gold and silver stocks removed from Korea during the colonial period, and other monetary claims. Korea also demanded title to all Japanese ships caught in Korean harbors by the Japanese surrender, as well as the return of fishing vessels taken to Japan in the interval between the Japanese surrender and the arrival of American Occupation forces. The Korean side also asked for return of all art objects "illegally" taken from Korea and now in Japanese museums, including items considered Japanese government property as well as those in private hands. Extensive lists of cultural properties, such as the contents of excavated tombs, paintings, books, temple sculptures, and other treasures taken during the entire colonial period, were prepared. The Koreans occasionally brought forward blanket war-reparations claims; at one time in 1952 their figure was about $2 billion. But the Japanese pointed out that since Korea had not been a belligerent during the war, reparations as such were not going to be allowed.

The Korean approach in these negotiations was similar to the Filipino or Indonesian approach to reparations; nothing the Japanese could do could possibly bring restitution for all the damage and hurt that had been done, but the claims were detailed and comprehensive and were scaled to the near-total destruction of Korean assets, not to Japan's capacity to pay. In the Korean case, however, the Japanese occupation had obviously lasted longer than anywhere else except Taiwan. There was a longer history of grievance, feelings of hostility were remorseless, and, at least while Syngman Rhee lived, the Koreans showed few signs of a willingness to compromise.

Nor did the Japanese give an inch in the negotiations. In fact, the Japanese delegate at the first talks insisted that Allied disposition of private Japanese assets in Korea to Koreans, which had been done before the Peace Treaty had been signed, was of dubious legality. His claim, which rested on a legal technicality, later was repudiated by the U.S. government, which reaffirmed that Japan had abandoned all claims to such properties when the Peace Treaty was signed. Put forward as a gambit in the bargaining more than for any other reason, the Japanese claim was not pressed, but it further infuriated the Koreans, who for years afterward liked to recall the Japanese claim that upward of 80 per cent of the real property in Korea had been created by Japanese and still rightfully belonged to them. The United States, in what was to become a familiar role, undertook to bring some reason into the discussions and mend the breach by inviting Syngman Rhee to visit Japan as the guest of General Mark Clark, then U.N. Commander in Korea. Rhee met Premier Yoshida at Clark's Tokyo residence and talked with some other Japanese officials, but without result. A few weeks after Rhee's return home, a Korean gunboat attacked a Japanese fishing boat in the straits of Tsushima, and a Japanese fisherman was killed. The first round of talks was broken off on April 24, 1952, just four days before the effective date of the San Francisco Peace Treaty.

The gunboat episode was merely the latest flare-up in a series of incidents connected with the so-called Rhee Line, which was by far the most provocative single issue inflaming Japanese-Korean relations in the period. During the Korean War General MacArthur had established a security boundary in Korean waters designed to seal off the peninsula. In January 1952 President Rhee took over this boundary and in 1953 proclaimed a "fisheries conservation zone" within a line drawn around the peninsula. Known to Koreans as the "Peace Line," it extended in some places as far as sixty miles offshore and took in rich sardine, mackerel, and other fishing grounds where the Japanese had operated for decades.

At a time when Japanese fishing rights in the North Pacific were in dispute with the Soviet Union and when mainland China was seizing Japanese fishing craft and imprisoning their crews, the Japanese reaction to the Korean demarcation line was very sharp, indeed. It was especially bitter in the western part of Japan, around the city of Nagasaki, which had been cut off from the trade with China that had once made it prosperous and stood to suffer from any suspension or curtailment of fishing operations in the sea areas adjacent to Korea. In 1955 the governor of Nagasaki prefecture described Syngman Rhee as "a madman, not a human being" and further declared, "If I were Foreign Minister, I would send all the Koreans back to Korea. Half of them in Japan are confirmed criminals." These were unusually strong words for a

Japanese politician to use, but Korea evoked strong feelings. The governor also echoed the views of many Japanese when he stated that "Japan developed Korea. We built dams and bridges and power plants, just as England did in India, maybe even more extensively. Why can't the Koreans feel toward Japan as the Indians feel toward Britain? What is to become of the families of Japanese fishermen captured by Korean patrol boats? Tokyo hasn't the courage to use its defense force." Leftists in the fishermen's union professed to believe that the "Rhee Line" was a plot devised by the United States to incite the Japanese to rearm.[35] On this, as on all foreign issues, there was an ideological split, with each side blaming the other or the United States; but the fishing dispute was not to be solved for many years. By October 1953, thirty boats with 500 fishermen were in Korean hands, and a stockade to hold them had been built in Pusan.

In the same month the second round of talks between Japanese and Korean negotiators broke down in Tokyo when a member of the Japanese team permitted himself to suggest that Korea had benefited from Japanese rule and made other statements offensive to the South Korean side. In the following years the two countries disputed possession of a group of uninhabited rocks in the Japan Sea called Takeshima (in Korean, Tokto), the Bamboo Islands, with the Koreans finally taking possession and building a lighthouse and the Japanese demanding that the matter be put before the World Court for arbitration. Korean-Japanese relations were nearly as barren as Takeshima's shores.

For most of the time between the second failure of negotiations in 1953 and Rhee's forced retirement in April 1960, no talks were held at all, in spite of American prodding of both sides. In 1956 Secretary of State Dulles visited Seoul and Tokyo without improving the atmosphere noticeably. Rhee interfered with trade with Japan or banned it entirely for long periods, at times refusing to allow U.S. aid supplies to be purchased in Japan, although that was the logical source for many such supplies. Travel of Japanese to Korea was restricted. In 1957 the London *Times* questioned

whether Rhee could accept the possibility of a fair settlement
with Japan, whose people "he has persistently denounced as un-
trustworthy and incorrigibly aggressive." [36]

In December 1955, the well-known Japanese Christian leader,
Toyohiko Kagawa, made an eloquent appeal in an open letter
to President Rhee, which was printed widely in the Japanese
press. Kagawa wrote:

> As Saul tried to kill David, the Japanese tortured Your Excellency
> and oppressed your people. In the name of Christ I apologize to
> your Excellency, and appealing to your Christian conscience, beg
> for your forgiveness. Forgive like the Lord who forgave His enemies
> on the Cross and bring . . . permanent peace between Great Korea
> and Japan.

Pressing his appeal, Kagawa drew examples from American history:

> There was a time when the United States was a colony of Great
> Britain. Angered by Britain's oppression of the colonies, George
> Washington stood up and fought against England to achieve today's
> independence. However, at present old hatreds are forgotten. . . .
> I wish the relationship between Great Korea and Japan would be
> like this.[37]

Kagawa's sentiments were noble, but few Japanese were disposed
so kindly toward "Great Korea"; most felt nothing but distaste for
Rhee's claims and were in no mood to apologize for the colonial
period.

The Japanese government no doubt agreed with the London
Times that the chances of better relations were poor as long as
Rhee was in power. In a more general sense, however, Japanese
leaders felt that time was with them. Their economic need for
South Korea was slight, but South Korea would sooner or later,
they thought, be forced to turn to Japan for help in its development programs. Japanese governments in that period felt little
obligation to make concessions in either the political or economic
sphere in spite of American pressure to do so. In 1959, for ex-

ample, when Rhee had shown that he would not accept repatriation of Koreans in Japan without cash compensation, the Kishi
government authorized sending to North Korea those Koreans
who wished to go there. This operation, justified by the Japanese
on humanitarian grounds, was supervised by the International
Red Cross, which screened applicants and conducted their registration. North Korean organizations in Japan painted a bright
picture of life above the 38th parallel, where jobs and opportunities to build a new society not present in Japan were said to be
awaiting every Korean who would return. The Japanese wanted
the Koreans gone for economic reasons; 75 per cent of those reg-
istering for return to the North were unemployed.[38] President
Rhee threatened naval intervention against the repatriation ships,
but aside from suspending trade for a time he took no action.
By mid-1961, about 75,000 Koreans had sailed for the People's
Republic in Soviet vessels from the port of Niigata on the Japan
Sea. (This was the first mass movement from non-Communist
to Communist areas on record.) But when the bulk of those
who wanted to leave had left, there were still at least 600,000
Koreans who had chosen to remain in Japan.

Strategic concern for Korea was as old as Japanese history. The
Korean peninsula before the war had often been described, in
a well-worn cliché, as a "dagger pointed at the heart of Japan."
Japanese, Chinese, and Russians had contested for control and
suzerainty there. Now Japanese power had greatly declined, and
the security problem was never far from the minds of Japanese
leaders from Yoshida's time forward. But the presence of U.N.
forces in Korea made it unnecessary for the Japanese government
to adopt new and different policies toward that country in a
hurry. Korea represented a danger near at hand, not "on the other
side of the river." But just as on China, consensus on Korea was
entirely unobtainable in Japan. Certain members of the "old
right" in the Liberal Democratic party were identified as a "Korea
lobby," just as some were known as the "Taiwan lobby." These
men had had commercial connections with Korea but were pri-

marily known for their strong anti-Communist stance; to Seoul they were the most palatable leaders of Japanese missions during the Rhee regime. Younger members of the conservative "new right," however, were opposed to any closer move toward South Korea on the grounds that this would jeopardize Japan's chance of having profitable relations with mainland China as well as with a reunified Korea. The Socialists demanded that relations with North Korea be normalized, and they fought restoration of normal diplomatic relations with the Seoul government unless the peninsula were simultaneously reunified. The government was extremely wary of forming any overtly anti-Communist relationship with South Korea, which might embroil it in America's wars and add to the conservative party's troubles at home. Rhee's intransigence was to be deplored; it was preventing his country from benefiting from closer economic ties, but it was also useful to Japanese politicians who believed it was in Japan's interest to sit tight and wait.

With Rhee's fall in April 1960, a slow thaw began in Japan-Korea relations. New "preliminary" talks were held that autumn, only to be attacked by the Korean opposition. However, Korea's economic need evidently dictated closer relations. Japanese companies were ready to move across the straits once government guarantees could be given. Investment surveys had been made by several large trading companies as well as by some smaller and less reputable ones. The Japanese proposed to build power plants, fertilizer factories, cement plants, and many other facilities. The United States strongly desired Japanese participation in Korean plans for both economic and political reasons, and the Japanese seemed ready at least to play a much greater economic role.[39]

After the military coup of May 16, 1961, and the installation in power of the strongly nationalistic General Park, the first serious long-range plans since 1945 for Korean economic development were drawn up, and new talks were begun with Japan. Initial Korean demands amounted to some $800 million in "reparations," plus return of cultural properties, and settlement of the residential status of the Korean minority. Japan's first offer was reported to be $70 million; the Japanese were particularly interested in settling the problem of the fishing zone. Demonstrations were repeatedly held against the talks in Tokyo and Seoul, and the Japanese Foreign Minister's automobile was mobbed during his visit to the Korean capital. But by early 1963, after nearly two years of desultory talking, a formula was finally reached for compensation for damage done under Japanese rule, and a treaty was signed on June 22, 1965.

According to the treaty, ratified by both countries later in 1965, Japan pledged to extend $500 million in government aid. Of this, $300 million was in outright grants, and $200 million in twenty-year loans at 3.5 per cent interest, with a seven-year moratorium on repayment. The loans were to be extended through the new Overseas Economic Cooperation Fund. In addition, the Japanese government agreed to facilitate private credits of another $300 million to South Koreans. All this compensation was made in a form that stressed economic cooperation, not reparations, a word already distasteful enough to the Japanese public and impossible to stomach where Korea was concerned. Besides the money settlement, a new fisheries agreement was reached that abolished the "Rhee Line," although the Korean side clung to this to the bitter end, changing its name to "National Defense Line" and infuriating the Japanese who at one point refused to talk at all until the Koreans conceded the issue. The treaty set a more normal twelve-mile limit for both countries and provided for joint operation outside those limits in the waters between them up to a catch limit of 150,000 tons yearly for five years. Japan agreed to return certain art treasures to Korea, even though it had earlier claimed that they had already been paid for. Finally, the agreement provided permanent residence rights for nationals of the Republic of Korea who had lived in Japan continuously since August 15, 1945, and for their descendants born up until five years from the date the treaty became effective.[40] Japan promised to make special provision for education, social security, and health insurance protection of Koreans becoming permanent residents.

In Seoul, students rioted against the treaty throughout the spring of 1965, and the Japanese Left in Tokyo did what it could to whip up another crisis of the 1960 type. But the treaty was signed and ratified without serious incident. A few weeks after the signing, on July 19, 1965, Syngman Rhee died at 90 in Honolulu, without having returned to his native land. Even though a treaty had been signed, much hostility remained to plague both countries. The truth of the matter was that in spite of the obvious benefits of cooperation for both sides, too long enforced familiarity before the war had bred mutual contempt. The Japanese Foreign Ministry liked to say that public opinion was so hostile to Korea that no friendly approaches were possible, but the Foreign Ministry did almost nothing to re-educate public opinion any more than it tried seriously to inform the public on other foreign policy issues. Its informational activities were especially meager where Asia was concerned. But this merely reflected the predilection of the leaders of the country themselves, who through most of the postwar period allowed deep-seated cultural prejudices to provide a pretext for not trying very hard to reach a better understanding with Korea. The relative lethargy of Japan's Korea policy up to 1965 was a reflection of emotional, cultural, and political distaste. Although economic relations would grow, the notion that they must necessarily be accompanied by a closer political relationship between Japan and South Korea remained to be proved. Such a relationship could assuredly not be forced on Japan but would have to be seen to serve its best interests, commercial and otherwise.

PART TWO

Japan and Asia, 1964–69

IV. The Level of Rhetoric: Asia as Seen from Tokyo

Japanese business firms abroad were the most conspicuous symbols of the national interest, but business alone did not determine foreign policy and was not the only voice through which the Japanese spoke their minds about Asia and the world. The alliance with the United States, involving military bases and a large foreign presence, presented Japan's leaders with intermittently explosive nationalist frustrations among those portions of the community critical of the government and its policies. The Security Treaty crisis of 1960, in which many nay-sayers confronted the advocates of the American alignment and business-as-usual, was the most dramatic manifestation of those frustrations. The crisis was not enough to drive the conservatives *per se* from power. But after the Tokyo riots, political events abroad, among them the Sino-Soviet split, the emergence of de Gaulle, and other symptoms of polycentrism in world politics, combined with prosperity and quieter times at home to turn the energies of many Japanese to a debate on national security and the national interest.

The debate cut across the spectrum of opinion from peace nationalists to the more conventional exponents of military power. Such subjects as nuclear weapons, taboo since 1945, were taken up by critics and commentators in the press and intellectual magazines, where terms had to be invented for "multiple option strategy," "second-strike capability," "nonproliferation," and all the other jargon of the new age. No real consensus on new political actions in Asia or anywhere else emerged from this debate up to the end of the 1960s, but behind all the talk could be discerned a reviving nationalism, in which Japan's economic influence in the world, now undoubted by all, suggested the possibility of new political roles, both as regards the country's position vis-à-vis the superpowers in the Cold War that now was believed to be breaking up (a theme often termed in Japanese the "East-West problem") and as regards relationships with the developing nations to the south (the "North-South problem"). And in a few minds, at least, these two areas of policy began to be connected in significant ways.

1. China and Japan's Security: The "East-West Problem"

Few ever doubted that Japan must one day play a larger role in the world. The argument turned on what this involved.[1] Participants in the debate were divided into a small but articulate group of "idealist" intellectuals, most of them university professors in Tokyo, and a somewhat larger group of "realists," including professors, lecturers in the Defense Academy, journalists, and others, who were beginning to make themselves heard more openly. Leaders of both groups had received all or some of their graduate education in the United States. Many were well known there, and most of their written views, if not their spoken feelings, were influenced by Western books and teachers.

"Idealists" justified their name by being generally unwilling to give up the image of Japan as a disarmed, neutral state. More than anything else, perhaps, they wanted to return to the Japan of August 15, 1945, the moment of surrender, when the alliance with America had not been made, the conservatives were in disarray, and Japan, by virtue of its experience of nuclear suffering, stood, or so some thought, uniquely equipped to influence the world through the force of persuasion and peaceful coexistence alone.[2] Beneath the opposition of the "idealists" to rearmament lay a deep-seated distrust, partly ideological, partly personal and visceral, of their own leaders, who were seen as the lineal descendants of bureaucratic reactionaries bent upon the exploitation of the people for capitalist-militarist ends. Some were moved to speak out against the government because of their knowledge of the intellectuals' failure to do so before the war. Resenting Japan's defeat and subsequent abject dependence upon America, some "idealists" found satisfaction in seeing America discomfited by the frustration of its Asian policies. Some were professedly Marxists, some self-styled liberals or humanists; all were Japanese, and all claimed to stand for what was best for Japan.

In the "idealist" view, Japan's close alignment with an intrusive, militaristic America increased the likelihood of general war in Asia and Japanese involvement therein. Some stressed the unconstitutionality of rearmament and wanted to abolish the self-defense forces. Others claimed that there was no need for defense, since Japan was not threatened, save through the possibility of retaliation against American bases. Once the bases were removed, peace would reign. They saw China as essentially unaggressive but provoked by an aggressive America. Still others maintained that defense was impossible anyway in a nuclear age; to align with America merely meant to threaten China, which was insanity itself in view of Japan's total vulnerability to nuclear attack: "China's nuclear development has, in fact, been expedited with great vigor so as to alleviate as quickly as possible the threat of America's nuclear encirclement."[3] Some Japanese "idealists," like some Americans, saw the United States as a failing power unless it altered its foreign policies, which may have worked in Europe but would not work under Asian conditions. Like some of their American counterparts, they lacked faith in the capacity of the United States to change in ways they thought desirable. Some had "given up on" American society and felt that Japan might better abandon such an elephantine ally and seek its fate in some sort of identification with "the people" of China or Vietnam. Their metaphors were sometimes mixed in the excitement of describing America's plight: "America the mammoth has had its heels nipped by a country as small as a mouse because her policy objectives in international politics have somehow run amuck. . . . Somewhere along the line the United States took the wrong turn, and in order to reach her destination she is inclined to push the accelerator to the floor." To which was added the admonition that "true national strength is the capacity to alter national objectives and maneuver national policies autonomously and freely. If, for example, America had the ability to withdraw from South Vietnam, her withdrawal would indicate a tremendous ability to discipline and control herself." [4] Some "idealists" in Tokyo gave encouragement to the peace movement in the United States and found sympathizers among Americans disenchanted with U.S. policies.

"Idealists" looked forward to their dream of the future, when American "nuclear intimidation" and Chinese "revolutionary extremism" would both be dissolved in an era of international good will and cultural exchange, and Japanese behavioral scientists would teach their Chinese counterparts the secrets of Western social science. This was revealing: their desire for detachment from the American tie as well as their assumption that Japan might have a tutelary role vis-à-vis China merely indicated their innate nationalism. To most Japanese some such role had always seemed natural. They talked a good deal about the energy of the masses and a kind of "international nationalism," in which Japan was prevented from taking part by its association with America. They may have dreamed of some sort of "moral equivalent" for the conventional accompaniments of national power; but they usually reserved for Japan a superior role in whatever future South and Southeast Asia were to have, and they showed little genuine capacity for putting themselves in the place of others. Their blindness to the real and practical problems of others suggested future difficulties for the Japanese in Asia.

Both sides in the debate perceived that the Chinese nuclear explosions beginning in October 1964 marked an ominous shift in the Asian power balance. As one "idealist" put it, they represented the "end of Japan's long-standing superiority over China in terms of national power." [5] In the words of a "realist," "by virtue of a single atomic test Peking upset Japan's traditional diplomatic, psychological, and military superiority over China." [6] The differences between them lay in how to deal with the situation that both recognized existed.

Some "idealists" experienced moral disquiet at the explosion of nuclear weapons in China.[7] For instance, in 1963, after hearing rumors that the Chinese were about to detonate a nuclear device, one professor at Tokyo University wrote what he described as "an appeal both to China's policy-makers and to the leaders of Japan's peace movement." He was deeply disturbed by the rumors, because to him a Chinese bomb raised the problem of Japan's collective guilt toward China in new and more agonizing form. The Japanese, he believed, could have truly fruitful relationships with the mainland only if they cleansed their consciences of guilt for what Japan had done in China during the war. But he knew that few Japanese had accepted such a need, much less acted upon it; most were diffident toward China, in spite of an interest in trade and some talk of cultural affinity. He saw that young Japanese felt no guilt for the past, and he feared that by building nuclear weapons the Chinese would forfeit their last remaining moral claim on the Japanese nation.

In any choice between moral obligation to China for past wrongs and the wider obligation to oppose all nuclear weapons, he chose the latter; but he regretted having to choose at all, and his thinking provided insight into the attitude of the "idealists," which could be criticized as rather patronizing toward China:

> When the leaders of any country make a decision to develop nuclear weapons they must be regarded as having degraded themselves morally. The decision of China's leaders, however, is of special significance, because it was the moral superiority those leaders displayed at war's end that made the Japanese people so keenly aware

of Japan's immoral actions and of the responsibility they must assume for them. It is no exaggeration to say that the moral superiority shown by Chinese leaders has been one of the main supports of postwar Japan's national conscience. Therefore, any moral degeneration on the part of Chinese leaders is bound to have an adverse effect on the growth of that conscience.[8]

The idea that the Chinese might have developed their weapons without reference to the moral categories of Japanese intellectuals did not appear to have entered the writer's mind. He hoped, by his own account, to influence the Chinese to cease their preparations for atomic testing and to accept his proposals for a comprehensive test ban and a denuclearized zone in Asia and the Pacific. In a postscript to his 1963 article, written after several more Chinese tests had occurred, he continued to hope that they would be stopped:

China does not have to continue until she has built a complete nuclear arsenal. She need not wait until *after* each test to call for a total ban on nuclear arms. She has another alternative, and that is to announce clearly now, *before* conducting further tests, that she is prepared to suspend all efforts to develop nuclear arms if the other nuclear powers agree to nuclear disarmament and a total ban on nuclear testing. This would put considerable pressure on the United States, the Soviet Union, Great Britain, and France to reach agreement. Although conditions have changed during the five years since I wrote this article, and although the specific proposals I make today may not be the same, I still retain my basic conviction that nuclear armament is not China's only alternative.[9]

The Chinese bomb may have caused some moral queasiness in Japan. However, the American bombing of North Vietnam beginning four months later, in February 1965, produced a much deeper anxiety among the "idealists," in which not only moral qualms but also an active fear for Japan's security, seldom if ever expressed where China was concerned, was very evident. Japanese public opinion was inflamed by reporting of the war in mass media hostile to the South Vietnamese government and deeply critical of American escalation. Fear of Japan's involvement in the war because of its commitments to the United States under the Security Treaty was intense for a time, and some of the same intellectuals who felt guilt toward China deplored the negativism of America's China policy, blamed the West for the whole evolution of Chinese intransigence, and scornfully attacked the failure of Americans to perceive that the long-drawn-out fighting in Vietnam was in essence a nationalist civil war.

"Realists" accepted the American alignment as a national necessity, at least for the foreseeable future. Some appeared genuinely to believe that only by adhering to that alignment could Japan have a chance to partake of a more creative and possibly a freer human society, one that would bring out the full potential of its members. To have this kind of world, they believed a stable domestic polity was essential; unarmed neutralism would only exacerbate social and political divisions within Japan and lead to the reappearance of some form of Japanism.

This did not mean that all "realists" favored full-scale rearmament. Some yearned for utopia as much as "idealists" did, and it was characteristic of the great majority of Japanese in the generation following the war to want to find nonmilitary ways in which to express the national will. A prominent academic "realist" eloquently framed his country's chief problem:

We are already on the threshold of an age where man can no longer be persuaded that the meaning of life lies in earning his daily bread. The release of man from slavery to his work is a revolutionary development that explains, in part, why many modern governments, especially the superpowers, attempt to convince their people of life's meaning by emphasizing common national goals. This emphasis on common national goals is designed to stimulate nationalistic feelings over and against the enemy on the basis of competition between vying social and political systems, of races to space, and of rivalry in armed might. Japan must not rely on such a facile solution to the problem of discovering man's meaning in the meaninglessness of post-industrial society. She must instead explore untried possibilities by continuing her historically unprecedented attempt to identify the nation's *raison d'être* with peaceful, noncompetitive values; we must be proud of the fact that Japan alone is attempting this and confident that we can succeed.

He then scolded the United States for its short-sightedness in having urged rearmament on Japan and insisted that "Japan's most effective role is not as a military power but as a model to which the developing nations of the world might look." [10]

His "realism" consisted in believing that Japan's security in a world that did not share its "unprecedented" search for "peaceful noncompetitive values" depended on sticking to the United States for the foreseeable future, which in turn meant maintaining the status quo in Asia. Japan, in his view, should have three main goals: to achieve domestic political stability, to "maximize" friends and allies, and to increase Japanese bargaining power. Attacking the "idealists," he asserted:

> . . . we can neither make allies nor minimize our enemies if we imagine that international politics is a kindergarten playground where we can hold hands and make friends with everybody. And we dare not make the mistake of trying to distinguish friend and foe on the basis of ideology, i.e., free versus Communist, capitalist versus Socialist, imperialist versus anti-imperialist, have versus have not, white versus colored, Western European versus Asian, etc. We must make our choice on the basis of economic, political and geopolitical national interest, and in doing so we must assume that Japan is (1) fundamentally a status quo power, (2) situated in the Asian cultural bloc, (3) an advanced nation whose high technical capabilities have brought her to the stage of mass consumption, and (4) a maritime state, which, as long as the U.S. Seventh Fleet controls the Western Pacific, is destined to remain under America's nuclear umbrella. [11]

Here sounded the authentic note of diffidence toward making open commitments on the basis of ideology as well as the pragmatic adherence to the American alignment that had characterized the world view of influential Japanese ever since Premier Yoshida's day. In phrases that put a premium on self-pity, "realists" described Japan as an "orphan" situated in the "dark valley" between the superpowers, but they perceived Japan's loneliness and cultural distance from the rest of Asia somewhat better than the more moralistic "idealists" did.

In the realist-idealist polemic the first stirrings of an awakening nationalism were verbalized. After October 1964 China demanded the attention if not the anxiety of all those concerned with Japan's security. Developments there reverberated in Japanese politics, overshadowing the war in Vietnam and providing fuel for the continuing security debate.

The estrangement of the Japan Communist Party (JCP) from Peking after years of close association followed on the failure of the attempted Communist *coup d'état* in Indonesia in September 1965. Japanese Communist leaders, more interested than they had ever been in their party's parliamentary chances, were appalled by the adventurism of Indonesian Communists and the Chinese inability to bail them out. Some JCP members pointed to the irrelevance of people's wars for Communist success in a modern society like Japan, whose cultural distance from China was now openly recognized on the Left. Like conservative businessmen, Communists deplored Peking's "irrationality." By contrast, the Soviet Union was increasingly seen to be a relatively benevolent advocate of peaceful coexistence.

As the Cultural Revolution progressed, the split between the Japanese and Chinese parties came into the open. Front groups like the Japan-China Friendship Association, the Asia-Africa Liaison Committee, the Japan Journalist Congress, the China Research Institute, the League of Returnees from China, and even the Association for Japanese-Chinese Buddhist Exchange broke in two, with pro-Chinese rump groups setting up "True Headquarters," which immediately received recognition and financial support from Peking. By early 1968 about 600 members had been expelled from the JCP for pro-Chinese sympathies.[12] The Chinese Communists made every effort to disrupt the JCP, even organizing rival branches in some of Japan's prefectures.[13]

Peking pressed invitations on sympathetic Japanese, paying special attention to youth: over 400 Japanese young people were invited, and over 100 were permitted to visit China in 1965, where they issued joint declarations of "fighting friendship" with their Chinese hosts.[14] One Japanese newspaperman, posted to Peking from September 1966 to September 1967, on his return wrote a bestselling account of his experiences, which included a description of how two visiting JCP members were beaten up by a gang of "Japanese Red Guards," children of other Communists who had been sent to Peking years before for their education and who now sided with the Chinese in the split with the JCP. The correspondent's book described the lengths to which some Japanese would go to keep in the good graces of the Chinese. One lady member of a Tokyo theatrical troupe read to her audience from Mao's thoughts in Japanese, and businessmen promised to demonstrate against the government after their return to Tokyo in order to assure further contracts.[15] In the period between January and June of 1967, representatives of "friendly firms" stationed in Peking issued at least six joint declarations of support for China. This earned them the contempt of one conservative writer:

> It was no surprise that among those friendly firms were some who publicly sold out their fatherland for profit, who sold out the spirit of Japan and bought Chinese acceptance by swearing loyalty to China. They were the running dogs of the Chinese Communists . . . who were given special position in return for supplying the Chinese with reports and materials. . . . The International Trade Promotion Council has become nothing but a subcontractor for the Chinese Communists.[16]

After the schism between the two Communist parties trade continued, but from late 1966 the confusion surrounding it deepened. In that year L-T trade amounted to $200 million, "friendly firm" trade to more than $300 million. This was larger than Japan's trade with the Soviet Union and far larger than that with Taiwan. The hope of closer economic relationships was kept alive by new negotiations following the expiration of the first L-T agreement in 1967. However, the Chinese never ceased to politicize the trade. Behind the bowls of fruit, the smiles, and communiqués lay many acid exchanges. When a Diet member belonging to the Kōmeitō, a Buddhist-affiliated party, informed a member of a Chinese mission visiting Tokyo that the popular Buddhist sect, Sōkagakkai, intended to proselytize in China, he was scornfully told to keep his faith-healing activities to himself. Industrial teams negotiating annual contracts regularly found themselves attacked by Peking for the Japanese government's pro-U.S. policy in Vietnam. Officials of Shōwa Denkō, a major manufacturer of chemical fertilizer, who conducted marathon trade negotiations in early 1968, reported that the Chinese side started with long harangues on Mao's thoughts and only much later got down to details of prices. Komatsu Engineering Company people, makers of agricultural machinery, reported the same. Some "friendly firms" were only too willing to comply with the ideological winds of the moment: The new "True Headquarters" of the Japan-China Friendship Association was reported to be composed mainly of representatives of such firms.[17] But trade faced increasing problems, and that it continued at all was evidence of the need felt for it by both sides, particularly by the Chinese. Reports were widespread in Japan of the failure of Chinese deliveries, port tie-ups, and the like.

The Japanese Diet delegation seeking a renewal of the 1963 agreement was forced virtually to give in to China and accept at least "in principle" the "three political principles" as well as the notion that economic and political relations were inseparable. These concessions, made by an "unofficial" mission, were promptly repudiated by the Japanese government, which denied that it could be bound by any Chinese "principles." Differing statements within the government, however, left some doubt about just how far the Japanese were willing to go politically for the sake of the trade. There was much pulling and hauling within conservative ranks, with some China-firsters urging the government to re-pudiate the "Yoshida letter," authorize deferred-payment plant exports, and otherwise take a more accommodating posture toward Peking. This, however, the Satō government refused to do. The L-T negotiations produced not another five-year agreement but a one-year arrangement. Chou En-lai warned the Japanese team that the future course of trade would depend entirely on Japanese behavior. By 1968 the "friendly firms" themselves began to feel the heat of Chinese disfavor when several of their representatives in Peking were arrested, at least one of them for espionage.[18]

The deterioration of relationships with China served to turn some merchants and businessmen toward the south. It also added to the already growing interest in the Soviet Union as a trading partner. More missions of top-level Japanese businessmen, econo-mists, and government officials visited Moscow, and more Russians came to Japan. There was nothing new in this, it was merely more noticeable after about 1964. The Russians had hinted at their de-sire to export electric power to Japan, presumably via an under-ground cable from Siberia. They had more than hinted at a pipeline from the Lake Baikal region to the Pacific through which cheap Soviet oil might be loaded in tankers for the short haul across the Japan Sea. Japanese who anticipated enormous energy imports in the coming years were naturally interested in these proposals. They were fully aware of the obstacles to Si-berian development, especially the scarcity of labor and markets. They knew that when the Russians said Siberia they meant the area just east of the Urals, whereas the Japanese meant the Mari-time Provinces. Yet the Japanese wanted to keep all their options open, and their isolation from China, though temporary in their eyes, turned the attention of some toward the option to the north.

One evidence of this was a carefully detailed study of Siberia issued by the Economic Affairs Bureau of the Foreign Ministry in October 1967.[19] This report had no illusions regarding Soviet mo-tives in courting Japan: "In view of the recent confrontation of China and the Soviet Union, it is reasonable to suppose that the

Soviet political objective is to remove Japan from the umbrella of the United States and at the same time to encircle China." The report raised various economic objections to the expansion of Japan's role in Siberia, among them the effect more raw materials purchases from Russia might have on Japan's trade with underdeveloped Asia; and it was not very sanguine about over-all prospects. In view of the history of Japan-Soviet relations and the territorial claims that still awaited settlement, too much was not to be made of Siberian possibilities. One Japanese economist estimated that even if a pipeline were laid from the Tumen oil-field to Nahodka and Japan were to use it to import 120 million tons of crude oil annually by 1975, that would amount to only 5 per cent of Japan's estimated total imports at that time.[20] On the other hand, it was reasonable to suppose that some amount of Japanese-Russian collaboration in Siberian development would continue and that it might increase, at least on a case-by-case basis. The most significant achievement up to this writing was a contract signed in August 1968 for export of $163 million worth of Japanese lumbering equipment in exchange for Siberian timber over a five-year period beginning in 1969.[21]

While academic "idealists" and "realists" debated the wisest course for the nation to achieve security, and events in mainland China grew more and more obscure, the Japanese government turned to its own stable of experts for foreign policy advice where China was concerned. Typical of the views of the more moderate China-watchers was a 312-page report prepared in late 1966 by a group of university professors, "realists" all, and distributed in mimeographed form by the Cabinet Research Bureau, a research and intelligence unit of the Premier's office in Tokyo.[22]

The authors of the report looked at China as if from a very great distance. They saw there aging leaders, desperately concerned with frustrating the neocapitalist trends that followed the failure of the Great Leap Forward in the early 1960s. They saw a degree of irrationality in Mao Tse-tung's insistence on ideology in the face of age-gaps, area-discrepancies in the pattern of party power, and the growing drift of the masses, with their desire for better conditions of life, away from the party. They saw an economy demanding rationalism and getting idolatry.

They believed that Japan, with its huge purchasing power and modern industry, inevitably had very great importance to China, especially in the latter's extreme isolation after 1965. In any interpretation of the relationship, China's need was the greater. Even if Japan's China trade grew rapidly, which was doubtful, it would not grow as rapidly as Japan's world trade. For this reason, although China would doubtless continue to try to use trade as a political weapon, its success was likely to be small. The influence of China on the political parties in Japan was, the experts believed, less worrisome than Chinese influence on the few businessmen who were traditionally dependent on the mainland, and than the psychological pressure of isolation from China on intellectuals and possibly on the people as a whole. The people's perception of China's importance to them could be greater than its real importance, and if the Chinese handled their nuclear program cleverly enough to threaten the Japanese, the effects of this pressure could be serious. But they saw no imminent national threat from China as long as Chinese leaders were preoccupied with domestic power struggles, which might continue for a long time.

The report predicted that Peking would have ICBMs by around 1975, but concluded that fear of retaliation by America's vastly greater nuclear strength would deter the Chinese from launching an attack on Japan. The alternative view—that if China attacked Japan with medium-range missiles, the United States would hesitate to retaliate out of fear of Chinese ICBM attack on the American continent—was entertained but rejected, on the grounds that China simply would not risk attacking first, and that its repeated announcements to that effect were designed to avoid foreign misunderstanding. Apart from nuclear attack, the report stressed that the state of Chinese armed forces was not such that Japan need fear direct invasion. China's naval forces were believed to be no more than adequate for coastal defense, whereas Japanese self-defense capabilities were quite substantial. On the other hand, Japan might possibly face a threat of insurgency in which disaffected Japanese might be supported in various ways by the Chinese. Changes in the status of Okinawa and Taiwan leading to the reduction of the American presence there might add to this threat; the possibility of guerrilla warfare against American bases in Okinawa could not be ruled out. How such a threat might develop was not spelled out, though the authors of the report reflected the concern of Japanese conservative intellectuals and politicians ever since Yoshida's day over the danger of subversion.

This 1966 report expressed the belief that neither the United States nor the Soviet Union wanted to change the power balance, and the reasons of both for wanting peaceful coexistence—a balance of terror in arms, relatively stable power spheres, and urgent internal problems—were likely to exist for some time. By contrast, China was seen as a kind of rogue in the world, seeking to alter the power balance but thus far failing to do so. Failure was attributed chiefly to the inflexibility and poor judgment of Chinese leaders. They had been in an excellent position early in 1965, having taken Vietnam as the key arena in which to prove Mao's theories of "intermediate zones" and people's wars against the metropolitan powers. But since then Chinese policy had collapsed everywhere in Asia and Africa. This was attributed in part to American military and political warfare in Vietnam, which, when the report was written, was believed to have had some degree of success in blocking North Vietnamese and Chinese aims. But a more basic reason for the failure of Chinese diplomacy was its total misreading of what the underdeveloped world wanted, which was neutralism and economic development. The Chinese revolution had had great appeal for other nationalist revolutions in their early stages; but by the mid-1960s those revolutions were mostly over; the first generation of leaders had foundered on economic problems, in the solution of which Mao's thoughts on revolution and war were less relevant than economic advice and cooperation from the advanced countries of the world, including the Soviet Union, the United States, and Japan. China's leaders had thus lost touch with reality in the "southern countries," whose future lay not in furthering theories of revolutionary struggle but in economic stability and higher standards of living.

Finally, the report concluded that while the next decade probably would not produce any great changes in the external balance of power in the world, the question whether China would be an internal threat to Japan depended in part upon Japan's own political evolution. The experts foresaw a steady erosion of the Liberal Democratic party's voting strength, continued factionalization of the party, and an apparent inability to transcend it, although factions were thought to divide somewhat more on issues than on personalities as formerly. One expert, a political scientist who analyzed the domestic political scene, believed that Japan was headed toward coalition government, which in ten years might find the Liberal Democratic party with 35 per cent to 40 per cent of Lower House seats, the Buddhist Kōmeitō with 20 per cent, and the non-Marxist Democratic Socialists with 5 to 8 per cent, governing together. If to this were added the rightwing factions of the Socialist party, a coalition comprising from 70 to 80 per cent of the seats might be formed, with the Communists and left-wing Socialists in opposition. This expert did not attempt to predict the chances of holding together such an unwieldly and disparate coalition, which would be an ideological and personal hash of everything from populist nationalism with religious trimmings to vague and varying versions of Marxism. He contented himself with the observation that the Buddhist mass organization, Sōkagakkai, which controlled the Kōmeitō, was fundamentally a phenomenon of the Japanese folk (*minzoku*) and therefore should cause no concern to the government in the future; and if such a coalition should be formed, he saw nothing to worry about as far as internal subversion was concerned. What really troubled the writers of this report was a recurrence of riots like those of 1960 in which the Chinese might possibly intervene with money, propaganda, and perhaps even arms.

The Cabinet Research Bureau's report and other writings by Japanese "realists" in the mid-1960s began to provide some political rationale for Japan's wider participation in the economic development of tropical Asia. For if one followed out the reasoning of these experts, Japan's economic cooperation would not only bring economic returns but would also respond to the felt needs of the underdeveloped periphery of China at precisely the time when China's revolutionary myopia had resulted in policy failures and retreat from the whole area. New Japanese initiatives in the area consequently could hardly fail to enhance Japan's position there.

Another group of "realist" commentators on defense and security matters nearer the right end of the political spectrum contributed to a series of books published in 1968 and designed partly to counter still another series, critical of government policies, that was issued by the *Asahi Shimbun*. This group included some "defense thinkers" and lecturers at the Defense Academy who had spent varying periods at think-tanks and research centers in the United States. Their books sold in small editions, and some members of the group were believed to be patronized by retired military officers of reactionary stripe. Their influence on their own government was uncertain, but their advice was being asked with increasing frequency.

Their writings were in effect a sustained counterattack on the "idealist" inclination to believe that America was to blame for Asia's troubles and that Japan's security lay in disengaging from America's alleged identification with anti-nationalism in Asia. Moreover, they assumed Japan's greatness, accepted the idea that there was no practical alternative to military power as the basis of diplomacy, and asked how Japan could satisfy its presumed urge for great power status in such a way as to avoid an expensive, dangerous rift with the United States. Some of them urged that Japan take over a much larger share of its own defense. All thought the country should do much more to contribute to the stability of Southeast Asia.

These "realists" had little use for the "idealist" emphasis on collective guilt and morality. They believed that having been the first nation to suffer atomic bombardment conferred no special moral superiority and sanctioned no unique role for Japan in history. They were suspicious of unique roles, and thought Japan would have used the bomb if it had had it first.[23] Attacked by "idealists" as reactionary, they felt that a peace Constitution like no other was an inadequate basis for national security policy in a precarious world environment. They talked coldly of national interest, asking whether the United States would have the will to go on defending non-Communist Asia after Vietnam [24] and wondering what signing the nonproliferation treaty would do for Japan's program of peaceful nuclear research, to say nothing of its chances of having nuclear arms. Few if any of them openly advocated nuclear weapons now, but there was very little doubt that at least some of the group looked upon their possession as a probability in the future. They wrote of finding and using a role of greater dignity vis-à-vis the United States, not merely of condemning American imperialism. In their view, the conservative government had used the peace Constitution and Japanese pacifism very cleverly for twenty years as a lever to get defense and technical assistance from the United States at minimum cost. Now they wanted Japan to use the nonproliferation treaty as a lever to negotiate separately with the United States and the U.S.S.R. for security guarantees and guarantees of peaceful access to nuclear energy as the price of Japan's signature.

Members of this "defense-thinker" group recognized that, with the exception of Japan, the peoples on the periphery of China felt threatened. The long-range answer to this fear was individual and regional defense by Asians of their own homelands. Protracted reliance on outsiders for a nation's own defense could only result in a collapse of the spirit. But, as one writer argued, "It is obvious that Japan can make no military contribution to the power balance in Asia in place of the United States. It must also be realized that the conditions for effective regional collective defense in the area are profoundly lacking." [25] For the foreseeable future, then, non-Communist Asia had no choice but to rely on American power. But Asia must also do much more to create firmer conditions for its own defense if it expected to rid itself of dependence on America. This meant social and political change from within and economic development to produce entirely new conditions of strength. Political and military intervention by the United States could have emergency effect but would never take the place of self-effort:

> Throughout the experience of the Vietnam war, America's military intervention has been a supplement to the South's own efforts, but it cannot take the place of those efforts. To oppose Chinese penetration via such people's liberation wars, Asians must themselves make stronger efforts for their own security. In the future, American military aid should be even more restricted. Aid from outside a country should be first of all for improving the means of political control and creating economic prosperity. Here is where *Japan must take over a part of the role of the United States; to help heighten feelings of security in Asia will mean stronger power to resist China.* Furthermore, economic blockade policies that prevent China from developing as a peaceful country and continue to look upon it as an enemy must be strictly avoided. A mixed approach is necessary that can respond flexibly to Chinese aggressiveness, while serving to restrict that aggressiveness.[26]

Quoting Secretary of Defense McNamara, the writer believed China would not have a second-strike capability for fifteen to twenty years, and he thought that an anti-ballistic missile system in the United States would so minimize the danger to the United States from China that Asians need not worry about whether the Americans would respond to an attack on them. He admitted that Japan, like the rest of Asia, could not rely one hundred per cent on America to protect it from a Chinese nuclear attack—which raised the question whether Japan should have its own nuclear weapons. He thought not. Even if the Constitution were revised and public opinion permitted nuclear weapons, no strategic nuclear capacity that Japan could foreseeably build would be absolute proof against a Chinese first strike and would merely replace America's vast nuclear power with a far less adequate Japanese substitute. The writer opposed all such weapons for Japan on the basic grounds that none of them would give the country as foolproof a system of security as would reliance on America. Japan might not be completely sure of the U.S. deterrent, but it ought not to try to develop one of its own unless and until it could be better than the American one. Moreover, development of its own nuclear weapons would inevitably have the effect of reducing the American commitment to help protect Japan.

He thus left the door open for nuclear weapons if the national interest should require it; he did not, as the *Asahi Shimbun* demanded, advocate an unequivocal and public rejection by the government of nuclear weapons as a matter of policy.[27] But like most Japanese commentators he was in favor of developing nuclear programs for peaceful purposes only and sticking to the U.S. Security Treaty for external defense for the time being. The author and his associates regarded Chinese nuclear weapons mainly as psychological and political tools, more dangerous to those nations not aligned with the United States than to those that were. Reliance on the United States was simply in Japan's national interest, as that was rationally and coldly arrived at. As one of his colleagues put it, sentimental nationalism of either right or left would not protect any country in the nuclear age, but would only lead to Japan's isolation in a hostile Asia.[28] Or, as another wrote, it required little courage for Japanese "idealists" to protest against the United States on emotional grounds, when they knew that they had nothing to fear from America. Such protests merely diverted the people's attention from a full attack on their own basic problems.[29] But to pillory America while expecting

American protection was still an acceptable mode of behavior to many.

Like some other "realists," this writer saw Asia's greatest need and first priority to be the creation of an environment in which China could live in peace with its neighbors and be returned from its orphaned state to fruitful membership in international society. It was here, and not in the military sphere, that he was very confident Japan could and should make a major contribution to the life of the area in the future. He criticized the government for its timidity in Southeast Asia, saying that the Satō Cabinet was afraid to present bigger aid budgets in the Diet, where they might provoke a battle with the opposition. But "after Vietnam," Japan should be ready to play a far larger role in the economic and political stabilization of the whole region.

Thus conservatives and progressives, "idealists" and "realists," debated the question of China and Japan's security and answered it according to their view of the world, who was evil, who good, or where the power lay. The conservatives tended to be *ad hoc* and pragmatic, as always. They were not unaware of danger: One professor at Tokyo University, who was among the ablest of the China-watchers, believed that the chances of rational action in Chinese foreign policy were no more than 50 per cent; the day might come when China would threaten nuclear attack unless American bases were removed from Japan. But, like most of his colleagues, he preferred to think of a brighter future, however distant, when Japanese technical assistance would spread to China and Mongolia to help "stabilize" Asia. It might take thirty years for his dream to come true. But like Premier Yoshida before him, he took long views on China; he was prepared to wait; and he doubted not that Japan would eventually have a key role in the economic development and consequently in the political life not only of Southeast Asia but of the Chinese mainland as well. In the meantime, Japan should undertake far more active economic aid programs in the countries on the periphery of China than had been attempted thus far.

2. THE "NORTH-SOUTH PROBLEM"

Until about 1964 Japanese foreign aid was given from commercial motives without much self-conscious relation to broader political objectives in Asia. One had to assume that the Japanese would one day play a more influential role there than was indicated by the apparent passivity of their foreign policy, but clear descriptions of that role were not to be had in Tokyo. "Aid" was given grudgingly, on stringent terms, with one eye on the balance of payments. Nobody wanted to throw away his hard-earned money on the undeserving poor of Asia. Most people with money to invest were beguiled by the chances of bigger profits at home.

Some economists and a few of the more thoughtful bureaucrats in Tokyo had for some years believed that the welfare of Japan must inevitably be connected with stability and modernization of the countries to the south; they urged greater aid to develop sources of strategic raw materials obtained from that area, as well as markets there. Next to North America, Southeast Asia was the most important source of many such materials. At the same time, the shift in the composition of Japanese exports toward capital-intensive products led economists to link Japan with Asian markets much in the way the United States was linked with Latin America and Europe with Africa.[30] Since non-Communist Asia was only one of many areas from which Japan imported raw materials and to which it sold heavy goods, economists stressing Asia's importance sometimes argued against themselves. Energy imports would indeed increase in the future, but most of the crude oil came from the Middle East, not Southeast Asia. In 1967 Japan's trade with the United States was greater than that with all Southeast Asia put together. If the Japanese economy had become global, as it clearly had, it could be "unwise and unrealistic for Japan to set up an exclusive economic bloc with its Asian neighbors."[31]

Those bureaus of the government responsible for economic

cooperation were less powerful than those concerned with more central domestic matters. An *ad hoc* committee on economic cooperation in the Diet was useful at budget voting time but otherwise dormant. The Diet had no standing committee on economic matters generally and no resources with which to secure expert advice from Japanese economists concerning foreign aid. No citizens groups wrapped towels round their heads and paraded in Tokyo or picketed the Diet chambers in favor of foreign aid programs. Little attempt was made to rally popular support for such programs: Japanese politicians were not in the habit of appealing directly to the people on foreign policy issues even when they could reach agreement among themselves. They acted and then informed the public. By contrast, they appealed constantly, at least in postwar times, to the good opinion of the mass media, and spoke to the people through those media on domestic issues where votes mattered. Thus Premier Satō on television in the summer of 1968 smugly quoted the predictions of American futurologists about Japan's world position in the twenty-first century and told his people that they "had never had it so good"; but nobody in the government went on the air to promote foreign aid.

The government had become involved in aid in the 1950s partly because it could not afford to forfeit the good opinion of the developed countries. Among other things, this included some modest programs of technical assistance. A small number of technical experts did valuable work overseas in Asia. They were as capable of hard work as any people, but really effective transfer of skills required more than the capacity of isolated individuals to demonstrate know-how and eat dried fish or drink local water in villages. It required more than the "will to serve," which was rare enough in any country. Until there was a concerted effort on the part of the Japanese government to make its technical assistance more systematic and to link it rationally with other forms of aid, few Japanese would care to risk their careers in Southeast Asia, where they were sure to suffer many inconveniences for dubious reward. But Japan's technical assistance, like its other aid activities, was often short-term, rigidly bound to projects that promoted plant and equipment export or to "development-import" schemes, and lacking in any centralized direction or well-thought-out objectives at home.

Some signs of change in this situation began to appear about 1964. The year before, Premier Ikeda had toured Southeast Asia and come back speaking more forcefully than any postwar Premier of Japan's role in Asia and the likelihood of much more important Japanese initiatives in the area. Some of this was political sloganizing reminiscent of his predecessors. But times had changed since Kishi's tours in 1957. Japan was gaining and feeling new confidence in itself. Ikeda had the wit and the luck to divert the attention of the people from street riots to more inspiriting plans to double the national income. National and individual income and living conditions rose spectacularly, and a new air of self-confidence and pride blew through the great industrial cities on the Pacific shore of Japan. The change of mood was not sudden, and actions had to be distinguished from mere verbalizing by politicians. But the new spirit could be unmistakably perceived behind the debate on defense and security described above, and it was symbolized by the Tokyo Olympics of 1964, an event which momentarily brought millions of Japanese to new consciousness of themselves as a nation and made them aware for the first time since the war ended of the essentially peacetime dimensions of their problems.

By this time, too, Southeast Asia was being discussed much more often than before in the mass media. Japanese television was a delicatessen of bizarre choices. One could have at the same hour a lecture on Pakistani economic development, a critique of Modigliani, or a *samurai* swordfight. *Sumo* contests ended with the playing of "Auld Lang Syne" on the loudspeakers. In the 1950s TV programs on Asia generally had been limited to such exotic subjects as minority people in the hill regions of India, Laos, or elsewhere; program managers all seemed to be anthropologists.

Now, however, problems more representative of the whole area were being explored far more fully and critically. For example, in a TV symposium of half a dozen college-age youth from all over the country in 1968, one girl said she had worked for years to improve the living conditions and social environment of Southeast Asians studying at her university, but felt she had failed. She attacked the student exchange program for its bureaucratic ineptitude but ended by criticizing the quality of those who came to Japan in the first place. Other young idealists on the program expressed their sense of the meaninglessness of Japan's aid programs: they deplored "mere economism" and lack of Japanese self-confidence and dignity in the world when compared with what seemed to them the more appealing nationalism of the countries to the south. They saw their own leaders as tired and soiled and thought they did little to improve their image with Japanese youth.

The press, too, greatly increased its coverage of Asia. In the 1950s, stories on Japan's mountain-climbing expeditions in the Himalayas had always been good copy, but what really concerned editors were problems of the Japanese economy, such as population control (the *Mainichi's* specialty) or land development (the preserve of the *Asahi*). Now editorial staffs took a new interest in the solemnities of economic growth abroad and made baleful predictions about the future of countries like Indonesia where, it appeared, disinvestment had been the rule for years. The *Asahi*, rising to its newly perceived obligations, in 1968 held a symposium on Asian development attended by leading economists in Japan and elsewhere. The *Mainichi* and *Asahi* both ran long series on Asian social, economic, and political problems, while the Southeast Asia correspondent of the *Asahi* brought out a pessimistic new book on the region, full of disapproval, as usual, of his government's policies there.

In 1963 Premier Ikeda spoke of Japan's ineluctably Asian location and grandly projected a larger Japanese role in the area, but he did not live to shape specific policies or to direct programs contributing to such a role. However, even before his death in August 1965, events were turning influential Japanese toward new policy recommendations for action to help solve the "North-South problem."

In 1963 Japan was admitted to full membership in the Organization for Economic Cooperation and Development (OECD). It had been a member of the Development Assistance Committee (DAC) of OECD since 1961, and before that a member of the predecessor Development Assistance Group. Joining OECD had great symbolic importance: it signified formal acceptance in the "club of rich nations"; Japan was the only non-Western nation in the club. It also assuaged a fear of isolation that had persisted in Tokyo ever since the European Economic Community was organized, when the United States appeared intent upon closer European ties. It ensured that Japan would be a party to all discussions of aid and balance-of-payments problems among the "have" nations.

At the same time, however, OECD membership involved responsibilities and obligations that were only half-grasped at the time but were brought home abruptly during the first United Nations Conference on Trade and Development (UNCTAD) held at Geneva in May-June 1964. In an atmosphere of diminishing geniality between developed and developing nations, when, in the words of one Japanese delegate, the developing countries acted like labor unions seeking wage raises and the response of the developed world as a whole was more negative than before, Japan found itself, characteristically, between the advanced West, which restricted Japanese exports in various ways, and an Asian-African world stridently demanding trading preferences and larger imports of its agricultural and industrial merchandise. The perils of being the "poorest member of the rich men's club" were described by a Japanese delegate: "Japan was in a delicate position because it joined with the Western European developed-nation group in all questions of substance and sided with the developed whenever there was a disagreement between groups, even though it had been selected to attend the conference as a member of the Asian group."

The same delegate was perplexed by the importunings of various Asian delegates:

One said, "Japan must understand the difficulties of us developing countries because it has only just reached a developed stage. In spite of this, why does it so often take a negative attitude toward our demands?" But actually Japan has a low per capita income and many other residual evidences of underdevelopment. To give preferential treatment to the developing nations' products will contradict policies toward our own agriculture and small industries. We cannot take the same nonchalant attitude as the most advanced nations toward these demands. This leaves us in a dilemma, but it is not easy to explain this to the other developing nations. Another Asian delegate said, "Japan has suffered discrimination against its own products by other members of the GATT. For Japan now to support GATT is absurd." This, too, is hard to get people in developing countries to understand: Japan has achieved international competitive strength and stands to gain more than it loses from liberalization of trade. Still another representative from a leading Asian country asserted, "If Japan trades with the West it can receive payment in cash for its exports. Not so with the developing countries. This may make it want to draw closer to the West. But it can hardly do without trading with the developing world, and should it not make greater effort to do so?" And still another Asian delegate: "It is not true of the majority of Japanese, but we have the impression that some of you have a tendency to look down on us. Can't you take a more sympathetic attitude toward problems of developing nations, or toward problems of the colored peoples, on emotional grounds?" [32]

The tone of such protestations had been familiar for years to Japanese attending international meetings. But in the first UNCTAD they surfaced in concentrated form; and the Japanese, now a member of OECD and about to be drawn deeper into the international aid competition, were made more uncomfortable than before. A sober lesson was drawn from all this criticism by the same writer:

The developing nations cannot but recognize the economic strength of Japan. We have plenty of opportunities to be invited to conferences as one of the principal trading nations of the world. But the elevation of Japan's economic position carries with it a widening of responsibilities in the political sphere. Our postwar policy of self-centered economism brought us back and developed us. But today [1964], when we rank fourth or fifth among the industrial nations in productivity, and when Japan's national income is equal to that of the entire 700 million people of Southeast Asia, things have reached a point where we can no longer act simply on the basis of the profit and loss of the Japanese economy.[33]

Criticism of Japan's aid activities and of its more general Asian attitudes thus began to awaken a few Japanese to the meaning of membership in the "rich men's club." Their country's obligations were made even clearer by the resolution of the first UNCTAD calling upon each developed nation to contribute 1 per cent of its national income to aid. No time limit was set on fulfillment of this pledge, and before Japan or many other countries had fulfilled it, new pledges of 1 per cent of gross national product were required to be made at later conferences. But the 1964 pledge, followed by the DAC resolution of 1965 calling on all donors to soften the terms of aid, introduced new slogans and new targets into Japanese economic diplomacy. At just the time when Chinese nuclear explosions and American escalation of the war in Vietnam turned participants in the security debate to writing about the urgent necessity for stability on the periphery of China, government officials concerned with economic cooperation began to regard a larger Japanese role as essential to the achievement of such stability, and as overdue; and they began to write papers in this vein.[34]

Weary of being criticized by both Asians and Americans at international conferences, Japanese officials began insisting that Japan put its century of development experience to work abroad for more clearly national ends and complained more openly of the passivity and expediency of the politicians. Escalation in Vietnam increased their anxiety, but President Johnson's Baltimore speech in April 1965 promising American money for foreign development after Vietnam gave them something new to talk about and respond to in terms of foreign economic policy. The Japanese government "welcomed" the speech and quickly offered to increase its contributions to the Mekong River development scheme. For the first time, the phrase "after Vietnam" entered the vocabulary of economic documents, where it remained to stimulate those with varied visions of Japan's future role in Asia.

Ideas for Japanese collaboration with others in Asian development that had lain dormant since Kishi's time reappeared in altered form. One of the most interesting was the Asian Development Bank (ADB), inaugurated in December 1966 under a Japanese president. Japan's decision to participate in the Bank, an institution designed to serve solely Asian needs, came as foreign criticism of Japanese aid policies was growing intense and coincided with the American search for more constructive policies of its own in Southeast Asia and urgings within the United Nations for such policies as the Vietnam war wore on. Such pressures led the United States to re-examine various schemes for regional cooperation that had been under discussion, e.g., among ECAFE officials in Bangkok, for years. Thus Japan's role in the Bank could hardly be considered apart from U.S. policy in the area.

It was too early, at the time of writing this, to evaluate the role of the Bank in Japan's over-all foreign policies. A regional organization, with thirty-one members from Iran to Korea, it was by its nature not susceptible to the control of any one nation. Nevertheless, from the first, nationalist feelings in Japan concerning the Japanese part in it were strong. The decision, by a one-vote margin, to locate the headquarters in Manila rather than Tokyo virtually reduced the Japanese delegation at the founding conference to tears. Giving the presidency to a Japanese hardly assuaged the sense of loss. Of Japan's importance in the bank there was no doubt, even though few loans had thus far been granted. Japan's contribution to the capital fund was by far the largest of any Asian member, and matched that of the United States. Indeed, Japanese contributions to a special fund for soft loans in agriculture to be administered by the Bank had not yet been matched by U.S. congressional appropriation. The President, an able former Finance Ministry official, appeared to be surrounding himself with some trustworthy Japanese sources of information: in 1968 both the Deputy Chief of Operations and the Chief Administrative Officer were Japanese. But this was his privilege, and Japanese nationals did not hold a disproportionate percentage of staff positions. There was no evidence of undue pressure being exerted from Tokyo where actual loans were concerned; on the contrary, official Japanese sources declared that the government was very sensitive to such charges, as well they might have been. The Bank was viewed officially as an auxiliary vehicle for the government's objectives, on the margin of but not replacing its bilateral programs of trade and aid. At the same time, the Bank could not but be regarded inside and outside Japan as one more expression of an increasing desire for influence and an impulse to leadership by the Japanese in Asia. Japan's financial presence was being felt in ways that China's was not.[35]

As usual, the Ministry of Foreign Affairs pressed for larger aid programs and a more important role in their implementation. This had been true ever since the conference of the Foreign Ministry officials in 1956. With the first UNCTAD and the 1 per cent pledge, the Foreign Ministry pushed harder, and in August 1967 the policy section of the Ministry's Economic Cooperation Bureau circulated a paper [36] which was important as a sign of changes in the wind.

Criticism of Japan by other members of the DAC and by the developing countries, the paper asserted, had led to demands in the Diet and elsewhere that aid programs be improved. Japan had a duty to transfer a portion of its prosperity to less fortunate countries to insure that they would themselves contribute to world prosperity. Whether or not 1 per cent was an appropriate figure was beside the point: it had been recognized internationally and had to be accepted. Japan could not expect to maintain its security and prosperity by its own economic power alone, but only when the countries around it were secure and prosperous.

After a few more such pieties the paper listed some problems of Japanese aid and made recommendations. It criticized the hard terms of aid and stressed that the object of improving terms was not simply to increase the quantity of loans and credits but to avoid destroying the recipient's economy: high interest rates and short-term repayment became an impossible burden, and debt servicing by the mid-1960s absorbed a substantial percentage of total aid received by South and Southeast Asia. More than 80 per cent of governmental aid extended by the other DAC countries was at 3 per cent or less, with twenty-five years to pay; but the best Japan had done was 3.5 per cent for twenty years, and there were only a few instances of such soft terms. The paper recognized that Japan's terms were hard because of high domestic money rates in Japan, but it urged the government to devise means of softening loans by widening the financial resources and terms of reference of the Overseas Economic Cooperation Fund (OECF), which was limited by its charter to functions that could not be fulfilled by either the Export-Import Bank of Japan or commercial banks. The paper pointed out that Exim Bank loans required at least 20 per cent participation by city banks; moreover, the Exim Bank drew no distinction between loans for developing countries and ordinary trading credits. As a result, public and private "aid" had become statistically and conceptually confused; it was problematical, to say the least, whether private investment and private credits could be called "aid" in any sense. The OECF should be used for a wide range of social improvement projects. Japan should also think of giving interest-free loans and grants, especially after the end of reparations payment in 1976. Multilateral aid via the Asian Development Bank should also receive greater emphasis. Nothing was said about contributing aid to over-all programs devised by the recipient countries; aid was still thought of in single project terms, in part because the Japanese lacked confidence in the ability of recipients to know what was best for them and plan for it, and partly because the commercial motives of aid could be best served by individually selected projects bilaterally agreed to.

The Foreign Ministry paper criticized the decentralization of aid policy-making and administration in Tokyo, where at least four government ministries pursued the subject from separate points of view; under these circumstances, decisions were nothing but time-wasting compromises. However, the paper came down against creating a new aid agency, pointing to the unhappy experience of certain unnamed foreign countries in this regard. Moreover, the Japanese bureaucracy was pervaded by such a love of checks and balances that no new agency would be likely to receive enough authority to succeed. What the paper did recommend, not unpredictably, was that aid policy should be the over-all responsibility of the Ministry of Foreign Affairs, and it urged that its own representative in the power battle over aid, the Overseas Technical Cooperation Agency (OTCA), be strengthened, with all Japanese technical assistance put under its control. The Ministry was dissatisfied with a situation that found the OTCA budget item listed under "export promotion." [37]

Finally, the paper observed that if aid was ever to gain the active support of Japanese taxpayers, most of whom were appalled at the idea of giving away money to others, it would have to be effective. This presented a dilemma. The only way to guarantee effectiveness was to be considerate of the feelings of people in recipient countries: people in South and Southeast Asia did not want Japanese exploitation, and they were suspicious of too much "structuring" of aid by donors. But without such "structuring," how was the aid to be effective in countries whose leaders themselves often had only a vague idea of what they wanted and why? One solution was multilateral aid, to which the paper recommended more study should be devoted. It then laid out a projection of Japanese aid that would fulfill the 1 per cent pledge by 1971.

The Foreign Ministry paper was one brief thrown into the growing discourse on foreign aid, and it naturally was designed to further the bureaucratic goals of its authors. Nevertheless, effects of OECD membership and Japan's new pledges were reflected in its language, which paid lip service, at least, to ideas of inter-dependence, obligations of donors, and collective security concepts in Asia. Nobody but its authors approved the paper, although one of its recommendations, revision of the OECF law, was soon afterward put into effect. Although the paper did not change the *ad hoc* approach to aid, it was one sign among many that the Japanese government was not satisfied with its aid activities and was searching for some rationale, extra-commercial if not supra-commercial, for them. The emphasis on efficiency was also notable. Arguments about Japan's economic need for tropical Asia, suggestions that with the collapse of China's policies and the diminution of Western influence Japan might move in with a greater presence—these and other matters were being debated and weighed, and they were no doubt of great importance. The desire for stability reflected the deepest interests of the Japanese in Asia, but it was efficiency that really excited them and that could produce a secular passion one saw not only in individuals in Tokyo but wherever Japanese were present throughout the region.

Another evidence of the Japanese search for new aid policies and methods could be found in the yearbook on aid issued by the Ministry of International Trade and Industry (MITI), the heart of the trade promotion activities of the government. The first of these annuals came out in 1963 and was at once recognized as the most detailed official source for the whole subject.[38]

The 1967 edition contained what by that time had become received doctrine in much of the government concerning aid. Written exclusively for a Japanese audience (no English translation was published), it stated that the purpose of aid was to supplement the efforts of developing countries to exploit their resources effectively in order to overcome the usual panoply of problems: overpopulation, inadequate food production, inflation, and so on. Only thus could the growing gap between developed and developing worlds be reduced. Since this gap not only prevented efficient use of human and other resources, but also made for political tension, none could refuse to accept the 1 per cent resolution. The MITI yearbook thus linked the resolution with Japanese foreign policy in general terms. Japan must take part in international development "within the limits of national strength. This will elevate our position in international society and increase our international responsibilities." Then, in a pitch to the commercial reader, the yearbook added: "We must recognize that economic development of those countries in Asia with whom our commercial relations are intimate will have a connection with the long-range development of our own economy. So, from the standpoint of international society and from our own standpoint as well, we must be active in economic cooperation."

The yearbook expounded upon Japan's low per capita income, its shortages of capital and so on, in the usual manner. This merely meant that aid would have to be concentrated where it would have the greatest effect; by giving consideration first to the readiness of other peoples to help themselves and by evaluating aid carefully, its effectiveness could be enhanced. The United States gave half of all the aid of the "free world," and gave it in support of ideological goals, on soft terms. France and England gave special concern to their economic and political ties with their former colonies. Just so, Japan's aid must have some characteristic mark or quality. It must bear upon a special area of the world, i.e., Southeast Asia, and must stress self-help and efficiency. The reasons for the focus on Southeast Asia were not hard to find: in addition to geographical propinquity and the fact that Japan was the only developed country in the area, the report stated that only 50 per cent of Japan's primary goods imports came from developing countries, whereas 85 per cent of the exports of those countries were primary products. Since those countries much preferred trade to aid in the first place, Japanese imports of primary products must somehow be increased. The yearbook showed no interest whatever in special preferences for imports of manufactured goods from those countries, as they all loudly demanded.

The MITI yearbook noted that technical assistance had to be increased. In 1966 such assistance was 18.8 per cent of the DAC average of total aid, but only 2.7 per cent of Japan's total. But what was most noticeable in the yearbook was the stress on self-help, which along with efficiency was becoming a key slogan in Japanese policy documents.[39] A paper prepared in November 1966 by an official of the Foreign Ministry's Economic Cooperation Bureau and delivered at a private seminar in Tokyo, stressed that loans should be restricted to countries with the ability to use them effectively; others should get grants, but these should be accompanied by Japanese technicians; and, if necessary, Japanese economists should help to draw up the economic development plans of other countries.[40]

Though the MITI yearbooks were circulated widely through the bureaucracy and were on public sale at government printing office retail stores in Tokyo and other cities, it may be wondered how many ordinary Japanese citizens ever read them. However, influential private organizations concerned with trade and aid were also busily engaged in preparing their own policy recommendations. In February 1968, the Japan Committee for Economic Development (*Keizai Dōyūkai*), a businessmen's association noted for its relatively advanced views, circulated a memorandum containing proposals for changes in the aid program to members of the Cabinet, Diet, and government agencies.[41] The memorandum described aid as one of the greatest tasks facing mankind in the second half of the twentieth century. The "North-South gap" was widening, and unless the developed countries contributed to the developing ones, world peace and prosperity would be totally impossible. Donors must act in a spirit of international harmony, each country giving what it could give best and most aptly, in concert with other countries.

The principal shortcoming of Japan's aid programs was seen

to lie in a lack of centralized coordination and responsibility in Tokyo. Therefore, to pursue more rational, long-range goals, a new Ministry or Agency of Economic Cooperation was considered essential. Such agencies had been set up in the United States, the United Kingdom, and West Germany. Some feared that a new agency would consist merely of cliques loyal to the various ministries from whence they came; but the goal should be to train new people for careers in aid work and to develop identification with that work alone. A new agency with its own budget could clearly identify funds for aid, instead of burying them in the budgets of other ministries. This would have the effect of forcing debate in the Diet, which would be reported in the press and would make the public far more aware of Japan's aid responsibilities than it had ever been. Aid could thus be a means of opening Japan to the world.

The memorandum made other proposals similar to those circulating in the government at the time. Virtually everyone agreed that the OECF was too restricted in its use. The memo suggested that it be used to control inflation, to "stabilize livelihood," and to carry out social development projects. Technical assistance should be increased, linked with other forms of assistance, and administered with more imagination and flexibility. The memo proposed an international agricultural development company to train Southeast Asians in farm management, animal husbandry, and other aspects of agriculture in which Japanese skills could be readily transferred. An International Management Cooperation Committee, modeled on the American Executive Service Corps, was recommended to provide management consultation to local business in developing countries. Such activities would also help Japanese get inside information on bidding and construction orders and assist the overseas operations of Japanese firms. The memo regretted that Japanese consulting firms had such short histories and such weak links with the World Bank and other international institutions. The Japan Youth Volunteer Corps could also spread the spirit of internationalism and service to others; it could "give dreams to youth" and should be enlarged.

The memo urged further liberalization of trade and capital transactions by the Japanese government and a basic shift in its policies from the principle of exclusiveness save in exceptional cases to a principle of openness, with exceptions where necessary: in other words, from an assumption of guilt to an assumption of innocence where foreign trade and exchange transactions were concerned. Asking the Japanese bureaucracy to do this was like asking a Puritan to give up original sin. The memo stressed the need for better export insurance, a fuller investment guarantee system, and a central committee on private sector aid to hear the grievances of Japanese businessmen overseas. It reiterated the need to move more small, labor-intensive Japanese industries abroad; to facilitate such joint ventures Japan should consider establishing something like the West German Economic Cooperation Limited Company. The private sector should also invest directly in local development funds abroad, and in development companies: an Asian Development Company with heavy Japanese participation was suggested.

Interest in technical assistance grew in the late 1960s and was especially marked in agriculture, matching the general shift of emphasis to this sector by donor and recipient nations alike toward the end of the first "development decade." Japan had engaged in small-scale agricultural assistance for many years. Between 1955 and 1967, it sent 488 technical specialists in all fields to Southeast Asia, including 120 in agriculture, the largest single category. Most of these went under Colombo Plan auspices; Japanese contributions under the plan were highly regarded abroad. In the same period Japan received 3,935 trainees in all fields from Southeast Asia, 794 of them in agriculture, again the largest category.[42] Japanese research in rice production in Taiwan before World War II contributed significantly to discoveries at the International Rice Research Institute in the Philippines in the 1960s, where new rice varieties started talk of a "green revolution" in Asia. Agricultural experts in Japan took an active interest in this research and planned new research programs of their own.

At a symposium on technical cooperation in agriculture held in 1967 under the auspices of the Kyoto University Southeast Asia Research Center and attended by government and private specialists, one of Japan's best known agricultural economists deplored the small scale of Japanese aid to agriculture in Southeast Asia. Sending experts, he said, had done more to raise interest in tropical agriculture in Japan than to influence agriculture in the region. With the exception of some new rice strains in Malaysia developed by Japanese plant breeders, little had been accomplished in any systematic way; efforts were dissipated in the vast ocean of need. He listed three principles essential to successful assistance to agriculture. First, aid should be given to those who help themselves. Like nearly all Japanese, what he most admired in others was the bootstrap spirit, "a quality of backbone, of hand to the plow, of acceptance of difficulties and the courage to face them in isolation—of pride and energy to make things new." [43] The role of foreigners must be merely to stimulate and supplement; if there was no real desire to develop, no amount of help would suffice. Second, effort should be concentrated on those things that could be done, always with the realization that all the elements of agricultural technology were highly interrelated. He stressed the interdependence of the many measures necessary to raise the technical level of rice farming: new seed varieties, insecticides, fertilizer application, irrigation, improved cultivation practices, better facilities for harvest storage and transport, mechanization, and so on. Third, agricultural development was a long-term affair. It was not something that could be accomplished in one year or five, whereas Japanese stayed too briefly on overseas assignments and seldom reached maximum usefulness; most went on two-year terms, spending the first six months learning the new environment and the last six months worrying about what they would do when they got home.

To implement these principles of self-help, concentration of effort, and long-term perspectives, he strongly urged that the Japanese stop playing such a passive role in the countries where their services were requested. Too often they had merely responded to the whims of politicians for this or that aid project without knowing or saying much about the feasibility of doing the things requested. But agricultural needs existed without much reference to political shifts in the region; short of major changes in the social and political system, the same needs persisted from regime to regime. It behooved Japan to use more initiative and to learn how to suggest that the appropriate measures be requested. This meant that Japanese must have far closer contact with people in Southeast Asian governments on both the official and the personal level. He then commented:

> Some Japanese think that if they put themselves into their work whole-heartedly in underdeveloped countries, the people will be naturally moved; and they place a high value on such spiritual ingredients. Behind the aid activities of Europeans and Americans in such areas there is, perhaps, a Christian spirit, or a pioneer spirit. The Japanese are, in fact, too economic-minded. But very few results are to be expected by stressing spirituality alone. What is more important is a high scientific and technical standard. In particular, for the technical development of agriculture, discipline is an absolute *sine qua non*. Nearly every successful result of our agricultural assistance has been achieved by men with strong discipline.[44]

In October 1967 one Japanese writer asserted that if Japan continued to tie itself too tightly to the United States in the technological sense, it would forfeit the chance to contribute something uniquely Japanese to the solution of the "North-South problem." (As an example, he mentioned cities without automobiles such as were being dreamed of by some urban planners in Tokyo!) He cited racial ties with Asia and the lack of them with America as grounds for not giving up the hope of a Japanese role. But men like the agricultural economist, the Committee for Economic Development businessmen, and the bureaucrats in the Foreign

Ministry or MITI were less concerned with racial differences and unique contributions than with discovering an efficient, orderly, disciplined means of bringing technical skills to bear in a way that would help others, but would also help Japanese business profits, advance scientific research, and satisfy larger demands for political influence in the world, not just in the Asian portion of it. The searchings suggested by the documents cited in this chapter have to do, basically, with the dimensions of a new nationalism, a sense of national purpose and scope, that was not yet clear around the edges but was being actively sought not only by academic "idealists" or "realists" but also by Japanese in many, many fields.

In addition to circulating policy memoranda the Japanese government took certain actions during this period to enhance its international position. In April 1966, quite without notice to the United States, the first Ministerial Conference on economic development of Southeast Asia was held in Tokyo with Cabinet-level delegates from Japan, Laos, Malaysia, the Philippines, Singapore, Thailand, and South Vietnam, and observers from Indonesia and Cambodia. The Ministerial Conference was not intended to compete with ECAFE, the chief international exponent of regionalism in Southeast Asia. But the Japanese, like some others, regarded ECAFE as too weak financially, too broad geographically, and too given to talking and writing reports without any further visible result. Thus the Ministerial Conference was designed as a more informal forum from which it was hoped some practical results in regional economic cooperation might eventually emerge.

From the first conference came a vice-ministerial meeting of nine Southeast Asian countries and Japan in Tokyo in early December 1966 to consider concrete proposals for agricultural development. Out of this meeting, in turn, came the idea of a special fund for soft loans to agriculture to be set up within the ADB, itself inaugurated only a week after the agriculture conference ended. The Japanese government later pledged $100 million to the special fund and had put up $20 million of it when this was written. Limitation of the fund's use to Southeast Asia reflected the Japanese focus on that area. Also from this conference came agreement to establish a fisheries training center in Singapore and a fisheries research center in Bangkok. Japan agreed to supply training ships, equipment, and staff, for which money was appropriated in the 1968 general account budget. Other suggestions for promotion of tourism, marketing of new products, and regional development programs for transport and communications came out of the second Ministerial Conference held in Manila in April 1967, and the third, in Singapore, in April 1968. The ADB President was present as an observer at the second and third of these conferences and received specific project requests for the Bank.

The Ministerial Conferences expressed a desire for some kind of regional forum in which Japan could have a major voice. (They also expressed the political ambitions of the Foreign Minister of the moment, who hoped to use foreign aid as a tool in his campaign for the Premiership.) In this period also, the Japanese government participated in the Asia and Pacific Council (ASPAC), begun on South Korean initiative in the summer of 1966 and including South Korea, Taiwan, the Philippines, Japan, Malaysia, Thailand, South Vietnam, Australia, and New Zealand. Opposition parties and some intellectuals in Japan spoke fearfully of ASPAC as a first step toward a Northeast Asian Treaty Organization; South Koreans and Chinese Nationalists appeared to wish to turn it into some kind of anti-Communist political and military alliance. But the Japanese government insisted on regarding ASPAC as a forum for economic matters only and occasionally suggested that Communist China might be invited to join some day. Up to this writing, ASPAC was little more than another regional body for discussion of economic problems. Its scope was modest and its future unclear. It appeared to have sprung in part from Korean jealousy of Japan's leadership of the Southeast Asian Ministerial Conferences.

By the late 1960s in the United States the dollar drain and

the Vietnam war were cooling public interest in aid and in Asia generally. In Tokyo what to do "after Vietnam" was being widely discussed. A few people may have had visions of filling the vacuum that they thought British and possibly American withdrawal from Southeast Asia would create. However, Japanese official policy was more cautious and noncommittal. In a speech to the third Ministerial Conference in Singapore, Foreign Minister Miki pointed to Japan's steadily increasing aid budgets and indicated that the Japanese government would continue to support regional co-operation in Southeast Asia; but he also stressed the need for closer regional association in what he called the "Asia-Pacific" area, meaning the United States, Canada, Australia, New Zealand, and Japan. Some saw Japan as the leader of a non-Western Asian bloc; to others the notion of Japan as a member of some sort of Pacific Community was more intriguing and expressive of the country's new world stature. Which role, if either, Japan would ultimately choose was as yet unclear and would be greatly influenced by what policies America adopted in the Asian region after the Vietnam war was settled. In the last chapter of this book I have speculated on these matters of future role. In the meantime, the Foreign Minister urged self-help on the Southeast Asians as the first prerequisite for help from the outside. In issuing ethical prescriptions, as in some other ways, the Japanese were playing a more positive role.

V. The Level of Action: Japanese Activities in Non-Communist Asia

Between 1963 and 1968 the total of Japan's foreign aid rose annually (see Appendix Table). It had not yet reached 1 per cent of national income, but more was being said about the necessity of meeting the 1 per cent pledge. Many who repeated this slogan did not stop to reflect on how inadequate it would be even when realized. That aid should fit into the development plans of recipient nations and not just serve the ends of the donor was also gaining some acceptance, although this had not become a governing concept by any means.

By 1968 economic cooperation had begun to be regarded by some key leaders as a means to Asian political stability as well as Japanese commercial profit. One saw this in policy recommendations in Tokyo as well as in Japan's membership in the Asian Development Bank and other organizations. In a wider sense, a variety of new events, including the announced withdrawal of British forces from South and Southeast Asia, the apparent American intention of cutting its losses in Vietnam, as well as predictions of enormous economic growth in Japan in the next decade, all stimulated wide speculation by Japanese and foreigners alike about the country's future role in Asia. But for such speculation to be at all meaningful it had properly to rest not just on what officials, businessmen, or other people in Tokyo said or were reported to have said, but also had to take into account the often confused and perplexing record of Japanese actions on the scene in Asia. What follows is a survey of those actions as seen and evaluated in the late summer and early autumn of 1968.

1. South Korea

The agreement between Japan and South Korea signed in June 1965 signified the end of the purblind chauvinism of the Syngman Rhee era and the beginning of South Korea's widening relationships with the world. By 1968 Seoul had established diplomatic links with nearly fifty countries, twice the number in Rhee's time, and had taken a much more open posture toward foreign investment. General Chung-hee Park led a government vigorously committed to economic development. Its performance was impressive, whatever might be said about its devotion to democratic principles. During the first five-year plan (1961–66) gross national product rose at more than 8 per cent a year. The second plan (1966–71) had to be revised to meet better-than-anticipated performance. The country still faced immense problems, the greatest of them its wholly artificial truncation. A menacing, implacable enemy resorted increasingly to guerrilla tactics below the 38th parallel; a large standing army in the south and substantial American forces were required to cope with this threat. Rural living standards were far lower than those in the cities, although peasants did not yet harbor guerrillas from the north but turned them over to the authorities. Shortages of power, transport, communications, and food were very severe.

The future of South Korea as a state was clouded by big-power rivalry in Asia, and its prognosis could only be guarded. Nevertheless, there was no doubting the energy of South Korean leaders and no need to disparage their accomplishments. In Seoul one could appreciate better than in Tokyo the good fortune of the Japanese people in having been able to industrialize before the age of ideological wars had set in. Yet Korea was clawing its way into the modern world. Over the front doors of the Seoul City Hall huge streamers exhorted the people of the city to perform "miracles from the sweat of four million," and one felt that a people with such spirit and such an ethic of hard work, who had already endured everything, would persist and somehow prevail. This was the context in which President Park's decision to sign the agreement with Japan had to be seen, and he showed courage in risking student riots to sign it. From 1965 on, his government exhibited a readiness to implement the agreement, and Japanese money and skills began to flow into South Korea for the first time since the Second World War.

Japanese activities could be conveniently described according to the provisions of the 1965 settlement. Under it, government grants of goods and services worth $300 million were payable over ten years. By mid-1967, $44 million of these grants had been paid for basic improvements in agriculture and fishing, including irrigation and drainage projects affecting 160,000 acres, livestock breeding and crop diversification schemes, farm mechanization, reforestation, tobacco production, marine products research and development, and construction or import of fishing vessels. Also scheduled to be paid for by future grants were river development studies, mining surveys, and plans for expansion of scientific and technological education. Small amounts of raw materials were to be given to Korea, where they would be sold to create counterpart funds for local currency needs of other development projects.

The agreement also provided for the equivalent of $200 million in yen credits, to be extended over a ten-year period from 1965. These credits, administered by the OECF, carried an interest rate of 3.5 per cent, with repayment in 20 years after a seven-year grace period—the softest terms of any Japanese credit to that date. By the end of July 1967, $38.6 million had been approved and $27.7 million paid. The money was earmarked for railroad improvements, expansion of machine industries, construction of water systems in two cities, transport and freight facilities, long-distance telephone expansion, a multipurpose dam, and harbor improvements.

In addition to government grants and credits, Japan agreed to expedite private deferred-payment loans at commercial rates to private enterprises in Korea up to a total of the yen equivalent of $300 million. Of this, two-thirds was supposed to finance the export of plants to be operational no later than the middle of 1970. By July 1968, export licenses had been issued for $274 million worth of this equipment in the following industries: cement, chemical fertilizers, plastics, acrylic fiber, fishing gear, and steam plants for power generation. A Japanese Ministry of Foreign Affairs report of June 1968, in comparing Japanese industrial loans with those made by other countries to Korea, showed that Japanese money was already participating significantly in a wide range of industries.[1]

It was impossible to determine how much private equity investment accompanied or followed the above loans, but the total was very small. The Korean government was cautious about Japanese capital investment and reluctant to sign double taxation agreements or grant rights of industrial ownership to Japanese. It appeared to prefer loans and technical licensing agreements that involved little or no equity participation. Evidence by late 1968 indicated that at least seven Japanese companies had directly invested in Korea: included in these were a lathe manufacturer with 49 per cent listed participation, a concern making elevators with 40 per cent, and others in shoes, textiles and food products, all small and with minority participation by Japanese partners. Twenty-two Korean individuals residing in Japan had officially-listed investments in South Korea, and many if not all of these were said to include Japanese capital or to represent dummies of Japanese firms. They held controlling interests in enterprises engaged in food processing, shrimp fishing, assembly of air-conditioning equipment, auto maintenance, and manufacture of construction equipment, plastics, and home appliances. Also listed were about fifty technical licensing agreements between Japanese and Korean firms involving cash or royalty payments for know-how and unknown amounts of equity.[2]

All this loan and investment activity was regarded by most observers in Seoul as merely the beginning of a much greater involvement of Japanese enterprise in Korea on an equity or license-and-loan basis or some combination of such arrangements. Some Americans freely predicted that Japan would dominate the Korean economy in due time. The Japanese commercial interest was primarily in Korean labor and the growing market there. Except for minerals north of the 38th parallel, the country was devoid of important industrial raw materials but possessed a substantial labor force, closer culturally to the Japanese than were any of the peoples of Southeast Asia and trained by Japanese in a variety of technical skills within the memory of a middle-aged generation. It was natural for the Japanese to look upon these human resources to some degree as an extension of their own labor force, especially as the latter grew more expensive, just as it was natural for the Koreans to want Japanese know-how and money but not their control. The possibilities for friction were obvious; but Korea had much to gain economically from Japan, and the Japanese government was concerned with maintenance of Korean economic and political stability in the face of the obscurantism and truculence of the Chinese and North Korean regimes.

In addition to government grants and public or private loans, small but growing amounts of technical assistance were being given to Korea under official Japanese auspices. Data provided by the Japanese Embassy in Seoul listed seventeen experts in the country for varying periods in 1967–68, in such fields as rice physiology and plant breeding, plant vaccine improvement, sericulture, hydraulic engineering, and livestock breeding. Korean sources complained that the Japanese had refused to supply silk-raising know-how that they had been invited to go to Japan to acquire.[3] Officials of the United Nations Development Fund in Seoul regarded highly those Japanese experts participating in its programs, in part because they were able to communicate fluently with Koreans over 35 years of age, most of whom had been forced to learn Japanese in school. Japanese were active in U.N. soil fertility projects, a deep-sea training center, fishery advisory services, a telecommunications training school, and the newly established Korea Productivity Center. For its preinvestment survey of the Naktong River basin in the southern part of the peninsula, described by one U.N. official as a "little Mekong," the Korean Ministry of Construction engaged the ubiquitous Japanese firm, Nippon Kōei. Japanese delegates to a conference in Seoul on trade and aid in late 1968 showed a great interest in supplying more technical assistance for development of agriculture. They promised to allow establishment of branches of Korean banks in Japan and to set up an automatic approval system for remittances by Koreans residing in Japan of up to $10,000 apiece. They also were interested in helping to electrify Korean railroads.

The chief economic problem between the two countries was commodity trade. South Korea had little to sell but labor, and Korean exports to Japan were less than a fourth of imports. Rice had been sent to Japan before the war but now was either in short supply at home or not wanted in Japan in large quantities. Japanese tariffs and quotas remained high on Korean agricultural products as well as on goods manufactured in Korea with raw materials imported from Japan. Trade was the subject of continuous, emotional negotiations: Koreans called upon Japanese to honor their DAC pledges and conform to UNCTAD resolutions for special preferences to Korean exports, but the Japanese were not yet ready to make major concessions that would lead to demands from all other countries in the same case. Some efforts were being made to develop new exports for the Japanese market; e.g., beef cattle interested the Mitsui and Mitsubishi trading companies in 1968. Eventually the Japanese would have to buy more semifinished and finished goods if they hoped to sell plant and equipment in Asia. But for the time being they were taking full advantage of their competitive position; the reduction of tariffs on pickled sea urchins could hardly be called a major development in the liberalization of trade. Japanese negotiators sometimes jibed at their Korean counterparts: if the trade imbalance was so serious, they asked, why did Korea keep on buying Japanese machinery? Such harsh mocking was typical of their old manner toward Koreans but was less obvious when they were trying to get something they did not possess, such as Philippine logs or Indian iron. Both sides knew the answer well enough: Japanese machinery was cheaper, its quality was good, and Japan was a nearby source. Some minor attempts were made to improve the balance of payments. In Pusan, across the straits from Kyūshū, Japanese television could be seen and a tourist hotel on the beach outside town catered to honeymooners, including a few Japanese. A ferryboat service between Nagasaki and Pusan was under discussion, but most Japanese tourists wanted to go to Hong Kong or Honolulu, not to Korea.

Korea was developing light manufacturing industries, some of them with Japanese help. These had already hurt the Japanese market for light exports to the United States, and Koreans wanted to compete eventually in heavy industrial exports as well. Japanese car assemblies in Seoul were required to contain a larger percentage of locally made parts each year: the Nissan "Shinjin" was 15 per cent Korean-made its first year, but by 1968 had reached 30 per cent. Japanese businessmen were vigorously selling their merchandise, as they were doing everywhere else; it was estimated unofficially that Japanese trading companies already handled 40 per cent of Korea's foreign trade on a worldwide basis. At the first International Business Machines Show in Seoul in August 1968, twenty-three of the forty-two exhibitors were Japanese firms, and Korean companies had Japanese as well as American, Swiss, German, Italian, and British partners. Japan and America were competing in the Korean market as elsewhere in Asia, even as America urged Japan to give more economic aid to the whole area.

Korean cultural aversion to the Japanese was still evident. People in Pusan and elsewhere spoke compulsively of the crudities and cruelties of the colonial period; they respected what the Japanese had done in Japan, but hated the memory of their domineering, arrogant behavior abroad. However, cultural distaste was becoming less important as a factor in Japanese-Korean relations than the rise of economic nationalism in Korea, which expressed itself in a dogged determination to maintain autonomy in the face of returning Japanese influence in the country. Whether or not this could be done was beginning to be debated in 1968. Some Korean officials declared that they were glad to have Japanese economic assistance, including investment, as long as these were offset by American influence; they expressed anxiety at the decline of American aid. Others insisted that they could and would cope with the Japanese and would not allow their own businessmen to sell out to Japan. Faced as it was by a direct threat to its existence from the north, the South Korean government wanted help where it could get it, but many regarded Japan as politically dangerous, liable to veer to the left at any time and make peace with the Communists at Korea's expense. Anticommunism was a burning, vocal passion in Seoul as it was not in Tokyo. When the South Korean Foreign Minister protested that Tokyo was trying to export plants to the north, the Japanese Ambassador hurriedly called a press conference to deny the charge. But suspicions persisted.

Japanese influence of all kinds seemed certain to increase in Korea, a much smaller, weaker country placed very infelicitously at the juncture of more powerful interests. Such influence would be based on the desire to stabilize and maintain South Korea as a buffer against larger enemies, as it had been maintained before, though hardly by the same methods. Japan sought no more colonial empires. At bilateral conferences the delegates sometimes spoke fulsomely of a "common Asiatic destiny" for both countries. These speeches had an old-fashioned ring but not much substance. Japan would be likely to try to keep ASPAC an economic organization for the time being and to avoid political commitments to South Korea in spite of an obvious strategic interest. If there we-e another war in the peninsula, people in Tokyo believed that Japan might send military forces to assist the Seoul regime; in some conservative circles, South Korea was more or less tacitly assumed to be within the legitimate sphere of operations of the Self-Defense Forces should such an emergency occur. It was hard to know what Japanese public reaction might be to such an eventuality. But barring that kind of crisis, the Japanese would go on as they had since 1952, hoping to allow the imagery of colonialism to fade, making no alliances that would foreclose their freedom of action with Peking or Pyongyang or muddy the political waters in Tokyo.

In 1968 the American presence in Korea was overwhelming. American dependents lived as they had for twenty years in compounds originally built for the families of Japanese colonial administrators. They would stay, for how long was not known, but most thought for a long time. Meanwhile, the Japanese had major contributions to make to Korean economic growth and they were definitely beginning to do so. Their ultimate role in the country was obscure even to them. But if, as was being predicted on both sides of the Pacific, Japan would dominate the economic life of the whole Asian area by the year 2000, they would probably have great weight with whatever government was in power in South Korea by that time, if not long before.

2. Taiwan

By 1968 Japan's reinvolvement in Taiwan had gone much farther than it had in South Korea. The pattern of Japanese activities in the two countries was similar: their money went into both to take advantage of cheaper, skilled labor and to protect markets for goods that were beginning to be produced locally. But Taiwan was farther along with industrialization than Korea; it had passed through land reform and begun to reinvest agricultural savings in manufacturing. Moreover, the record of Japanese colonialism, largely under naval auspices, had been somewhat less harsh than the army's administration of Korea. Whereas the Japanese before the war thought of Korea as a strategic corridor to Manchuria or a buffer against Russian expansion, they regarded Taiwan as an agricultural storehouse and spent much energy on research in many fields, some of which were to pay dividends after the war. This is not to say that colonialism in Taiwan was a picture of contentment. But it would have been inconceivable to find a night club audience in Seoul singing old Japanese folk songs and bursting into cheers afterward, as happened in 1968 in Taipei. In Taiwan, as almost nowhere else in Asia, it was possible to find at least a few people who remembered the Japanese era with something approaching affection, if not with joy.

As in Korea, the American aid program in Taiwan, which with Chinese hard work and ingenuity produced remarkable economic progress, began to be sharply reduced in 1965. In April of that year Japan and the Republic of China signed a yen credit agreement providing for the equivalent of $150 million to be extended over five years for major economic improvements. Of this, $101.3 million was an Export-Import Bank of Japan credit for machinery exports, repayable in 12 to 15 years at 5.75 per cent. The remaining $48.7 million was extended through the OECF at 3.5 per cent, repayable in 20 years. The Exim Bank portion of the credit was earmarked for bridge and harbor improvements, fertilizer plant construction, and a number of other industrial projects; the OECF portion was allocated to construction of a multipurpose dam and reservoir on the Tsengwen River in Southwest Taiwan and a new harbor entrance at the major southern port of Kaohsiung.

The influence of the yen credit was quickly felt. Japanese machinery exports to the island rose from $48 million in 1964 to $94 million in 1965, one year ahead of similar but even more dramatic expansion of such exports to Korea.[4] The effect on the trade balance was immediate: while Taiwanese exports to Japan, almost all of them agricultural products, remained around $140 million and declined slightly between 1964 and 1967, Japanese exports to the island rose from $140 million in 1964 to $206 million in 1965, $230 million in 1966, and $315 million in 1967. Like South Korea,

Taiwan appealed to Japan to buy more agricultural produce, but pork imports continued to be barred, and, aside from bananas and canned pineapples, little or no fruit was being purchased abroad.

With plant exports came investment. Japanese investment in the island had been tiny, a small fraction of the American total, but beginning in 1965 private money from both countries flowed in to help replace U.S. aid funds. The Chinese government actively encouraged this, allowing up to 100 per cent capitalization by foreign interests. By the end of 1967 a total of 171 cases of Japanese investment had been approved by Taiwanese authorities. Of these, all but 39 were post-1965, 81 being approved in 1967 alone. The total approved amount was approximately $29 million, or 12 per cent of all foreign investment in Taiwan. Only one Japanese investment exceeded $1 million, a synthetic textile plant to be built by the Teijin Rayon Co. with an initial commitment of $6.5 million. The rest averaged less than $500,000 and were in a wide variety of consumer goods fields, but especially in pharmaceuticals, electrical home appliances, textiles, metal goods, and chemicals. Japan was exporting its small and medium industries to Taiwan to sell primarily in the local market. By comparison, up to 1968, American investment amounted to 99 cases for a total of $127 million and was centered in processing of raw materials and parts for re-export to the United States. Americans and Japanese had thus far avoided much direct competition in Taiwan itself, though some Americans regarded the Teijin Rayon plant as a disturbing exception.[5]

Chinese officials declared that they were trying to avoid over-concentration of industrial investment that would glut the market in any one field, but they had not been entirely successful. For example, many Japanese drug makers had rushed in and were getting in each other's way. By 1967 Japanese and Sino-Japanese ventures controlled an estimated 30 per cent of the Taiwanese market for electrical and electronics products. In both categories, however, Chinese-owned companies were still more important, and overseas Chinese investment in Taiwan was nearly four times as large as

Japanese. Japanese equity, as distinct from loans connected with investment, was difficult to determine but probably amounted to at least two-thirds of total Japanese investment. Nearly 150 Japanese firms (compared with less than 50 American) had licensed know-how in a huge number of processes. The list was as diverse as Japanese enterprise itself: fluorescent lamps, watt meters, radios, condensers, rubber tires, biscuits, scooters, insecticides, refrigerators, boilers, plastics, plate glass, canvas shoes—in these and a host of other fields Western know-how originally adapted by the Japanese over many years was filtering into Taiwan.[6]

The Chinese in Taiwan had mixed feelings about the expansion of Japanese economic influence. They wanted Japanese money and skills, which many insisted they could have without accepting economic control. Rules and regulations for investment required that local "value added" begin at 40 per cent and increase annually to at least 70 per cent of products involving foreign parts and processes. Automobiles were an example: the Chinese criticized the Philippines for allowing assembly of cars from imported parts completely and indefinitely. One Chinese economic official, a mainlander, defended the policy of inviting Japanese money into the island. Japan, he said, had put more into Taiwan than into any other country in Southeast Asia. (The Japanese Minister in Taipei was proud to agree with this.) Japanese investment was raising local skills and providing employment, and what was already being called their penetration would be carefully controlled, in spite of a few examples of overcompetition in the local market. Like other Asians, he wanted to use the Japanese for all they were worth, and he and some of his colleagues in the Chinese government did not attempt to conceal their desire to involve them more deeply in Taiwan and to give them a stake in the place in order to make it harder for them to abandon it politically. At the same time, he and others spoke of the Japanese in typically cavalier Chinese style, referring to Tokyo industrialists of considerable international importance as "that little fellow at the Chamber of Commerce," or "that fellow at the Expo in Osaka." Other Asians seemed to

have trouble remembering Japanese proper names. But behind the
glib, self-assured conversation of some Taipei officials, particularly
those who came from the mainland, a strain of bafflement about
the future could be detected. Their rhetoric was sprinkled with
conditionals: "as long as the Vietnam war goes on and Satō is
in power, Taiwan has nothing to fear from Japan." But the future
beyond Vietnam was an enigma, like the future of Taiwan itself.

That Chinese from the mainland wanted to involve Japan more
deeply in the island for purposes of self-preservation merely revealed their insecurity. Many mainlanders, like many Koreans,
were obsessively suspicious of Japan's supposedly neutralist tend-
encies and feared the worst, recognition of Peking. On the other
hand, Taiwanese Chinese, including some politicians who were
waiting for the day when they would inherit power from the mainlanders, sought to use the Japanese to advance their own interests.
As one American on the island put it, they were "in bed with the
Japanese." They shrugged off the notion of a Japanese military
role in Asia in the future and belittled Tokyo's political influence,
professing to believe that Japan was so wholly dependent on America that Taiwan had nothing to fear. Some did not attempt to
conceal their fondness for Japan: one Taipei resident, a graduate
of Waseda University, spoke sentimentally about Tokyo, boasting
that Japanese newspapers were the world's best. But he added that
most people in Taiwan thought little about what their relationship
with Japan should be; they were living from day to day and making
money, with Japanese help or without it. Some businessmen dis-
missed as nonsense the idea of a Japanese swing to the left. They
wanted to make money and intended to do so without worrying
much about being taken over by the Japanese. Some of them
described themselves as anti-Japanese but were wined and dined in
Tokyo and paid under the table for contracts. Others admitted
Japanese influence would be profitable for Taiwan even though
Japanese themselves were still disliked. Thus one could find a
wide range of attitudes toward Japan.

Some Taiwanese professed to see evidence of what they thought was a new nationalism in Japanese social gatherings and spoke of the *Hi no maru* spirit—a reference to the Japanese flag, hence nationalistic. However true this may have seemed to them, to an American observer the attitude of some of the more important resident Japanese in Taipei was less nationalistic than perplexed. How were they to deal with the black-and-white political world of the Chinese or the Koreans? How could they project the reality of their own society, with its modern complexities and its relative openness, in such still very authoritarian realms as Seoul or Taipei? Here, as throughout Asia, one felt the agonizingly awkward position of the Japanese, located in Asia but not wholly of it, half developed, half not, being dunned and threatened, courted and cajoled from Seoul to New Delhi and beyond, fumbling to behave in the way prestige and profit required but without much real stomach for the exercise. How were they to deal with former colonies now immeasurably proud of their achievements, less interested in talking of Japanese technical assistance to them than of their own technical assistance to others, urgently insisting to visitors that they—Koreans or Taiwanese—would soon compete with Japan industrially and would never go back to the status of suppliers of agricultural produce alone? How to communicate individually where being Japanese meant one could once impose one's demands but could do so no longer, and where disparate, isolated individuals were left to make their way as best they could with only the vaguest of guidance behind them? One saw their dilemma with especial force and poignancy in the area of technical assistance, where the individual, if he went on a government assignment, had not even a company to support him. United Nations representatives from one end of Asia to the other agreed that Japanese technicians were better in groups than by themselves, and, like members of the Youth Volunteer Corps, were better at demonstrating visual or manual skills than at explaining them orally or administering projects that required contact with a large number of local people.

All over Asia there were these solitary Japanese, like the expert in agricultural machinery who had spent years in Manchuria or the rug weaving specialist who had learned his skill in Afghanistan, and who both were now advising small Chinese companies in Taiwan. Many of them had it in their blood to live overseas and in this were not unlike many Europeans or Americans. But their difficulties of communication were immense. Often not even the native humor of the Japanese, with its rich vein of ridicule, could come through to others because of the language barrier, or personality difficulties, or because other Asians regarded them shallowly as imitation Westerners. If only, one often wished, Asians had some cement to hold them together and give them a sense of belonging to a single region instead of being, as Sun Yat-sen said foreigners called the Chinese, a sheet of loose sand.

In both Seoul and Taipei, claims of Japanese association dating from the colonial era coexisted with more recent and powerful claims of Western, largely American, relationships. The Japanese political presence in Taiwan and South Korea was inconspicuous and circumspect. To some extent Japan profited from the American presence and used it as an excuse for dealing with both countries and re-establishing itself in both. Any reasonably balanced reading of the situation could only lead to the conclusion that Japanese influence in Taiwan would be very great in the future, especially so long as the island maintained an identity separate from the Chinese mainland. With a third of the island's trade already with Japan and Japanese investments growing, any other forecast was unwarranted. This had little to do with Taiwanese efforts to increase Japan's "stake" in the island or with the American yearning to develop stronger ideological motivations concerning aid in the Japanese mind. The Japanese perception of Korea and Taiwan simply implied a leading role, if not a paramount one, for themselves in both places. They were coming back heavily in a commercial sense. Japanese trading companies in 1969 were reported to handle more than half of Taiwan's exports to third countries.[7] The mainlanders, some of them, in Ezra Pound's phrase, men "on whom the sun has gone down," were uneasy about Japan, fearing its political inconstancy. Taiwanese Chinese were glad to have the Japanese, meant to use and control them, but were not wholly certain that they could. As far as the short-term future of Japan's relations with Taiwan was concerned, the Mayor of Taipei was probably correct when he remarked that "the real decisions will not be taken in Tokyo or Taipei, but in Peking and Washington."

3. THE PHILIPPINES

In 1968 Japan was the Philippines' second largest trading partner, with about a third of total Philippine exports and imports, compared with the United States' 45 per cent. In Manila it was being predicted that in five years Japan's share would be larger than America's. Japanese goods and money blanketed the country. Along the Manila waterfront huge billboards offered the Mitsubishi trading company's services "worldwide for your every need." A growing share of Philippine trade with third countries went through Japanese hands. The Manila press daily carried advertisements for Japanese patent medicines, hair pomades, and motorcycles fitted with garishly decorated side-cars to suit the tastes of young Filipinos. Japanese radios, washing machines, television, and other consumer goods were offered in department stores on the Escolta, and Japanese drugs would soon compete with American and European products.

It was reliably estimated that between 8,000 and 9,000 Japanese businessmen resided in the Philippines. Since no Treaty of Friendship, Commerce and Navigation provided them legal protection, they did business by virtue of executive directives issued by the President's office, which gave them privileges not specifically barred by the Constitution and other laws of the country. This was not enough to interest many Japanese in joint ventures. Philippine minimum wage laws also made such enterprises less attractive than they were in South Korea, Hong Kong, Taiwan or Thailand. The half-dozen joint ventures in operation in 1968 included an iron pelletizing plant capitalized at about $1 million, 90 per cent Japanese-controlled; a food seasoning plant, 27 per cent Japanese; a mill to make galvanized iron sheets, 20 per cent; and a piano factory, 40 per cent. Japanese firms also owned a small share (about 5.5 per cent) of the Philippine government's integrated steel mill in Iligan on the northern coast of the island of Mindanao.

Japanese interest in the Philippines was primarily in resource extraction, which involved extension of loans to such industries as timber and sugar. There was less Japanese money in mining, although interest was high in copper and chrome. Iron ore imports from the Philippines were important in the 1950s and early 1960s but dropped sharply as ore deposits became depleted and less economical to exploit.

The case of timber was especially instructive. Without the Japanese interest, the logging industry in the Philippines would hardly have developed as it did after World War II ended. Japanese deliberately set out after the Occupation to develop the market for plywood products in the United States. Their methods were interesting. They made little effort to master the technique of log extraction, which involved unfamiliar soil and terrain conditions and the use of heavy, wide-tread, light-flotation machinery, not much of which was being built in Japan at that time. (By 1968 such heavy equipment was substantially underselling American makes.) The Japanese preferred to avoid, as much as they could, contact with local laborers, with whom personal relations, especially in the early 1950s, were often awkward. Instead, they loaned money to local log extractors and took payment in a share —10 per cent or more—of production. Half of the total Philippine production was exported, and Japan took four-fifths of that. Logs were shipped in Japanese vessels to Japan, where workers in Shimizu or Nagoya, the centers of the industry, turned them into plywood. Their woodcutting and glueing techniques were known the world over. Wood for door-skins and other plywood products went to America; saw-wood was largely sold at home, where in the 1960s sawmill technology improved and wood-drying kilns were built after the lumber industry had gone through a period of depression. Waste products mills were built near the plywood plants; nothing was thrown away; and it all made money for many years in the triangular trade. By the late 1960s Taiwan and Korea were competing with Japanese plywood, and Japanese plants at home had begun to move overseas.

The timber business was a good example of the kind of design-and-improve ability for which the Japanese were famous. The total amount of Japanese loans to the timber industry in the Philippines could not be known; neither was it known for certain how much Japanese equity was involved in the industry or how much of it was associated with American money. However, the Mitsubishi Trading Company had substantial capital stock in an important Philippine firm, the Aguinaldo Development Company, and Japanese funds were said to be heavily involved in at least two other Western-owned companies in the timber trade. A pattern of loans followed by equity involvement appeared to be common: Filipino entrepreneurs unable to meet their loan obligations offered shares to their Japanese creditors. In Manila one heard incredibly high estimates of total Philippine indebtedness to Japan; some thought the figure might reach $3 billion. (Total American investment was worth about $1.5 billion.) The Japanese interest was probably much less than that, but how much less could not be known unless the network of loans was exposed to view.

The United States officially welcomed the Japanese involvement in the Philippines. Some Americans were glad to have them or anybody else to help share attacks from Filipino nationalists. Others were impressed by the rapidity and extent of Japan's economic return to the country but had no personal interests at stake. Some American managers of companies based in Manila were worried by Japanese competition, but their parent organizations in the United States were usually far more interested in the American market than they were in the Philippines, especially as the American preferential position there dwindled. Whether or not preferences will be extended after the Laurel-Langley agreement expires in 1974 was unknown.

Some Filipino politicians appeared to think they would receive loans on softer terms from Japan once Japanese investment in their country had grown large enough. Filipino negotiators came to Tokyo with a shopping list. In 1966, for example, they presented loan requests "rounded out," in their own words, at $100 million for such things as 20,000 two-room schoolhouses, estimated to cost $20 million, irrigation pumps and pipes, pilot rice farms, bridges, fishing wharves and cold storage plants, refrigeration and food preserving plants, and fertilizer factories. They asked that these, as well as the Manila Railroad extension, be financed through the Overseas Economic Cooperation Fund, insisting that since the OECF was being used for loans to Thailand, Malaysia, and other countries, the Philippines should get "equal or better terms." [8]

A note of desperation could be detected in these maneuvers. In the late 1960s the Philippine economy was deteriorating. Reparations had been badly wasted and were half paid. José Laurel, Jr., chairman of the Philippine Reparations Mission in 1966, implicitly admitted the failure of the program when he declared to Japanese officials that President Marcos had decided to "channel the greater portion of reparations to the government sector for procurement of monumental and lasting projects." He blamed the failure of reparations to produce such projects on the lack of peso funds with which to implement them and demanded that the Japanese supply such funds to assure successful utilization of future loans. Ignoring criticism of poor performance in the past, Laurel told the Japanese that Marcos needed more loans and a speeded-up reparations schedule "so that his massive four-year socio-economic development program may be achieved." Laurel's menacing arguments were reminiscent of the earlier reparations negotiations:

. . . some quarters are unwilling or reluctant to consider extending to the Philippines other forms of financing from sources like the Overseas Economic Cooperation Fund or Export-Import Bank of Japan similar to those extended to the other Asian countries like Korea, Taiwan and others. To deny the Philippines similar assistance is likely to be interpreted in my country as a discrimination.

He stressed the difficulties surrounding ratification of the Treaty of Friendship and tried to get loans in return for ratification:

President Marcos needs the helping hand of everybody, including Japan. I sincerely believe that the Japanese government can help effectively by supplying President Marcos with tangible arguments to win over those who are against the treaty. . . . And the best tangible arguments that Japan can supply would be in the form of economic cooperation and assistance extended in the true spirit of neighborly helpfulness rather than in the rude concept of barter which is repulsive to the Oriental sensitivities of our two peoples.[9]

Japanese officials were less concerned with "Oriental sensitivities" than with the risks involved in loans to the Philippines. In their view, the country had squandered reparations, and they had no intention of approving loans at 3.5 per cent for long-term projects of dubious feasibility, especially before a treaty protecting Japanese interests in the Philippines had been ratified. The Japanese side was adept at dodges and innuendoes of its own; it hinted at the danger of opposition attacks in the Diet if it gave in to some of the Philippine wishes. The two sides thrust at each other, but Filipino negotiators knew only too well where they stood and knew also the perils of trying to force ratification of the treaty in the Congress in Manila. President Macapagal had tried to do so in his day, only to be jumped on by his rival, Ferdinand Marcos, who called the treaty a threat to Philippine sovereignty. Now that Marcos was President, his opponents in the Senate would use the treaty against him at every opportunity. Beyond political opportunism, many people in the Philippines honestly feared that the rather loose language of the treaty draft would open the way to unrestricted economic penetration of the country. By 1968 three of the six bills proposed to plug holes in the treaty and protect the Philippines from "aliens" (except Americans, who were specifically exempted) had been passed, but others, such as a measure giving the National Economic Council a veto over Japanese investment and another barring government purchases from alien firms, were still pending.

As was suggested earlier, reparations were not a total loss, in spite of the graft that surrounded them. In a few cases personal enrichment was accompanied by some good to the country or to portions of it. For example, on the east coast of the island of Cebu, about 35 miles north of Cebu City, a local political boss built a cement plant, a factory making paper bags to hold the cement, a drydock to build barges to haul the cement-filled bags to market and bring back sugar cane, and a mill to extract sugar from the cane. Put up by sixteen Japanese engineers with equipment supplied under reparations, the whole project gave employment of a sort to several hundred people. The road from Cebu to Danao, where the plants were located, was paved with locally-made cement. Cement was sold to the government for use in Mindanao and the Visayas. The owner was a Congressman who had been on the Reparations Commission in the 1950s; his wife was mayor of Danao, a town of 30,000 people. Their complex was described by Americans in Manila as a case of "dynamic despotism." The setting somewhat resembled a Graham Greene novel: armed guards checked traffic in and out, Japanese engineers on the job lived without their families in dirty, pretentious quarters isolated from contact with local people. Only one of the sixteen spoke any English. Yet cement was in great demand for road building and construction, and the Danao complex supplied a significant portion of it. The owner's wife professed to be pleased with Japanese technical assistance and thought that "in due time" Japanese with families would be living in Danao. She recalled that before World War II there had been a Japanese department store in Cebu and said that feelings of hatred engendered by the war had almost completely disappeared. One could not be sure of this, however; another less powerful local citizen laconically volunteered the information that his uncle had been decapitated by a Japanese soldier with a bamboo knife.

In Manila, many Filipinos wavered between self-deprecation and defiant overconfidence when they spoke of Japan. Many blamed the United States for most of their national difficulties. This was a sort of tic; they accused America of neglecting Filipino interests after the war, which contributed, or so it was alleged, to Japan's rushing into the "vacuum." Moreover, the "vacuum" was ubiquitous; all over Southeast Asia Japanese were said to be ready to move into it. Some Filipino intellectuals noted that the Japanese were saying they would protect the Filipinos from the Chinese Communists and were also claiming to understand Filipino nationalism better than the Americans ever had. Such tactics, they rather shrilly asserted, would never deceive anyone; but intellectuals of strongly nationalist bent had for many years been ambivalent toward the Japanese and uncertain how their influence and presence in the country could advance Filipino desires. Others in Manila repeated stories of the war and the resistance that had been told over and over for twenty-five years. They clung to the heroism of that period and were full of irony about the Japanese, accusing them of flooding the country with merchandise, as if that in itself were evil. They were even more bitter about Americans, and their bitterness was blended with self-pity as they thrashed about in a painful search for national and personal dignity in a society and polity in which they had in varying degrees lost faith. Some who had been friendly earlier to America and Americans now were hostile or remote, declaring that Washington was behind Japan's supposed rapaciousness.

In addition to purely commercial activities and technical assistance stemming from reparations contracts, Japanese were making efforts in the cultural sphere that were somewhat broader in concept than the flower arrangement classes for politicians' wives that had characterized their efforts in the 1950s. A well-appointed

Japan Information Center on Taft Avenue in Manila offered free Japanese language lessons to the public, including some who had learned the language earlier and who now wanted to do business with Japanese partners. Films were shown, including some of the best Tokyo commercial productions, and a film mobile unit traveled the provinces from time to time, once at least venturing into rural Mindanao under protection of an armed guard, who turned out to be quite unnecessary. The Center's director, a young Foreign Ministry official on loan, interestingly enough, from the Economic Bureau of the Ministry, asserted that his goal was to get more of the Filipino "masses" to know Japan. He was in favor of playing down economic diplomacy and thought Japan should make a greater public relations effort. He bemoaned the fact that after a severe earthquake in Manila, when Shell and Caltex had come forward with contributions to help the homeless, Japanese business firms had contributed nothing; as he put it, "it isn't in their ethic." He also professed to be disturbed by what he called (in English) the "human gulf": "Japanese are interested only in getting, not in giving." His Center was a clean and pleasant place, and his assistant, who taught Japanese language there, also gave courses on the Japanese economy at a local university.

The younger generation of officials included some persons of this sort, who modeled their cultural programs to some extent on USIS. Sixty-odd members of the Youth Volunteer Corps also were scattered over the country in 1968, and the Philippine government had asked for 200 more—always the cry was for more! more!—to assist with vegetable cultivation projects, bambooware crafts, sericulture, tea culture, and so on. The emphasis of the Corps was on technical skills, but some also served as gymnastics and swimming and track coaches at the University of the Philippines. Many of these young people were graduates of technical schools and a few had finished a university in Japan, though seldom one of the best. Talking with them one was reminded of the sharp generation gap in Tokyo and its outreach into Southeast Asia. As a young Japanese plant physiologist put it, with mild amusement and some dismay, elderly Japanese visitors occasionally still spoke of Southeast Asia as the *Nanyō*, a term meaning South Seas and evoking images of Zero fighters, PT boats, and vegetable patches on bypassed Pacific islands of a generation ago, which were as strange to young Japanese as to young Americans.

Senior Japanese officials in Manila wondered what Japan's role would be in the Philippines, say by 1980, when worldwide Japanese imports and exports might each reach $50 billion annually and flood the area. One of them, at least, had read Myrdal's *Asian Drama* and had not yet recovered his buoyancy. He saw the main local problem to be the unavailability of labor: people were not so much underemployed as they simply could not be prevailed upon to work. Their values were not appropriate for industrialization; they were indolent and corrupt—such observations quickly turned into stereotypes—more so in Indonesia and Vietnam, perhaps, but enough so in the Philippines. This official had not had his faith shaken in the desirability of modern technical societies throughout Asia, but he was convinced that the Philippines would "never" have heavy industry; the most it could achieve would be a few import substitution industries. He scoffed at the idea of Japan's filling a "vacuum" left by American departure: Japan, he thought, could hardly do more than buy and sell now and for the foreseeable future; yet the Philippines would not want to have its raw materials exploited forever but could manufacture nothing else to sell. He believed that in a hundred years Southeast Asia might resemble Latin America today, and he envisaged a role for Japan that resembled the United States's role in Latin America. To him this promised repeated and endless frustrations and failures. He compared the Foreign Ministry's periodic Ministerial Conferences on the economic development of Southeast Asia with the Alliance for Progress and was equally pessimistic about both.

To this senior official, Korea was of far greater importance to Japan's national interest than all of Southeast Asia. Even if the

Malacca Strait were blocked in some future crisis, Japan could get its oil by other routes; but Korea was strategically crucial, and he thought more appreciation of that fact was needed in Tokyo. Philippine nation-building seemed nearly hopeless to him. There were two bright spots: rice production and road-building. But he saw the day coming when Japan might overrun the country economically and might as a result be in a position to exercise great political influence as well. He had no real clue as to what that would mean. Japan, he thought, must remain uncommitted to the area ideologically, but he had no really clear idea of what this involved, either, and no blueprint for his country's foreign policy. The one thing that he was sure had to be avoided above all else was a collision between America and Japan in Asia.

Other thoughtful and responsible Japanese worried about the failure of Philippine leaders to make any really concerted efforts to redistribute wealth and create a national economy. They realized that reparations had hardly touched the *barrios*, having profited only the land-holding elite. They perceived that elite to be hostile to any serious effort at social or economic change, merely using the Philippine version of elective politics to preserve its own position as it had done throughout much of the modern period. Family meant more than nation; or, rather, a few families felt themselves responsible for the nation; in their own minds they *were* the nation. The Philippines was an incorrigibly verbalizing culture, drunk on its own rhetoric, more Latin American than Asian to many Japanese. Beauty contests seemed, unaccountably, to interest more people than nation-building. A small entrepreneurial class was emerging, but too often it was more eager to invest in real estate in the old familiar way, as the half-empty office buildings of Makati suggested, than to reinvest profits in productive facilities that would employ more people. Too many Filipino entrepreneurs were figuratively smoking their opium pipes [10] in their mansions in Forbes Park and disregarding the crying need to raise Filipino purchasing power and build a real middle class.

In sum, to Japanese as to Americans the situation in the Philippines was less hopeful than it had been some years earlier. The economic environment was relatively stable but was shot through with corruption. Businessmen could be dealt with if they could be separated from politicians, but political interventions made the country a poor place in which to do anything but sell goods and mine resources. The political system was somewhat more outward-looking than in many other parts of the region, but this was changing; nationalism blocked much Japanese equity investment and was reducing other foreign investment as well. The Japanese were trying to strengthen or renew their connections with families of the Philippine elite who had become entrenched at the trough of patronage during American colonial rule, and they were also developing new relationships. They were being most circumspect; there was little evidence of any overt Japanese political influence in the national government. Some Filipino journalists liked to charge that such-and-such a politician was kept by Japanese interests; there may have been some truth in this, but it was impossible to prove, and the Philippine press was notoriously sensational. In any event, hatred of the Japanese, though waning, could still be used for political purposes, as was done in 1968 when the mayor of Manila abruptly banned all Japanese business operations within the city limits. (Most merely moved across the line into Makati.)

Broader efforts at cultural diplomacy were being made, and the treatment of individual Japanese had obviously improved. The first ship salvage workers in 1956 had to be quartered in compounds on the Manila docks surrounded by barbed wire and guarded by men with guns. By the mid-1960s Japanese moved freely through much of the country, in pairs or groups but also singly. Some scholars did useful work on rural problems, although plans to establish Japanese model rice farms in Mindoro and Leyte were criticized as being too late by some Filipinos, who observed that "we know the mechanics of good rice farming now," and who thought the venture showed a "straining for goodwill, which was neither necessary nor practical." [11] Japanese history and related subjects were taught at the University of the Philippines, and a handful of Filipino scholars concerned themselves with "Asian studies." Japanese restaurants had opened, Japanese brand-name signs written in English dominated Dewey, renamed Roxas, Boulevard. In the hotels of Ermita and Malate, Japanese and Okinawan tourists bought trinkets of mother of pearl, pineapple cloth, or Philippine gold, but in the embassies in the same district, as in the ministries in Tokyo, the question of Japan's role in the Philippines' very uncertain future was a subject of perplexed discussion.

4. INDONESIA

Before 1965, reparations were the bridgehead over which Japanese returned to the Indonesian archipelago. They catered to Sukarno's personal tastes without regrets and even with some relish. In 1968, one Cabinet Minister in Tokyo expressed pride in his country's Indonesian record; he thought Japan's wartime policies there had been generally good and beneficial, despite intermittent cruelties. He was proud of the stimulation Japan had provided to the nationalist movement. He regarded Sukarno as a friend and thought that the Japanese were closer to Indonesians in temperament than to any other Asians except the Chinese. Certainly they were closer to them than to the Thais, while toward the Indians the Cabinet Minister felt a positive antipathy.

As indicated earlier, Japan was the last of the non-Communist countries to give up on Sukarno. The Mitsui and Nomura interests in particular were active in Indonesian matters during his time. Their principal political agent was Shōjirō Kawashima, a conservative leader of the older type in the mainstream of the Liberal Democratic party; the last yen credit before the 1965 coup attempt, granted in April of that year and amounting to $37 million worth of textiles and other consumer goods, was known in Tokyo as the "Kawashima credit." Except for a small amount of textiles it was unfulfilled when the September uprising occurred. Even after that, however, Japan tried to keep contacts open, giving an emergency food grant of $2.5 million in March 1966 and another emergency credit of $30 million in May of that year.

With Sukarno's departure from power, Japan's relations with Indonesia entered a new phase. A different group of men, mainly army officers and their academic advisers, emerged to have a try at running the country. Most of them had little experience with Kawashima or other Indonesia-cultivators from Tokyo; the academicians were more familiar with professors from Harvard, Wisconsin, or Berkeley, especially the last, where many of them received their training. At the same time, the Japanese government found itself drawn into an international attempt to rescue Indonesia from almost complete collapse. A continuing lack of agreement within Japan about what policies were most desirable at any given time was responsible for the uncoordinated and orderless appearance of Japanese activities on the scene. This led in turn to a variety of criticisms by Indonesians and others regarding Japan's trade and aid and to much pulling and hauling among Japanese themselves. But after the shock of the 1965 coup attempt had been fully felt in Tokyo there could be no doubting that Indonesia was increasingly seen to be vital to Japan's long-run political interests in Southeast Asia, as well as to its long-run economic interests in the region.

Japanese interest was signified by the Foreign Ministry's initiative in calling the first conference of the members of the consortium to aid Indonesia in Tokyo in the fall of 1966. There Japanese delegates found themselves under pressure to give aid on soft terms to stem the grotesque inflation and help stabilize the Indonesian economy. Bureaucrats in MITI and other ministries who, when they spoke of "aid," meant the sale of Japanese goods, reacted negatively to demands for stopgap assistance to Indonesia. They seemed unable to realize that there might be merit in holding Indonesia together for the sake of collective security even if profit margins suffered for the time being, and they preferred to talk of their own dollar problems.

The Indonesia aid issue was debated heatedly in Diet committees, where, in 1966 and later, conservative rivals of Premier Satō charged giveaways while the Socialists loudly deplored Japan's "imperialistic plottings" in Southeast Asia. However, the Foreign Ministry worked hard to counter the opposition to aid, pointing not only to Indonesia's vast unexploited riches but also to its great strategic importance and the dangers illustrated by the coup attempt, which they warned might be repeated in the future. Some officials now urged that the politicians look at Indonesia with new eyes. Its new leaders were apparently—one could not be absolutely sure—trying to open the country to the world on a scale unprecedented since 1945. At least the World Bank, teams of American economists, the Ford Foundation, and other Western organizations were moving into the country. A foreign investment law had been passed, although the climate for investment was still risky. In other words, there were clear reasons for not being left at the post in the international competition for influence in Indonesia merely because of bureaucratic niggardliness and what amounted in some places to a neurosis over the balance of payments. Some such arguments were brought to bear, along with other more concrete points concerning Japan's present and future energy requirements, its interest in offshore oil concessions, in Borneo timber, Celebes nickel, and so on.

After all these and other pressures from outside the country had been exerted, the Japanese government finally decided to make a grant of $10 million, a 20-year loan of $50 million at 5 per cent, and to refinance $38 million in previous loans secured by reparations, all to count as Japan's 1967 contribution to the aid consortium. United States monetary aid approximately equaled the Japanese contribution, and a pattern was established, to the trepidation of some officials in Tokyo and the pride of others, whereby America and Japan would each give about one-third of the total decided upon each year, with the remaining members of the consortium making up the rest. Japan's contribution differed from its previous yen credits in that the $50 million loan was made available to the Indonesian government essentially as program aid, with its use to be determined by Indonesians, rather than for export of Japanese plant and equipment for individually-contracted projects. The Indonesian government used the money to issue certificates which were valid for import of desperately needed goods to help control inflation.

In this way Japanese fertilizer, textiles, electric equipment, chemicals, spare parts, and other necessities entered the country. No allotments for engineering or other industrial projects were included in Japan's 1967 aid, since the Indonesian government had no local funds whatever to spend on them. In 1968, after another round of protracted negotiations, Japan pledged a total of $110 million, of which $80 million was to be given in that year and $30 million in 1969 (without prejudice to regular 1969 contributions). Of this, $65 million was for program aid, $5 million for rice, and $10 million for project aid to be applied to dam construction projects in Java and Borneo that were begun but not finished under reparations.

A private Japanese commercial source estimated that of the 45 substantial projects originally authorized under reparations, half were unfinished in 1968. Like other businessmen, the source believed that aid should be concentrated first on completing those projects on which Japanese construction had already begun, and only after they had been completed should Japanese aid be coordinated with the over-all aid policies of the Indonesian government. The same source frankly explained his own understanding of Japan's aid to Indonesia:

> According to Islam, the rich have a duty to give to the poor. But basically . . . the charm of a market of 100 million people is great, and resources of oil, timber, and non-ferrous metals . . . play a great role in maintaining our economy. If we cut off aid, Japanese goods may be banned and it may be difficult to protect those resources.[12]

So much for the formal framework of Japan's aid, which clearly was on the point of becoming a vital ingredient in new Indonesian economic plans. But what about the actual presence of Japanese there, and what about their attitudes toward Indonesia, and Indonesian attitudes toward them? One received the same impression of commercial aggressiveness as in the Philippines. No treaty of friendship, commerce and navigation had been signed, and therefore branch offices of Japanese companies were not legally authorized to operate, but the Bank of Tokyo, Japan's largest foreign exchange bank, in early 1968 opened a branch in the same building with the Japanese Embassy and Japan Air Lines; a large JAL advertisement stood in front of the Embassy, leading one American to wonder what would happen if Pan American put up a similar sign at the U.S. Embassy. Some 58 companies had several hundred representatives in Djakarta, where there was a Japanese school and a Japan Club, and where a copy of the private telephone directory of Japanese residents compiled by a Bank of Tokyo staff member was one of the most prized documents in Indonesian-Japanese relations.

Production-sharing schemes in oil, timber, and nickel were still the most notable commercial projects in which Japanese were involved. The first and last of these, especially the last, were going fairly well. In addition, after Sukarno's fall two Japanese firms acquired oil-drilling rights offshore of north Sumatra and southern and eastern Borneo. Japex Indonesia, which began exploration in 1966, was organized by the official Japan Oil Resources Development Corporation; Mitsubishi Shōji, Mitsui Bussan, Marubeni-Iida, Nippon Kōkan, and Sumitomo interests also subscribed capital to this undertaking. Kyūshū Oil, the other Japanese company, was at least 50 per cent subscribed by Yawata Steel. These ventures operated under terms similar to the production-sharing formula for north Sumatran onshore wells, but much of the responsibility for actual drilling operations was vested in the Japanese, in the hope that some of the bickering, pilferage, and inefficiency that had plagued NOSODECO from its inception could be avoided.[13] Full-scale drilling operations had not yet begun in late 1968; Western oil companies supplied Japan with most of its Indonesian and other oil. New discoveries in Alaska and elsewhere meant that Indonesia would continue to be forced to compete with other sources of supply. Political uncertainties also had something to do with the slow pace of Japan's advance. But in view of the immense Japanese need for energy in the present and future, their Indonesian oil explorations were of greater significance than their other activities in the country. And if there were large strikes, the whole pattern of Japan's oil procurement might be changed in an important if not a decisive way.

In addition to production-sharing, a number of Japanese-financed schemes were in various stages of completion or were being planned, mostly the latter. In the last days of the Sukarno regime so many Indonesians were competing for import commissions from Japanese that there was little foreign exchange left for other more productive enterprises. Those days were over, at least for the present. Japanese had interests in tin mining, shrimping, and pearl fishing. Some of their projects had proved abortive or were in their early stages. A scheme to open 175,000 acres in southern Sumatra to rice and corn production fell afoul of local politics and unrealistic costs. Mitsui Bussan began a more modest feed corn project on 10,000 hectares; Mitsui held 51 per cent, local interests 49 per cent. Sumitomo Shōji also planned to grow corn in Java, but poor transport and communications were serious drawbacks to such plans. A substantial investment was reported about to be made in an oil refinery in Sumatra to be built by Sumitomo, and Japanese were also involved in a fertilizer factory. More such investments would likely be made in the near future, although just how far the Japanese government was prepared to go was not clear. One Japanese writer lamented that Japan's ventures lacked the scope and strength of Western concerns like the Freeport Sulphur Co. or International Nickel, both heavy investors in Indonesia; but he ended on a rather combative note: "Japanese businessmen have an energy that does not have to be defeated by Western capital. That energy will be tied up with the reconstruction of Indonesia, and will take part in this great enterprise that will rewrite history." [14]

There was no doubting Japanese energy, particularly that of those large corporate businesses that through their very presence spoke for the national interest. In October 1968 Japan fielded the largest and most impressive foreign business mission to visit Djakarta since 1945. Sponsored by the Indonesian Committee of *Keidanren*,[15] the mission's leaders were a senior industrialist and a banker of the first rank. Each morning for ten days its older members were bowed out of the Hotel Indonesia (built by Japanese reparations) by their subordinates and went off in a fleet of Mercedes-Benzes with motorcycle escort past a display of Japanese flags to consult with Indonesian businessmen and government officials. The mission was designed to assess the chances of Indonesian viability and ascertain investment opportunities. Its results were uncertain. Some local Japanese saw the visit of such important men as a portent of large-scale investments in the near future. As one put it, he might soon have to stop trying to interest his home office in investing and start persuading the Indonesian authorities to permit it. Not all were so sanguine, however.

One Japanese banker in Djakarta spoke of developing Indonesia as the American West had been developed, through private exploitation unrestrained by bureaucratic controls. He thought Japanese companies should form close links with different local army groups. This would result in economic and political disorder at first, and much capital would flow out of the country. But he claimed that eventually money would flow in again, and a balance would be reached without government manipulation and interference in the economy. He criticized the new Indonesian government's economic advisers and their Western associates, who, he said, were governed by the "macroeconomic thinking of the International Monetary Fund," whereas what was necessary was to develop Indonesia through "microeconomic action" in the private sector. In this sense he thought the activities of Japanese adventurers during the Sukarno era had not been all bad in spite of the rascality of some of them; and he and some of his colleagues in Djakarta were disappointed with the *Keidanren* mission, which instead of telling the Indonesians which field Japan was prepared to invest in, merely inquired what fields they wished to favor. This was too passive an approach for the banker, who, like some other Japanese in Djakarta, grumbled that the Japanese government would probably not authorize any important investments in the near future.

Like some Filipinos, a number of Indonesians bitterly criticized the Japanese government's lack of interest in helping them to develop their country and believed Japan wanted Indonesia's raw material resources and nothing else. They accused Japan of limiting aid to projects narrowly connected with its own plant exports; and they desired Japan to invest in manufacturing that would provide employment and train Indonesians in a variety of new skills, the kind of process that they saw going on in Taiwan. In return, they promised repatriation of profits and other incentives. Baffled by the Japanese slowness to respond to their proposals, they wondered how to appeal to them. In some of these men there was an almost pathetic desire to discover how to influence the Japanese; they were even driven to seek clues to this from visiting Americans.

Each side wanted to take from the other, and each was prepared to extract as much as it could, but neither would give itself away without some very specific *quid pro quo*. Charity was not noticeably present in the oil business: when the Indonesians asked for more advanced oil technology, the Japanese suggested that the cost would be a piece of the industry. At the University of Indonesia's agricultural institute in Bogor, the director asserted that he needed staff and would accept Japanese, but that he had had no offers. It was not difficult to imagine the wasted opportunities that resulted from such a psychology.

A handful of Japanese who had been associated in one way or

another with Indonesia before 1945 had returned after the war
and were present in 1968. Like old hands in other countries, they
were less ready than newcomers with glib answers to Indonesia's
problems and the question of Japan's relations with that country.
Their views were rather dark. One Japanese student of Indonesia
who was respected by both Americans and Japanese spoke wanly
of the ignorance of the country on the part of his own Embassy
officials, who knew neither English, Dutch, nor Indonesian well
and had never met, much less got to know, many of the professors and generals who were now in power. No Youth Volunteers
had yet been sent, no effective technical assistance centers established, although surveys were being made by able people in the
field of agriculture. Conversely, Indonesians, this scholar declared,
saw Japan as a source of consumer goods and entertainment rather
than as a place to respect culturally. They regarded the Japanese
language as a passport to nowhere, except possibly a job in a
Japanese company; it was not a world language and would never
be. Most Indonesians preferred to learn what they wished to know
directly from Europe or America, not to have their information
filtered through often murky and inarticulate Japanese sources.
If only, he lamented, the Japanese could get out of themselves
an inch or two, and not be so hopelessly tense and opaque in
social relationships. The few exceptions had to carry a heavy burden everywhere; and while he welcomed the appointment of one
of them as an economic adviser to the Indonesian government, he
feared that one man, however able and forward-looking, might
end up ground to a powder between warring Japanese and Indonesian bureaucracies.

Another long-time official of the defunct Yokohama Specie
Bank with more than twenty years in the country noted glumly
that Japan did less business with Indonesia than with California.
He claimed that the Asia Economic Research Institute sent out
people to do research who could speak neither Dutch nor Indonesian. He confessed that he had become more interested in the
Indonesian past than in its present and asked where were the

histories of Indonesia in Japanese. No one in Japan wanted to know about the past. Rather the question most often asked was, "Is it more profitable than somewhere else?" He criticized Japanese technicians who refused to adapt to local conditions: "Japanese manufacturers of rat poison have no business telling Indonesians how to kill rats until they have come here and seen whether Indonesian rats are bigger than Japanese ones." The same complaints about the rigidity of Japanese technical experts were heard in the Philippines.

Still another old Indonesia hand was the Japanese resident representative of NOSODECO in Djakarta, who had been in the country during the war, had helped settle reparations, and was valued for his negotiating skill. He described NOSODECO candidly as a pilot project designed not only to secure oil and expand Japan's small supply of oil technicians but also to extend Japanese political influence and make Indonesia to some extent dependent upon Japan. As far as trade was concerned, such dependence was already considerable: Japan bought most of Indonesia's bauxite exports as well as substantial percentages of its oil, natural rubber, timber, and nickel output. The balance was presently favorable to Indonesia, as was also the case in the Philippines and Malaysia, other raw material exporters. Like the banker quoted above, he deplored his government's stinginess and the web of restraints it put upon the operations of Japanese business abroad, but like most of his fellows, he implied that the Japanese interest was great and would increase.

If Indonesians asked for more Japanese investment and had trouble communicating with them, some Americans hoped that participation in the aid consortium would make for a more clearcut awareness by Japanese of the political implications of aid and a greater commitment to a sense of common purpose in giving it. They spoke their wish that Japan would adopt more "farseeing" aid policies. They were apparently not putting this in terms of "saving the free world" or trying to act as a fairy godmother to the Japanese. But they complained that, by contrast with its aggressive businessmen, Japan's officials seemed timid, passive, and inert. But this was deceptive; although Japanese purposes may have coincided with the West's in Indonesia, they tended to be pursued separately, always with a sense of Japan's peculiar status as a half-developed, intermediate, essentially solitary power, with financial and structural problems of its own that set narrow bounds on its ability to help others even if it wished to do so.

Japanese and Americans were isolated from each other in other ways in Indonesia, as they were everywhere in Asia outside Japan itself. Over-all amounts of aid were pledged in international meetings, but implementation of aid programs was in most cases bilateral. On-the-spot coordination of such programs was not all that it might have been: the American Embassy sometimes heard about what Japan was doing in Indonesia as rapidly from Washington or Tokyo as from Japanese sources in Djakarta. Some Americans judged that Indonesian feelings against the Japanese were still so strong that for America to push any harder for Japanese cooperation in specific projects would cause Indonesian resentment. Other Americans pointed to the keen Japanese-American competition in business and wondered whether there was a contradiction in urging a larger aid role on Japan.

Japan may have been gathering options, from Siberia to Southeast Asia, Australia or India; but Indonesians, too, were trying to keep their options open. They would try to avoid too heavy an influence from Japan but use the Japanese where possible as a hedge against the Chinese. Their ambivalence was obvious; uneasy with their new, outward-looking posture and their newly opened economy, some leaders in Djakarta felt nostalgia for the era of controls, circuses, and inward-looking nationalism. As one Japanese remarked in late 1968, "Suharto has given the people no dreams, not even a single building. His chance to show what he can do will not last forever."

A few Japanese in Tokyo and Djakarta saw that Indonesia would eventually be a market for much more sophisticated types of machinery and heavy goods, of which reparations had provided only a foretaste. Some day, perhaps sooner than most people thought, makers of machinery and chemicals would find it profitable to establish overseas operations in Java. But that time was not yet, and the essential Japanese activity in Indonesia remained resource exploitation. The memory of the war was fading, and the war had not, in any case, provoked the same response toward the Japanese as it had in the Philippines. Collaboration to many had been an active means of patriotism. The military occupation as it unfolded was cruel and disillusioning, leaving the people with hostile feelings toward Japan, but they also remembered that it was Japanese who had made return of the Dutch impossible. Like the Filipinos, many Indonesians professed to fear Japanese economic penetration and to be determined to prevent it. The general tone of the relationship was not warm, in spite of some individual exceptions. One found in Japanese documents on aid to Indonesia the same lugubrious tone that characterized all their writing about countries that lacked the same cohesiveness and rage for secular order that they themselves possessed. As in Manila, so in Djakarta Japanese Foreign Ministry officials were deeply perplexed about the Indonesian future and Japan's relationship to it. If there were any well-laid plans for Japan in Indonesia, they were being very carefully guarded. Meanwhile, officials hoped without much confidence that their aid money was not being poured down a rat hole.

5. Singapore

In Raffles Place, fronting the harbor in the heart of the city of Singapore, stands an immense granite monument dedicated in three languages to the civilian citizens of Malay, Chinese, or English descent who lost their lives during the Japanese occupation of the colony. Erected in 1966 by the government of the new Republic of Singapore, it is as impressive a reminder as any in Southeast Asia of Japan's past actions and attracts tourists from many nations, including bands of American sailors on shore passes.

Across the green, beyond the Anglican cathedral in its Victorian treaty-port setting of broad lawns and hedges of tropical flowers, a steel scaffolding holds aloft a huge neon sign advertising National home appliances, manufactured by the Matsushita Electric Company, one of Japan's most famous business concerns. The National sign is slightly, but only slightly, less tall than the monument.

In 1968 Japanese commercial activities in Singapore were growing with impressive speed, and memories evoked by the war monument, while they would remain below the surface for a long time to come, were being rapidly overshadowed by a whole new array of business relationships. That this was occuring was due largely to the outward-looking, energetic policies of the new Singapore government, which had decided to try to build local industries for export in order to soak up heavy unemployment and put the city-state on a different basis from the days when it could live entirely on entrepôt trade. Although the process was in its early stages and its ultimate success was unclear (in 1965 manufacturing accounted for only 13 per cent of GNP), the government actively encouraged foreign, including Japanese, investment by laws allowing full repatriation of capital and profits, tax incentives and other measures, even as it raised barriers against the import of products that could be purchased locally.

A so-called blood debt for Japanese actions during the war was settled in 1967, when the Japanese government agreed to loans and grants amounting to $17 million in lieu of reparations. Following this, new Japanese capital began to enter the island to participate in government-sponsored industrial projects or to set up joint ventures with local Chinese partners. Accurate investment statistics were hard to come by. Official Japanese sources indicated that as of April 1967, 29 cases of equity investment had been approved in Tokyo, totaling $10.4 million. In Singapore itself, estimates of Japanese investment ran as high as $80 million by October 1968, and Japan's over-all commercial involvement was second only to that of the United Kingdom. On a visit to Tokyo in late 1968, Prime Minister Lee Kuan Yew stated that Japanese investment equaled 10 per cent of total foreign investment, and he invited more of it. Actually the percentage may have been larger. The three-to-one imbalance of trade in Japan's favor he dismissed lightly as a passing phenomenon that was destined sooner or later to turn to Singapore's advantage.[16]

Most Japanese manufacturing activity was focused in the Jurong industrial estate in the southeastern corner of the island, where the largest single cluster of industrial plants in Southeast Asia was under construction. Some, like the Bridgestone Tire factory, had been started in anticipation of sales in the Singapore-Malaysia common market; after Singapore's withdrawal from the Federation in August 1965 they were forced to seek export markets elsewhere. Other enterprises either in operation or planned included a cement plant, a motorcycle assembly plant, and a cotton yarn spinning mill.

Probably the most interesting and certainly the most important single Japanese venture in Singapore to date was the Jurong shipyard, a joint enterprise of the government's Economic Development Board and Ishikawajima-Harima Industries, the giant Japanese shipbuilding firm. Incorporated in 1963, about 51 per cent of the shares in the shipyard were held by IHI, 49 per cent by the Singapore government and several private Chinese interests, all of them relatively minor. Financial and operational control of the yard was vested firmly in Japanese hands. An initial loan of around $4 million had been provided by the Exim Bank of Japan. (The Japanese general manager scoffed at the OECF as a source of credit for such projects, saying that although the Fund had been set up partly to help ailing Japanese industries abroad with soft loans, "if you let them know you are in trouble they won't lend you a yen.")

In October 1968, when I visited the shipyard, a Japanese manager and more than a dozen senior staff from IHI-Japan were on the scene, as well as more than a score of junior engineers and a larger number of shop foremen sent out from home without their families for two-year periods to work alongside Singaporean Chinese workers. The manager, an engineering graduate of Tokyo University, had been with IHI since 1945, had conducted feasibility surveys for shipyards in Brazil, and advised Indians on a yard in Calcutta. He was a completely self-assured and able person, more fluent than most Japanese in English, possessed of a sharp sense of humor and on close terms with key Singapore officials. He spoke wryly of the days, just twenty years ago, when his company, which now builds some of the world's largest supertankers, had been limited to boats of 200 tons or less by decree of the American Occupation.

The Jurong shipyard was the first stage in a design to make Singapore the most important ship repair and servicing center between the Persian Gulf and Yokohama. Employing nearly a thousand workers, it was already able to handle ships of up to 90,000 dwt, and a new drydock that would take 100,000 tonners was under construction. By unloading their oil in Japan, cleaning their tanks at sea while steaming south and putting in at Jurong for necessary repairs en route to the Persian Gulf for more oil, tankers might save several days' demurrage in Japan, which even with relatively high labor costs in Singapore could mean a saving of many thousands of dollars per voyage. Furthermore, the yard had plans to expand its shipbuilding as distinct from repair operations in order to develop all-round training opportunities for local workers and lead eventually to creation of a full range of subsidiary industries. After four years of operation, mainly as a repair center, the yard expected to pay a 10 per cent dividend at the close of 1968. The Transportation Ministry in Tokyo had backed the project from the start, and the general manager at Jurong commented rather acidly that the Finance Ministry's anxiety about it would be assuaged as soon as it paid a dividend, though hardly before.

Japanese were commonly criticized for their preference for short-term loans and their reluctance to transfer resources to Southeast Asia. But the Jurong shipyard was a longer-range investment and one that involved a Japanese stake in the future of Singapore and the whole region. Its senior managers were some of the best men Japan or any other country had to send overseas. Embodying the vigor and venturesomeness of some of the most successful representatives of postwar Japanese capitalism, they praised local Chinese as diligent and ambitious, and were sanguine, even buoyant, about future prospects for Singapore. When asked how the project fit over-all Japanese objectives, one of them replied, "I don't know whether or not it is best for Japan ultimately but it was best for the business, and we felt we had to go ahead and do it." Like some other visionaries, they saw Singapore primarily as a servicing and repair center for all of Southeast Asia. They thought the day might come when Americans, Japanese, and others would mine the ocean floor for iron and other minerals between Singapore and Saigon, as they were beginning to drill for the oil there. In the coming age, long "beyond Vietnam," Singapore might be an industrial out-station for the Western powers and Japan, never big enough, perhaps, to compete seriously with home country industries across the board, but able to flourish by its servicing facilities and support a range of import substitution enterprises, as Hong Kong had done, but on a larger scale.

But there was more to the Japanese interest in Singapore than this suggests. Their concern with the place, and indeed with the whole Indonesia-Malaysia-Singapore area, was at least as much strategic as it was commercial. In Singapore, the two interests could hardly be separated. Japanese oil companies already were using the island as a staging base for their offshore drilling operations in Indonesia. Through Malacca Strait came 90 per cent of the oil that kept Japan's economy running. By the late 1960s navigational hazards in the Strait made it difficult or impossible for the largest supertankers to transit while fully loaded. Plans for dredging were being pushed. Meanwhile, Lombok passage and other straits were alternatives, but they raised problems of the interpretation of coastal waters with Indonesia. And British forces were apparently withdrawing from Singapore.

These matters were being carefully discussed in Tokyo, where there were published reports of Defense Agency plans for construction in the 1970s of naval escort ships and other vessels that could convoy tankers if that should be thought necessary. As early as April 1968 unsensational journalistic sources predicted:

> . . . the sphere of the Maritime Self-Defense Forces is bound to be extended to the Strait of Malacca . . . political conditions in areas linking South Korea, the Philippines and the Indo-China peninsula are still extremely unstable. The same is the case with the Middle East. Under the circumstances, how to protect Japan's economic interests in these areas naturally becomes an important problem. . . . It is no longer possible for Japan to devote itself to economic growth under the aegis of U.S. military force.[17]

With only a few weeks' stockpiles of oil in Japan and an equally small amount at sea at any given time, the importance of assured navigation through the Singapore area was obvious. It could of course be argued that convoying tankers was a more expensive and politically inflammatory strategy than finding some other way for them to reach Japan. But this issue was a natural one for that minority of people in Tokyo who insisted that only full-scale rearmament could provide the technological incentives for industrial growth that would make Japan a truly great power.

As elsewhere in Southeast Asia, the Japanese in Singapore left others pretty much alone and were left to themselves for the most part. A query as to whether they had been admitted to a well-known club brought the response from an Englishman that none had asked to be and furthermore that none would ask. One was led sometimes to wonder what the Japanese had to do to exorcise finally the burden of distaste that still was manifested toward them in various ways. Yet this may have been an irrelevant question. The fact was that money and time were washing out the stains of the past, as they were everywhere in Southeast Asia. The Japanese had their own clubs, their own schools; if there was little ecumenism, neither was there much evidence of open anti-Japanese feeling, and that which remained was less directed at Japanese in particular than it was a part of the general anti-foreignism that was characteristic of the whole region. At any rate, speculation about the plight of Japanese who were disliked could cause one to overlook the essential fact that Singapore, like Taiwan and Korea, was on the move, and anti-Japanese sentiments were being dissolved in a golden stream of commerce and investment. If ventures like the Jurong shipyard and some others were any guide, the Japanese were certain to participate in Singapore's future in a significant, if not a paramount way, and they were already preparing their positions, cementing relations with local Chinese merchants and officials, while the influence of mainland China was at least temporarily on the wane.

6. MALAYSIA

North from Singapore, Japanese were engaged in a wide range of activities, from investment in manufacturing, usually with Chinese partners, to natural resource exploitation, construction of dams and irrigation projects, and Youth Volunteers Corps assistance to agriculture and vocational training. Most Japanese activity dated from late 1966, when a yen credit for $50 million worth of goods and services was granted to the Malaysian government for project aid in its first Five-Year Plan. Two-thirds of the Malaysian credit was extended through the Exim Bank of Japan at 5.75 per cent, with repayment in from 15 to 18 years, the remainder through the OECF at 4.5 per cent, with repayment in 20 years. Projects included the Malaya Railroad, a telecommunications network, and the city water system in Penang. In 1967 the Japanese government settled its "blood debt" to Malaysia, paying the equivalent of $8.3 million in ships and other capital goods in lieu of reparations. Private deferred-payment loans increased from $3.1 million in 1965 to $17 million in 1966, as Japanese firms began to come in under the "pioneer industries" law to protect local markets and open new ones. Malaysia was somewhat more remote from the Japanese consciousness than either the Philippines or Indonesia and was regarded as having less potential as a market or source of raw materials. Nevertheless, in 1967 Japan's log imports from Malaysia, mostly from Sabah, nearly matched those from the Philippines and amounted to almost half of total imports from Malaysia. The remainder consisted principally of tin, rubber, and iron ore. Japan's overall trade balance with Malaysia was heavily adverse, imports being three times as large as exports in 1967.[18]

Some 300 representatives of Tokyo or Osaka firms were busy in more than 30 joint ventures, including a National home appliance assembly plant and a food seasoning plant, Ajinomoto Malaysia. A branch of the Bank of Tokyo in Kuala Lumpur was doing a brisk business lending to these and other new ventures. A tin smelter with a capacity of 1,200 long tons monthly was owned principally by Ishihara Sangyō, the same trading company that had been involved in the Perdania Bank in Indonesia. The Peony Blanket Company, a Japanese-backed concern, turned out 10,000 low-grade blankets monthly. The Pan-Malaya Cement Works had Japanese money in it, as did the older Malayan-Nozawa Asbestos and Cement Company. A toothpaste company, 58 per cent Japanese-owned, made Lion brand dentifrices and cosmetics. The Malayan Weaving Mills specialized in bleached cotton fabrics and had heavy Japanese participation. Japanese equity investment by 1967 totaled perhaps $22 million, or about 10 per cent of all foreign investment in the country, and was increasing.

The Malayawata steel mill in Prai, opposite Penang on the peninsula, was 39 per cent Japanese-owned (including Yawata Steel's 20 per cent and numerous other Japanese companies with smaller shares). With a paid-in capital of $31.1 million, Malayawata went into operation in late 1967 and lost money heavily in its first year. It burned old rubber trees for charcoal for the furnaces and employed around 1,000 workers but had problems with the small local market and the "Malayanization" of management. However, a second-stage blast furnace was scheduled to go into operation in early 1969. Like NOSODECO in Indonesia and the Jurong shipyard in Singapore, Malayawata was described by some local Japanese as a long-term investment by which Japan hoped to establish a base in the Malaysian economy and which could widen Japanese influence throughout Southeast Asia.

In Kuala Lumpur, Japanese residents opened a school and a club in 1967. Young businessmen lived in suburban flats, drove to work in Volvos or Toyopets, talked gravely about Malaysia's wasting assets, and drank Scotch heavily in Chinese nightclubs. They were building new plants: for example, Nisshō-Iwai, a result of the recent merger of two old trading companies (anticipating the planned merger of their parent firms, Fuji and Yawata Steel), was putting up a factory that would make plastic-wrapped, insulated copper communications cables. Most of the funds for this came from the Furukawa Electric Company, an old, established cable manufacturer, and from local Chinese sources. The latter controlled the share capital, but the Japanese had the managing director and would effectively run the enterprise. Plans had been made for a band saw factory to supply saws to loggers and to the plywood veneer plant which Japanese expected to set up soon under prodding from the local government, which complained that not enough value was being added to raw materials before they were taken out of the country. Some Japanese in Kuala Lumpur admitted that the Malaysian government was not as easy to silence with bribes as the Filipinos or Indonesians were; as one of them observed in a matter-of-fact way, "the Malay top echelon is only just beginning to be corruptible now that it has been in power for more than a decade." Stories of the business subterfuges of young Japanese executives were the staple of bar gossip all over Southeast Asia. They were criticized but also admired by other foreigners because the Exim Bank of Japan was a government institution and could offer loan terms that could not be matched by other countries' businessmen.

Japanese firms also trained local personnel in Japan and sent technicians from home on a scale and on terms that were quite impossible for Western firms to match. Malays irked these young Japanese businessmen by their European-instilled notion that a college degree conferred the right to a higher salary whether the holder could perform efficiently or not, and removed him from the indignities of manual labor. Chinese, by contrast, were regarded as just as hard-working, if not as skilled, as Japanese.

The young Japanese businessmen, graduates of universities like Hitotsubashi or Keiō or Waseda, believed that Malaysia must industrialize to solve its rising unemployment and its overdependence on the export of primary products, the prices of which had been falling for years. But their prognoses were gloomy, and they complained of nationalism, meanwhile wishing they were in New York instead of Kuala Lumpur and dreading transfer to even less desirable places like Djakarta or Calcutta. In some of their homes only the whiskey had taste; one found the inevitable living-room suite with its chairs squared off round a glass-topped coffee table and the children huddled before TV in the corner. The loneliness of expatriated businessmen was very marked as they complained about the Bank of Tokyo's high interest rates or deplored the inexperience of Japanese in negotiations with Malays for joint ventures. Few Japanese had much real stomach for any kind of jointness with others; yet they were there, and for the long term, too, investing carefully to protect their sources of raw materials and markets. Malayawata may have lost $4 million in its first year but it was persisting and expanding. Japan had to get behind tariff walls if it expected to avoid great difficulties in the future, and it was an open question whether Japanese were any more exploitative or greedy than businessmen of other countries. They were accused of bidding low on "pioneer industries," then stalling on plans to build factories in order to protect their exports while preventing rivals from setting up operations. But the pay-off and squeeze were part of the life of business and politics in Southeast Asia, and some who complained of "unscrupulous" Japanese behavior could be supposed merely to be jealous of their success.

Another kind of Japanese activity in Malaysia that was of great potential benefit to the country was work on the damming of the Muda and Pedu rivers in the extreme north of the Malay penin-sula, along the Thai border northeast of the town of Alor Star. Sponsored by the World Bank, which provided 70 per cent of the funds, the Muda River project involved construction of two dams, a diversion tunnel in the upper reaches of the rivers and irriga-tion channels downstream that would allow irrigation and winter-cropping of 260,000 acres of rice-plain in Kedah and Perlis states and bring Malaysia nearer to self-sufficiency in food. The project was international: the canals for carrying water to the plain were being built by a Swedish concern; to build the dams, tunnel, and reservoir, two Japanese construction companies, Kajima and Taisei, jointly received the contract; and site investigations and technical services were provided by an English consulting firm. Begun in 1966, the project's total construction costs were esti-mated at about $70 million.

No other enterprise brought out better the positive aspects of Japan's activities in Southeast Asia. The contrast with the sad loneliness and the wheeling and dealing of traders in Kuala Lum-pur was dramatic. The setting of the Muda project was in sparsely inhabited and poverty-stricken hill country, where banditry and guerrilla warfare were endemic and tigers were shot on the dam sites at night. At the peak of construction, 130 Japanese were housed near the two dams alongside the families of English en-gineers. Forty Japanese children attended an improvised school with some English children, and English and Japanese wives ex-changed domestic know-how. Their families shared a swimming pool; a small club was opened with bar and dining room and a TV set that could pick up Singapore. Seventeen hundred local workers were employed on the project. Malayawata provided some steel, while cement was brought in from Ipoh to the south. Construction machinery was imported from Japan, the United States, the United Kingdom, Austria, and elsewhere. Some if not all of it would eventually be left in the country.

The Japanese in charge, an engineering graduate of Tokyo University, had been in the naval engineering corps in World War II and had been stationed in Rabaul, where he helped build the airstrip and later grew sweet potatoes to stay alive in the closing months of the war. In 1968 he declared flatly that he never wanted to hear the word war again. Forty-eight but looking sixty, he had been with the Kajima Construction Company since the war and had built large dams in Japan. He regarded the two on the Muda River as small by any reckoning; one was a rockfill affair 200 feet high and 800 feet long, the other one smaller. But he and his associates were highly skilled professionals who knew their work down to the last detail. One of them, an engineer who also had worked on the Balu Chaung hydro plant in Burma, remarked that local workers had not believed until they saw it that the Japanese plan for the diversion tunnel would work, "but of course it did." The language barrier was no serious impediment to understanding between Japanese and English engineers. Here, a few hundred miles from the site of the "Death Railway" and the "Bridge on the River Kwai," Englishmen in shorts stood with Japanese colleagues atop a dam on a jungle river and consulted long and earnestly over details of its construction for the benefit of the Malaysian economy. When I visited the project in October 1968 it was nearly completed, and water for irrigation would flow in the winter of 1969–70.

A cable plant in Kuala Lumpur and a dam in the jungle involved different skills, different people, and perhaps somewhat different motives. But all that that meant was that there were many different kinds of Japanese in Asia, as there were at home. If some were joining hands to collude in bidding for joint-venture contracts, others were sweating it out to mine copper or logs in north Borneo, while still others were enlisted in the Youth Volunteer Corps: 46 of them were in Malaysia compared with 550 Americans in the Peace Corps there. The Volunteer Corpsmen came from diverse backgrounds and were engaged in a variety of activities. One young lady, for example, received a subsidy from the Ministry of Education in Tokyo to teach the Japanese language at the University of Malaya in Kuala Lumpur. She had been born in Taiwan, where her father was a specialist in tropical agriculture. She thought that Japan had to know Southeast Asia "in order to live," and said "I wanted to *do* something." Yet she felt that Malaysia had little original culture, and she wished to visit Thailand, where she believed there was more art and a richer history. A strong, modest, though not very well-informed person, she was a graduate of a Japanese women's university and was a Christian, as were some other Japanese in Kuala Lumpur. One wondered whether the Volunteer Corps favored Christians, or whether Christians simply were more likely to be interested in such assignments.

Five of the Volunteer Corpsmen were assigned to a government vocational training school on the outskirts of Kuala Lumpur, where they taught manual trades to Malaysians. One was a ship's carpenter; others taught welding, woodworking, and electronics maintenance. These young Japanese were between 25 and 28 and came from technical high school or provincial university backgrounds. They gave various reasons for joining the Youth Volunteers. One wished "to understand Southeast Asia and promote Japan's development"; another "wanted to get outside Japan and look at its island culture." He resented the term, *shimaguni konjō*, or "island-country feeling," which was applied pejoratively to the Japanese personality and attitudes by many Asians. A third young Volunteer said he wanted to go abroad once, since only once would it be possible and it was best to do it while he was young. Unlike the young business executives, they seemed content to be where they were, and their relations with the Malay official in charge of the school were good, in spite of their poor

English and his nonexistent Japanese. But they had many complaints, which they vented eagerly, almost explosively, to a foreign visitor who could speak Japanese with them and who tried to communicate. They had not time enough to train students properly; there was no national standard of qualifications to train them toward; texts and other materials were scanty, and so on. Yet they saw value in what they were doing, and one of them spoke approvingly of a former officer of the Imperial Japanese Navy who was assisting Malays to build a small shipyard on the east coast of the peninsula. Another reminded me in straightforward fashion that they had an advantage over me in Malaysia in their skin color: at the Muda River project a Japanese engineer had made the same point. There was no denying this sense of racial awareness just as there was no point in seeing anything sinister about it.

Japanese political motives in Malaysia were never expressed except in clichés about peace and stability, but stability was in fact their goal throughout the region. The government of Malaysia had shown no special desire to form security arrangements with Japan but insisted rather that ASPAC, to which it belonged, remain merely an economic association. The Chinese in Malaysia were somewhat more anti-Japanese than the Malay majority and Chinese had been behind the "blood debt" issue. When that was settled in 1967, Premier Tengku Abdul Rahman told local Chinese that Malaysia would make no further demands on the Japanese. Malaysian security arrangements were with the Commonwealth, and it was expected that even with British withdrawals, Commonwealth ties would remain strong and Australian forces might replace the British to some extent at least. In 1968 various formulas were being talked about for American-Australian-British cooperation in the future security of the area. Although there was also growing discussion and speculation about a naval role for Japan, it was too early to talk about stationing Japanese military forces, especially ground forces, overseas.

Whatever political role Japan might play in the future of Malaysia, one came away with the renewed conviction that it was through increased technical assistance that the problem of Japan's human isolation from the rest of the world might best be solved and that however difficult the transfer of skills might be, this ought to be worked at and encouraged far more than it had been, without sentimentality but also with a better appreciation on all sides of what the Japanese could teach as well as learn. The Muda River project was only one small example of this fact.

7. THAILAND

Japanese activities and profits in Thailand multiplied as the Vietnam war progressed and Bangkok experienced an economic boom. The city suffered an astonishing sea-change, losing most of its charm. Its *klongs* were filled in for roadways, its trees cut down for hotels. The results were predictable: immense traffic jams and air pollution in one of the sultriest urban locations on earth. Thousands of Americans roamed the streets, where "Florida" bars and "Miami" hotels stood alongside "Swedish massage parlors." To satisfy the rising demand from swarms of people lured from the backward hinterland, hundreds of new businesses sprang up. Perhaps 10,000 Japanese traders and entrepreneurs were resident in Thailand in 1968, most of them in Bangkok. As in South Korea and Taiwan, Japanese business had moved in to take advantage of cheap labor and an expanding market; however, the process had gone much the farthest in Thailand.

Japan's commercial influence began to burgeon about 1964. In 1961, when I first visited Bangkok, it was scarcely visible. In February 1963 new legal incentives were offered to foreign investors by the Thai government. In May of that year, agreement was reached between the two governments on Thai claims arising from wartime yen issued by Japanese occupation banks. Japan agreed to pay the equivalent of $27.7 million annually for six years in goods and services, mainly ships, rolling stock, and textile machinery, to settle these claims. Payments were to be completed by May 1969. In the same period, deferred-payment industrial loans began to flow into the country; in 1965 these totaled $36 million, of which 18 loans, for $10 million, were for automobile assembly plants. A year later the total of industrial loans had risen to $46 million.[19]

In 1968 the Japanese cumulative registered equity investment was worth about $27 million. Unregistered investment totaled another $50 million at least, and if to this were added loans of one year or longer, the aggregate of Japanese investment was probably somewhere between $150 million and $200 million, or about the same size as American capital investment in Thailand.[20] Japan by October 1968 had contributed some 11 per cent of all equity investment in the country, as compared with 66 per cent classified as Thai, 6.8 per cent as American, and smaller percentages of overseas Chinese and other foreign investment. As elsewhere, Japanese joint ventures were typically small-scale, often involving Chinese partners and financed as far as possible from local currency resources. Nowhere were their activities welcomed more freely, and nowhere were stereotyped attitudes toward them expressed more often.

There were at least ten automobile assembly plants in the Bangkok area, six of them wholly or principally Japanese-owned, some of the rest dependent upon Japanese technical assistance. In 1968 these ten companies imported nearly 9,000 passenger cars "for assembly purposes," along with another 10,000 trucks and buses. A report by a private American automotive expert indicated that most so-called car assemblies required very little capital investment in Thailand. Vehicles were legally imported in what was described on manifests as "completely knocked-down" condition, but this was misleading. Actually, sub-assemblies were brought in that could be fastened together with the simplest of equipment. The bulk of labor had been performed at the parent plant in Japan; local plants painted trims and did other minor tasks. About the only parts made locally were batteries, springs, and tires, and some of the latter could be imported more cheaply. The report estimated that more than two-thirds of all vehicles sold in Thailand were imported in such "built-up" condition, and that the number of employees engaged in such work would more than double if built-up imports were restricted and more of the assembling done locally. One car assembler guessed that his locally made components did not exceed 7 per cent of the finished car.[21]

How much the Japanese were to be criticized for taking advantage of Thai laws allowing import of car sub-assemblies was a nice question. Unlike the Chinese in Taiwan, the Thais had not yet begun to require a larger annual value-added component; as one official noted, Thailand was "still an adolescent trying to make herself attractive for investment." A more relevant criticism often made by Japanese themselves was that too many assemblers had crowded into the limited market.

There were other examples of Japanese-controlled enterprises. Japanese money dominated the textile industry, in which mills financed by Japanese loans spun synthetic yarn from Japan-made fiber, then wove and finished the yarn in various fabrics. Such companies as the Thai Toray Textile Company, a subsidiary of Tōyō Rayon, were supervised by Japanese technicians, with Thai foremen trained in Japan. Textile workers, mostly women, received wages much lower than those currently paid in Japan and lived in free or subsidized housing near the factories. Japanese-style fringe benefits and other characteristics of industrial paternalism were exported to Thailand, and in some respects the conditions of early industrialization in Kobe or Yokohama were reproduced there.

Japanese were involved in other industries. The Matsushita Electric Company had six plants in its Bangkok compound engaged in assembling radio and TV sets, electric fans, batteries, and other consumer goods. Some raw materials were local, but most were imported. For batteries, the tin plate for outer casings, steel-zinc blanks for inner casings, paper, contacts, carbon centers, and some of the manganese came from Japan. (When their own processing plants begin in the near future they will be expected to use more Thai manganese.) Production capacity of this plant was about 1.5 million batteries a month, but output was far less. In 1968 half of the production was being exported, most of it to East Africa. Here again, workers were mostly girls, who earned an average of 600 baht a month (the equivalent of $30 or 10,800 yen), much less than wages for comparable workers in Japan.[22] Japanese were also involved in a steel mill, a glass plant, a caustic soda plant, and a wide assortment of other enterprises.

One interesting Japanese venture in Thailand was the development of yellow corn for animal feed. Corn had been grown on a small scale in the north and northeast for a long time, but it was not until the United States built the "Friendship Highway" north from Bangkok and opened up the hinterland that produce could be brought to an outside market economically. In the mid-1960s Japanese trading companies moved in, taking over from Chinese traders or subcontracting with them for collection and delivery of the corn crop, and selling machinery and seeds to farmers. Corn was an ingredient in chicken and cattle feed in Japan, where demand for such feeds grew rapidly from the late 1950s. By 1966 Japan had gained a monopoly of the Thai corn trade. (However, Japanese imports of corn from Thailand amounted to only 20 per cent of their total corn imports; the rest came largely from the United States.)

The governments of Thailand and Japan were both pleased that something had been found to help improve the great imbalance of trade, which saw Thai exports to Japan falling steadily in relation to imports, until in 1967 the former were only $160 million and the latter $341 million. Other than corn, Thailand exported little that Japan wanted: in 1966, $28 million worth of natural rubber, $11 million of rice, the same amount of hemp, and a smaller amount of iron ore. By contrast, Japan sold Thailand $120 million worth of machinery, $66 million of metal products, and sizable quantities of textile goods and chemicals. However, Japanese corn operations were strongly criticized by Americans and others in Bangkok. It was asserted that the pricing formula agreed to annually by the Thai Board of Trade and the Japan Feed Trade Association was disadvantageous to Thailand, because it gave the Japanese unreasonably long bidding options. Fixed monthly deliveries were set up against a future crop the size of which could only be guessed and which gave the Japanese a chance to buy up the whole crop at falling prices if the crop exceeded expectations, as it sometimes had. Under free market conditions Thai traders might sell corn at $52 a ton, as against $55 for U.S. corn; the Japanese, however, were not satisfied with the free market price but demanded further discounts because of low quality of grain or for other reasons. It was further charged that Japanese traders refused to buy ground grain, preferring to grind it in Japan. It was difficult to know the truth of these and other charges of Japanese economic imperialism.

Japanese Foreign Ministry officials in Bangkok liked to draw parallels between the late Premier Ikeda's "double-the-income" plans of the early 1960s, which according to one Embassy official had "stopped the left-wing in Japan," and Japan's economic cooperation programs in Southeast Asia, which "must stop Chinese communism." One of them described the 1966 Ministerial Conference on economic development as "one of the very few times in the last century when Japanese diplomacy took the initiative in anything." Aid, in his view, had a strong political motive behind it. But in the conversations of such officials a cynical note was also often heard. Aid was a sop to make trade seem better balanced. The Agriculture Ministry in Tokyo refused to allow more agricultural products into Japan, so the Foreign Ministry had to go begging to the Finance Ministry to get aid funds in order to avoid political consequences with the Thais. In the long run, subsidizing exports would make more money for Japan than giving aid, but trade imbalances were too extreme to allow much more of this. Young Embassy officials perceived their role as mediators between the strident demands of people in Southeast Asia and the parochial diffidence of the Japanese people at home, locked in their island of self-concern and heedless of the political consequences of their ignorance of the developing world. They could sometimes develop this theme to the point where the listener became uncomfortable, almost expecting tears. These never came, and conversations were generally rescued from bathos by a return to the more robust theme of profit.

At the Economic Development Board, Thai officials responsible for planning spoke of wanting more Japanese companies to move from Yokohama or Kobe to Bangkok, where they would be closer to raw materials, abundant labor, and a larger market than was available in Hong Kong, Singapore, or Taipei. They saw that Japan was already doing this but wanted the process to move faster: they thought Japanese should "move up the ladder" economically and leave room more rapidly for Thais to take over the less complex industries. Some Japanese economists urged the same thing. Thai planning officials thought Japan had no choice but to accept the notion of more value added abroad. The question was when and how. They admitted that Japanese control over joint ventures in which they took part was often pervasive but insisted that local participation was increasing. More and more Thais were taking management roles and exerting influence: "Thais like to get their way subtly," one declared. They claimed that Thailand would look after itself, would use Japanese to offset Chinese or Western interests, and said they lost little sleep over trade imbalances with Japan as long as large U.S. spending for Vietnam continued and the over-all balance of payments was favorable. If they feared Japanese economic imperialism they showed no signs of it.

Other Thai sources were not so sure: they criticized their own economic planning officials on grounds of their inexperience and lack of sophistication, noting that the postwar generation of Western-trained officials had had little experience with Japanese. Some observers in international agencies with headquarters in Bangkok saw the Japanese as hard-bitten types who would commit themselves to others only on their own terms. This view was pervasive in Thailand as elsewhere: the Japanese may have been no worse at sharp commercial practices than others, but somehow they seemed worse. Their clannishness and self-centeredness, it was asserted, would defeat their purposes if these included building a long-term position against Chinese competition.

Japanese technical assistance and more purely intellectual activities were also criticized. Kyoto University's Southeast Asia Research Center set up a branch office in Bangkok in the early 1960s to gather data in such various disciplines as political science, history, anthropology, and the natural sciences. In 1968 the young man in charge was a plant physiologist working on new rice strains at a government experiment station. He and his wife were attractive people who appeared genuinely interested in their assignment. Yet the Center, like the rest of Japan's activities in Thailand, was attacked by Thai professors on the grounds that it was returning most of the results of its work to Japan. It had begun a "Thai project," involving "in-depth" studies of the ecology and social structure of central Thailand, yet the Center was said to have no visible connection with Thai universities, and its research products were translated into neither English nor Thai.

Many such criticisms had some basis in fact. They also threw light on the three-cornered relationship that was developing among Japanese, Americans, and Thais in Bangkok. The Thais showed little cultural hostility toward the Japanese. The Sino-Thai governing class felt some anxiety over their heavy commercial penetration but meant to balance that against other foreign influences and had considerable confidence in its ability to do so. The Thais expected to have a distinguished future, not under Japanese control. They felt little ambivalence toward the Japanese as liberators, since there had been nothing to be liberated from. Nor did they share the residual hatred felt by the Filipinos. The Japanese were not primarily operating or trying to operate through local channels that went back to the war period. Rather, like everybody else, they approached the government, found a local partner, and tried to form business ties with people who had political influence or access to it. (A few Thais were still around who had deep contacts with Japan going back to the war, including, as it was said, horizontal contacts, but these were the exceptions.) Japanese succeeded because of the cheapness, nearness, and quality of their product, better credit terms, and other commercial reasons. The Thais would buy from them and use them in every way for their own purposes. They had no more illusions about them than they had about any other people.

Most Japanese, for their part, were trying to make money. Some thought in terms of building a position against China, but nearly all talked of how they were still disliked and distrusted. This feeling often persisted even in places where there was little or no reason for it. Japanese felt little affinity for Thais such as some professed to feel for Indonesians. One Japanese asserted that Thais could have little self-respect because they showed so little respect for others. A handful of Japanese taught their language in Thai universities, but most Thais, like most other Southeast Asians, were more interested in learning French or English. A small number of Thai students had gone to Japan, not always without difficulty: eleven girls who won government scholarships to study nursing in Japan had to wait until the Labor Ministry in Tokyo could be persuaded that they would not constitute an invasion of foreign labor. One professor at Bangkok University of Medical Science was not optimistic about their trip, saying that even if they learned how to use modern equipment there would be none when they returned, and moreover, the Japanese language would not be of much use.[23] Except for getting a job in a trading company, learning Japanese was a dead end.

Americans in Bangkok seemed to be intrigued with Japan's potential for helping to build stronger non-Communist societies in Asia, but they showed little fondness for Japanese individually or corporately. Most disturbing was the negative Japanese image: Thais and Americans alike found them grasping, selfish, and remote, and this stereotype, which of course ignored the differences

between individual Japanese, made it that much more difficult
for the good qualities of each people to be communicated meaningfully to the other.

8. JAPAN AND THE MEKONG PROJECT

Japanese were active not only in private commercial ventures in
Thailand but also in a wide range of international agencies and
organizations with headquarters in Bangkok. Perhaps the most
important and certainly the most dramatic of these was the
Mekong scheme.

The goal of that project was and is to manage and develop the
resources of the Mekong River, one of Asia's greatest streams, for
power, irrigation, flood control, and navigation in the lower basin
of the river, which extends 1,500 miles from the Burma-China
border to the South China Sea. The river flows through or forms
the boundary between portions of four nations, Laos, Thailand,
Cambodia, and Vietnam. It is almost totally uncontrolled and
even unbridged. Its basin is home to diverse peoples in varying
stages of economic and social development, the overwhelming
majority of them very poor. Banditry and insurgency are chronic,
and large-scale warfare has affected wide areas of the watershed for
years. Under the circumstances no project could be more likely
to engage the idealism or the skepticism of people in many nations.

The decision to undertake the development of the Mekong
River grew out of a recommendation adopted by the Economic
Commission for Asia and the Far East in 1957. The governments
of the four riparian countries agreed to establish a Coordinating
Committee to supervise the project, and in due time the Committee agreed to appoint a career U.N. official as its executive
agent. A technical and advisory link with the United Nations
and its agencies was thus established, assuring the Mekong Committee of access to international expertise and a variety of financial resources. Soon after the Committee came into existence and
the report of the first and most basic survey mission had been

made, governments of the "donor" nations began making pledges of support to the project. France, the United States, Canada, and New Zealand had pledged various technical services and funds by the end of 1958, and in December, Japan entered the project, offering to undertake a reconnaissance survey of the major tributaries of the Mekong Basin and to contribute $240,000 toward the costs of such a survey.

From the outset, the Japanese saw the project as a way for plant exporters and construction companies to make money and, beyond this, as something in which Japan could not afford not to participate if it expected, as it obviously did, to count in the area. An informal steering committee known as "Mekong International Japan" was set up in Tokyo, including among its members such key figures in Southeast Asia policy as Ataru Kobayashi, former head of the Japan Development Bank, later president of Arabian Oil, and the man behind oil exploration in Indonesia; Kyūtarō Ozawa, a member of Japan's House of Councilors and President of the International Engineering Consultants Association; and Ryōtarō Takai, former President of the Tokyo Electric Power Company. Advisers included the ubiquitous Yutaka Kubota, of Nippon Kōei, and such well-known technicians as Dr. Kōichi Aki, chief of ECAFE's Bureau of Flood Control and Water Resources Development, and Dr. Saburō Ōkita, the man responsible for Japan's long-range economic plans in the Ikeda era. One key interest group pushing participation in the project was the Japan Electric Power Development Company, a quasi-governmental organization which by the late 1950s had turned overseas for markets for its electric power generating equipment.

Work on the tributaries survey commenced in early 1958, and the Japanese report was issued in September 1961. Survey parties included representatives of construction and power companies, governmental agencies, trading companies, and the Japanese press. Kubota headed all three phases of the survey, which covered general and extensive reconnaissance of thirty-four major tributaries in all four riparian countries and took the Japanese teams into some of the wildest and most dangerous terrain in Southeast Asia. The report concluded that two huge dams on the mainstream and five lesser ones on the tributaries would bring vast new areas under irrigation and control flooding and improve inland navigation along mainstream reaches as well as on some tributaries. It selected four of the latter as most promising for development. As it happened, one tributary was in each of the four riparian countries.

The tributaries survey became one of the key reference documents for further work at the preinvestment stage by the Mekong Committee. Following the survey, Japan's contribution to the project steadily grew, although it remained a small part of the total for some years. Several scholarships were given to train specialists of the various riparian countries in Japan. Japanese engineering firms undertook other feasibility studies, including important ones on the mainstream at Sambor and Prek Thnot in Cambodia and the Nam Ngum tributary project in Laos. Much of Japan's technical assistance in the project was financed through allocations under the Colombo Plan. By 1964, nineteen countries and fourteen international agencies were participating in the Mekong scheme. In that year Japan's pledges totaled $832,000, out of a total of $18.2 million pledged. Thus far the Japanese had given nothing for construction, but representatives of Nippon Kōei, the Electric Power Development Company, OTCA and other agencies were very much on the scene and were mentioned more and more often in annual reports of the Mekong Committee. These reports also began to mention in 1962 the possibility of establishing an aluminum industry in the Mekong basin, if bauxite were ever discovered in commercial quantities.

In 1965 the first dam construction in northeastern Thailand was completed. Engineering designs for the Nam Pung dam were Japanese, and construction was carried out under supervision of a Japanese firm. In the following spring Japan agreed to invest in its first major construction project, the Nam Ngum dam north of Vientiane, Laos. Funding was arranged as part of the bilateral economic and technical cooperation agreement signed between

Laos and Japan in lieu of reparations. Nippon Kōei was designated to oversee construction. By 1967 Japan's total pledges were $16.8 million, exceeding West Germany's and exceeded only by the United States and Thailand.[24]

The Japanese government, pressed by big business and the Foreign Ministry, clearly had made up its mind to become a major factor in Mekong development. In Bangkok in late 1968, members of the Committee noted that Japan had put up money for the Prek Thnot dam in Cambodia, while the United States had not yet done so. The Japanese government also had urged the Committee to appoint as associate executive agent a Japanese Foreign Ministry official. (There appeared to be room for more Japanese at the administrative level of the Committee headquarters; in the 1967 report no Japanese name appears in the table of organization listing the 35 top jobs.) The Foreign Ministry was taking the initiative to enhance Japan's role in the venture, which had the potential of transforming the face of Southeast Asia if order there were ever established. This might take decades, if not generations, but some Japanese, at least, were interested in getting in on the ground floor of the process.

Attitudes toward Japan's part in the project were diverse. In Bangkok, Japanese technicians were regarded by their Western colleagues as less parochial than the French. One high Mekong official, a Thai, thought Japanese could be used very well where quantitative data were sought, especially in early stage reconnaissance and feasibility studies, but he was rather condescending toward them: "We gave them the small tributaries, because they will take risks where Westerners won't; they will go upcountry and even get captured by the Viet Cong." But the same official thought Japanese findings would have to be qualitatively refined before the stage of negotiation for financial support of any project was reached. Futhermore, he was certain that "the Japanese are in it for themselves. They have the long-run aim of establishing an economic foothold in the region, and we must balance them against other foreign powers." This attitude was perhaps more characteristic of the Thais than of the Laotians, Cambodians, or Vietnamese. At any rate, a certain prejudice against the quality of Japanese technical services could be discerned, at the same time that they were credited with having some definite advantages. Their work was more punctual than that of Americans, somewhat less thorough but more flexible, less specification-bound. Japanese engineers might say that a dam should be thus and so on the basis of all previously known flood records, whereas the U.S. Bureau of Reclamation would insist on meeting more rigorous formal requirements on the basis of drillings or technical details of rock formations in order to make the risk of flooding even less likely. Japanese enterprise was widely admired for its risk-taking just as it was often resented for its aggressiveness and unscrupulousness. One Mekong official in Bangkok commented wryly that a man like Kubota could arrange for appointments with top politicians in Tokyo much more quickly than the Japanese Embassy could.

The implications of Japan's participation in the Mekong project were still unclear in 1968, as indeed was the whole future of the project. One detected a certain ill-defined uneasiness in some Western quarters in Bangkok when Japan's role in the project was mentioned, as though there might be well-laid plans for a new co-prosperity sphere built around exploitation of regional resources. On the face of it, there was great doubt about whether all the power generated by the planned dams could ever be used by the riparian countries themselves. This was merely one of the many dubious aspects of the project; sour estimates of its future were easy to elicit in Bangkok. At the other extreme were the dreamers, who saw a new era of regional cooperation coming "after Vietnam," and who foresaw that Japan's positive contributions could outweigh any possible chances of exploitation that might be afforded in future. The dreamers, some of whom were also supreme egotists, projected an unparalleled technological future for the whole region, in which one sometimes wondered where a place might be found for the aspirations of the people themselves. In any event, the Mekong project was one more clear evidence of a growing Japanese presence in Southeast Asia.

9. INDIA

Up until early 1969 Japan, as a member of the aid-India consortium, had extended a total of the equivalent of $465 million in eight separate yen credits to India.[25] These amounted to about 60 per cent of all such credits given by the Japanese government, although they were only a small portion of total foreign assistance to India. The first five credits were spent for Japanese machinery and services for two large fertilizer plants in Uttar Pradesh and Gujarat, an alloy steel plant, and other smaller factories for manufacture of cables, chemicals, bearings, and other products. Most of the total went to finance public-sector enterprises. The sixth credit, signed in December 1966, and the seventh, in September 1967, were mainly for commodities and a small amount of capital goods necessary for completion of earlier projects. In these years it also became necessary to reschedule repayment of the first (1958) yen credit.

About $90 million in deferred payment loans was also made available through the Export-Import Bank of Japan to Japanese suppliers. Projects included development of iron mines at Kiriburu and Bailadilla in eastern India, rail and port facilities, and sizable quantities of textile machinery, as well as a fertilizer plant at Kota in Rajasthan, and a number of ocean-going ships.

Out-and-out grants to India were extremely small, amounting to about $1 million, and were used to establish centers for the training of Indians in the use of small machinery (at Howrah, near Calcutta), a fish products processing center (in Kerala), and a scattering of demonstration farms—eight in all—in various parts of the country.[26] Most such grants were made as a part of Japan's contribution to the Colombo Plan and involved dispatching technicians to India: in all, about 65 experts were sent and 315 Indians trained in Japan in the period 1952–69. In addition, small amounts of rice and fertilizer were shipped during the severe droughts of 1966 and 1967.[27]

Between 1958 and 1965 Japan's exports to India nearly tripled, from $85 million to $204 million, and the balance was favorable to Japan. The composition of exports also changed, with machinery rising from a quarter to two-thirds of the total. Japanese technical know-how was licensed by Indian private firms, representing the export of processes originally acquired from the West and now being transferred to less developed countries. Between 1957 and 1968, 250 such licensing agreements were signed, representing about a tenth of the total of such agreements completed by India. But of these, less than a fourth involved any equity participation, such participation as there was being very small, amounting to only $12 million by 1968. The Japanese government had very little interest in encouraging private companies to invest in India; only four small investments were made in 1967.

Japan's commercial and industrial activities in India presented a classic case of the frustrations suffered by two peoples with different values and methods of achieving their goals.[28] Japanese descriptions of projects financed by yen credits helped bear this out. For example, nearly everyone agreed that the fertilizer plant in Gujarat was a success. It was constructed by three Japanese companies on a turnkey basis, meaning that all aspects of the construction work, including the foundations, were a Japanese responsibility and involved no negotiation with local concerns. This arrangement was regarded as ideal by Japanese, especially in India but not exclusively there. The plant was put up and operating in 20 months, with a capacity of 100,000 tons of urea and 250,000 tons of ammonium sulphate. According to Japanese accounts, such speed was "unprecedented . . . the construction progressed extremely smoothly." But at the other yen-credit–financed fertilizer plant at Gorakpur in Northern India, the story was different: "Construction was delayed exceedingly, with the result that the building cost far surpassed the original estimate. The delay in the construction work was attributed to red tape in-

volved in the construction of a state-operated plant as well as to
the inconvenient location of the plant. Moreover, since the business contract did not specify the turnkey job system, the Japanese
construction firms could not go beyond the furnishing of the
plant and over-all supervision of the construction work." [29] At
the alloy steel plant at Durgapur, incompletion of the foundation work meant a 14-month delay in beginning the installation
of machines. Insurance premiums payable in rupees increased after
the devaluation in 1966. The operations of the sheet mill were
delayed by shortages in raw materials. The foundations were
badly poured; the plant layout was too rigid; strikes halted construction. More seriously—and this was a complaint heard throughout the Japanese community in India—no real study was ever
made of market demand for steel. As a result, inventories piled up
and production never was able to approach the break-even point,
much less full capacity. This happened in other industries: licenses
for plate glass mills were granted to new companies despite the
fact that India-Asahi Glass and one or two others already were
satisfying the total anticipated demand. A fish canning enterprise
was set up to sell in the Bombay fish market, but, "due to the
absence of a change in the eating habits of the Indian people," the
consumption of fish dropped and the company was saved only
when it found shrimp on the Malabar coast and began packing
them for export to Japan.

A whole range of other problems baffled Japanese trying to
operate in India. They might be allowed to come in and set up a
plant, only to be denied the right to import necessary raw materials or spare parts, which were either higher priced in India
or totally unavailable. This got so bad that portions of the later
yen credits were earmarked for import of Japanese materials to
keep such plants going. Indian government policy required
Indianization of management in what seemed to many Japanese
an unreasonably short time. For example, all crew members of
shrimping boats had to be replaced by Indians in two years or
less. Six of the Japanese company's twelve boats registered in

Cochin were manned exclusively by Indians: "The result is that the efficiency of these boats dropped considerably." In the case of iron mining, Japanese engineers were bewildered when Indians allowed harbor facilities from which the ore was to be shipped out to become silted up, just as they were baffled by the high price of moving the ore from mine to shipping port because of the poor transportation network.

Projects controlled by the central government in New Delhi were generally regarded as less successful than those run by the states. A porcelain plant in Mysore State had 20 per cent Japanese capital participation and was put up with Japanese technical assistance. In Kerala a Japanese company had 30 per cent of an electrical equipment concern, which was successful for a time but suffered from the drastic curtailment of equipment investment by electric companies in the mid-1960s. Other plants were forced to cut back production or close down entirely for similar reasons. A watt-meter factory in Bangalore virtually monopolizing the Indian market was set up by Japanese in the late 1950s. By 1967 it was run entirely by Indians and most of the components were made in India, but the economic crisis of 1966–67 forced cancellation of licenses for import of the remaining crucial parts.

It could be argued that all such difficulties were predictable and were no different from those experienced by other foreigners attempting to operate in India. But what set the Japanese apart most sharply from at least some other foreigners was their near-total preoccupation with commercial opportunity, as well as their inability to understand or empathize with Indians. If there had been more of a commitment to Indian development for extra-commercial reasons, the relationship might have had more resonance. But this was expecting too much, and until very recently conditions grew steadily worse in India. Economic performance failed repeatedly, and the Japanese, valuing performance above all else, grew more perplexed, discouraged, and impatient. Most of them did not know how to deal with Indian leaders, who were still divided over issues of ideology and pragmatism.

They did not know how to respond to the remark of one of the top leaders that "Japan is a big country economically. India is big in other ways." To many Japanese this was a strange, irritating remark. In their modern experience economic achievements were the *sine qua non* of all other bigness. When an Indian bureaucrat insisted on spreading irrigation water that might have been sufficient for a million acres over a much greater area on the theory that more people would receive at least some water, Japanese consultants regarded this as an irrational, pre-modern act. With the Thais there were no such problems, or so they said. They were pragmatists, and the Japanese could deal with pragmatists. But Gandhian socialism and Hinduism they could not grasp, just as they were baffled by the absence of a spirit of entrepreneurship: after more than a decade of searching for local sources of funds, India-Asahi Glass, the largest Japanese enterprise in the country, was still more than 99 per cent financed from Tokyo.

The failure to share ideals led to petulance on both sides. One Indian industrialist was incensed when, on a tour of Tokyo, he asked a Japanese company their production figures and was told that they were classified. This led him to fume that the Japanese were out to get what was in it for themselves and nothing else. Such readiness to regard another people as detestable, no matter how one was provoked, was inevitably disabling to the spirit. On the other hand, Japanese sometimes behaved in an extremely heavy-handed fashion toward Indians. At a conference in Australia, Japanese intellectual delegates of the "idealist" school who were given to writing of their moral guilt toward China revealed no comprehension of Indian problems and even suggested that India could hardly be described as an Asian country at all. This produced an agitated response from an Indian professor, who haughtily reminded the Japanese that Buddha had been born in India; and he went on to accuse the Japanese of being little more than stooges of the United States. But this missed the Japanese point: being the birthplace of Buddha had little or nothing to do with being Asian in their minds.

Japanese had gone to India in some numbers after the early yen credits hoping to sell machinery, mine iron ore, and set up plants to get behind Indian tariff walls. These might almost be called their natural activities. Many of them were already discouraged in the early 1960s; there was an element of resignation in Japanese contributions to consortium aid, just as there had been in payment of reparations to Southeast Asia. Technical experts on consulting missions for private business or the Japanese government also entered India, where some of them did valuable work, yet even so, a degree of disenchantment was evident. In 1961, after a visit to Calcutta, I wrote of an interview with a Japanese small-industries consultant:

> His points were simple ones, and he put them simply. Indians, he said, always will say they know how to do a thing, whether they do or not. Try to tell them how, and they say they know. This leads to mistakes and maybe will ruin a machine. Tell an Indian sweeper to sweep up and he will sweep up, perhaps; but he doesn't know what his sweeping has to do with anything else. Because he is a sweeper only, he performs an isolated act, he does not feel integrated in a productive process. Just so India is importing machinery from all over the world, but Indians are not changing their mentality to absorb and integrate the machinery in a new industrial society. They are merely copying machines without changing their own thought processes. And caste gets in the way at every stage: the man on the lathe must have another to bring him his materials and a third to clean up the mess he makes around his machine.[30]

By 1968, Japanese pessimism had deepened. In spite of some hopeful signs in agriculture, India's economic decline and stagnation over the previous five years had caused a waning of what hope there had been among Japanese there that the country would achieve solvency and make its way into the modern industrial world. Interest in India declined as interest in Southeast Asia increased. New credits flowed into Indonesia after 1965, and more Japanese money found its way to Malaysia, Thailand, and elsewhere. By contrast, many pointed to India's unhealthy dependence on foreign aid, which the Japanese found offensive to their deepest instincts regarding self-respect and self-reliance. They thought that the Indian government had not made a really urgent effort to end such dependence. Instead of attacking its immense problems, the Indian Parliament frittered away its time debating whether or not to impose prohibition, just as the government lost opportunities to develop offshore oil resources while it tried interminably to decide whether it really needed foreign help in the process. Japanese still criticized what they regarded as too much emphasis on heavy industry and argued that too great a dependence on U.S. surplus food shipments had reduced local incentives to produce or reform the pre-modern structure of the rural community. They saw without pleasure that their credits to India would have to be refinanced, perhaps indefinitely, and wondered whether they would ever be completely repaid. As one Japanese writer put it, "Providing loans via the consortium does not always help in realization of Japanese objectives both with regard to terms and the amount of the loans." [31]

Cooperation had its limitations, and India was exotic, beyond the periphery of the consciousness of most Japanese. Why was the West so intrigued with the place, why did it seem to have such a stake in India? This puzzled many Japanese, even those sophisticated enough to know the answer. The Japanese-Indian equation was worth pondering. Just as a few perceptive Japanese realized that they lacked an ingredient of "pioneer spirit" or "Christian mission" in their aid activities in Southeast Asia, so they sensed that their relations with Indians were on a different footing from those of the West. On one level Indians showed respect for Japan's modernizing experience. The Japanese were Asians, and they had succeeded. As one Indian put it, they could not but be respected because they "produce everything." They had achieved the production hope of the rest of the Asian world. Yet they were condescended to constantly by Indians, who saw them as opaque, uncommunicative members of an essentially derivative civilization. The Confucian ethic of worldly probity did not get its message across to the Hindu. Technology could be transferred, but human understanding was a more difficult matter. Thus Japanese engineers flew into Palam Airport at New Delhi, often arriving in the black of night, traveled by night train to projects such as the new fertilizer plant they were building for Delhi Cloth Mills at Kota in Rajasthan, lived there in a hostel in a group, never went anywhere till the job was done, afterwards flew in a group for a brief, ritual visit to Srinagar, then flew back to Delhi, and took off for Japan without having done much more than unload their expertise. Only in rare instances did Japanese stay in India long enough or live on terms allowing them to come to know Indians personally. One of the most interesting of the few who did was a teacher who spent several years in New Delhi, and he was a Communist who wrote a book full of direct perceptions of Indian life sandwiched in between pious excoriations of the inequities of Indian society.[32]

Some Japanese saw that in the long run, no matter how deep their present disappointments and frustrations, India was important to Japan and would be more so in the future. Key officials of the Foreign Ministry, believing as they did that Japan's best interests still lay in close ties with the West, conceived that Japan, like it or not, must play a role in helping to promote Western objectives in the Indian subcontinent. They perceived that India was passing from ideology to greater pragmatism, but no new Indian foreign policy had yet been found in the wake of Nehru's death and the shock of the Chinese border fighting. Indian officials were jealous of Japan's obviously growing influence in Southeast Asia, but they had not yet decided what to do about it; internal politics was in flux and foreign policy was on a day-to-day basis. Yet with pragmatism growing at the center as in the states, it stood to reason that in five to ten years the Japanese presence in India would increase and that the transfer of the skills and money Japan had to give, once the Indians decided to receive them, would accelerate. Japan might then feel that it was at least dealing with India on a basis of more rationality, whether its primary goal was to sell merchandise or to check unfriendly influences there. Those who shared this view assumed that Japan's alignment with America would last for at least another decade. They did not constitute an "India lobby" so much as they simply believed that India would have a future somehow and in any case was greater than the smaller nations of Southeast Asia. The notion that India and Japan might unite in a political alliance directed against Communist states was not implied. The Japanese were much more likely to want to retain their freedom of action vis-à-vis the Communist world. But Japanese Embassy officials sitting in New Delhi and reading their European newspapers spoke and wrote of the need for much more discipline, self-help, and more realistic long-range planning, in which Japanese might legitimately take a larger hand. They had serious qualms about Soviet influence in India. They believed that there should be a larger Japanese role in decisions on use of aid funds in the Indian sub-continent. They wanted to tie aid ever more tightly to trade, and they thought a larger portion of future yen credits should be made available to Japanese joint enterprises. It was no accident that the chief delegate to the Round Table Conference on Indian-Japanese problems convened in New Delhi in 1968 was the President of the Fuji Steel Company.

VI. Conclusion: A Look at the Future

Many different Japanese versions of the Asian future exist, but all of them presuppose a wide material gap between Japan and the rest of the region. One recent projection, derived from a composite study of past performances and the targets of national plans, forecasts a per capita gross domestic product of slightly more than $6,500 at 1960 prices for the Japanese people by the year 2000. By then Taiwan, Hong Kong, Malaysia, Singapore, and South Korea will have reached $1,000 per capita income and will have joined the "developed" nations. Thailand will stand somewhere between $500 and $1,000; Cambodia, Ceylon, Laos, Pakistan, the Philippines, and Vietnam, $300 to $500; while in Burma, India, and Indonesia per capita income will still be less than $300 a year.

This projection by the Japan Economic Research Center sanguinely assumes that "each country will make the utmost efforts to attain the most efficient economic growth plans" and that governments "will follow a wise policy to harmonize the welfare of the people with economic efficiency." It recognizes that "a great war or serious economic crisis" would wreck all prospects of hopeful development of the poor states of Asia. Given these profound reservations, however, it predicts that agricultural production will increase so much and population growth be controlled so well that "the ghost of Malthus . . . will probably disappear in A.D. 2000." Industrialization will enormously stimulate intra-regional trade, which has been quite stagnant since the end of World War II. National economic plans will be replaced by regional composite planning and duplicative import-substitution industries by an intra-regional division of labor. Thus regional economic integration, while not yet fully achieved, will have become a possibility and will have been preceded by the growth of subregional developmental groupings with a greater measure of reality than they have so far exhibited. "Under pressure of world opinion, developed countries will no longer offer financial aid to developing countries as a means of their own political, economic and military expansion." United Nations agencies like ECAFE will be more powerful, less noted for talk without effectual action, while such projects as Mekong basin development, the Asian Development Bank, the Asian highway and seaway, and other schemes as yet undreamed of will flourish and strengthen horizontal connections among Asian nations. Japan's importance to the area is taken for granted: "if the Japanese economy should lose its growth potentiality, the take-off of the developing Asian countries would be seriously retarded. . . ."

According to the blueprint, by the year 2000, foreign aid will be administered multilaterally through international organizations. Its purpose will be "to build up a welfare world." Creation of this kind of world, the projection recommends, should be the chief aim and underlying philosophy of Japanese foreign policy for the remainder of the century. The study is cautious regarding the future of mainland China, pleading a lack of reliable data. It believes that the chief source of China's economic difficulties has been the erratic nature of its policies and concludes that if Chinese leaders follow a consistent course either of offering "material stimulus," i.e., giving some private incentives for production and capital accumulation, or of "spiritual education," i.e., enforcing self-sacrificing restriction of consumption, and if either course can be carried out with some success, China will slowly develop into a modern society, with the result that "except in the worst case (where civil wars continue, agricultural production does not increase, and excessive defense efforts are continued), the economy of China in 2000 will reach the level of the Soviet economy in the 1950s. By that year, its [China's] economy, which has so far been controlled by politics, will come to control politics." [1]

The above projection may be no more than the wish-fulfillment of some Tokyo technocrats. It is certainly not shared by many Japanese, whose pessimism and bewilderment regarding the short-term Asian future have been amply demonstrated by this book. It does, however, represent an extension to the whole Asian area of the rather bland but hopeful version of welfare capitalism, or "progressive conservatism," that has gradually come to color Japan's own domestic economic policies, especially in the last twenty years. Japan today is run by economic managers, nearly all of them still of the prewar generation. The only political figure of even quasi-charismatic proportions in the postwar period was Yoshida, but he has long been gone from the scene and his successors are skillful but unheroic technicians: bureaucrats, businessmen, or politicians who were themselves once bureaucrats or businessmen. Few stand out as individuals—the politicians with their arcane factionalism perhaps better than the others, but all mean to stay in charge and, in the process, to become as modern as their problems. This can be seen in the increasing emphasis on rational social policies that one finds in the language of their plans and of their domestic programs, as well as in their slowly increasing assistance to others. The conservative leaders of the Liberal Democratic party will not satisfy those with apocalyptic visions demanding immediate gratification. They may, on occasion, discourage those who wish for a more rapid liberalization of Japanese society. But they preside over their tasks with immense skill and are far more representative of their people than most Asian elites; furthermore, they are the best thing in sight on the horizon of Japanese politics.

How these men deal with the confusions of their own society, not to mention the crises that occur abroad beyond their control, and how they pass power to those younger than themselves, will tell much about how Japan acts in the international sphere. One can estimate their economic abilities with some accuracy and have some assurance when reflecting on the traditional strengths of the social system that contributed to industrialization up to now. It is quite another thing to predict what foreign policies the Japanese public wants and will accept, or indeed how important domestic opinion will be in the shaping of such policies. But there is abundant evidence that whatever foreign policies are chosen in the future will have to have the support or at least the working assent of an increasingly middle-class society, full of traditional Japanese qualities, to be sure, but more and more characterized by the pervasive influence of mass media and by other physical and psychical phenomena common to industrial urbanism: pollution, blight, cynicism toward the electoral process, intellectual alienation and student protest, the weariness of unrealized, unrenewed ideals, or the absence of ideals altogether. The conservatives will have to cope with a generation that is increasingly unable to recall World War II and that is at base uninterested in origins; a "cool" generation, to which Japanese imperialism has little or no meaning, but which, though it is "pacifistic," is only marginally more liberal or international in outlook than its elders; a generation, in short, that expects prosperity to continue and is ravenously technological, but has never fought for its own freedom or anyone else's.

The question is not whether Japan should play a larger role in Asia. Such a role is inevitable, in my view. The question is the manner and spirit of the role. This is where attitudes and policies come together in action and where the real meaning of Japanese modernism will reveal itself in events.

It is clear that a policy of close alignment with America since 1952 has paid off handsomely for Japan, allowing it to concentrate on its formidable entrepreneurial and trading skills and to reaccumulate wealth and considerable economic power. Such has been the legacy of decisions taken in the Yoshida period: Japan has become the "peace and production hope" of non-Communist Asia, and its economic accomplishments continue to astonish the world. At the same time, the mainstream of the conservative elite has sought to maintain a "low posture" politically in Asia, re-building trust in its intentions while avoiding regional political alliances that might jeopardize its future relations with China. This policy has led to charges that Japan has had a free ride at America's expense, which is, in a sense, true; Japan's importance to the United States fully justified the ride. A weak, neutralist Japan, its economy subject to manipulation by China or the Soviet Union, has not been in the American interest since World War II. Japan's "low posture" in Asia has also led to criticism that the country has not been "doing its part," which is more doubtful. But, what-ever the justice of these feelings, the Japanese have known their true value to the United States, and they have used their ties with America as well as their "peace Constitution" with great skill, taking advantage of their inability as well as their unwillingness to contribute Japanese lives in Asia's wars since 1945. Today the con-servative mainstream wants to prolong the American alignment, with some modifications, for an indefinite period beyond 1970. As one Japanese diplomat put it, "The Anglo-Japanese Alliance came to an end, but ours with you must not." Why should they want it to end, when it has brought them so much profit and stability in spite of recurrent political turbulence?

In the last few years the conservative government has felt pressure from rival political organizations as well as from within its own ranks to make alterations in the pattern of reliance on America and to respond to the repeatedly expressed desire of the people for some less dependent nationalist posture in the world. Much of this pressure has been vague, diffuse, hard to describe when it could be discerned; the stunning effects of defeat in World War II on public opinion long made it difficult to sense what new imagery of nationalism was emerging. On one issue there has been some consensus: the government of Premier Satō has virtually staked its future on the return of Okinawa to Japanese hands; and it now (late 1969) appears that this issue will be settled by some formula of reversion reasonably satisfactory to both sides in the not distant future. Okinawa has had great importance to the military policies of the United States that have prevailed up to the present. The island's bases have been regarded as vital to the support of U.N. forces in Korea and important as a staging area during Vietnam operations. But return of Okinawa to Japanese sovereignty has become a symbol of real national independence in Japan. In addition, the Japanese government in 1970 and thereafter is likely to insist upon continued reduction in American bases and other installations, which still number over 100, and the removal of those that remain as far as possible from the awareness of the public.

Beyond these short-term adjustments in the pattern of military relationships with the United States, little consensus on actions in Asia is to be had; but there are signs in the press, the political parties, and the intellectual community that more and more Japanese will tolerate and even welcome a more assertive leadership than they have had for many years in the field of foreign policy. The difficulty lies in describing just what this means. Fortunately, a great diversity of opinions is held and expressed, from innocuous suggestions by a few liberal internationalists for creation of private Japanese foundations to play a larger part in overseas development programs or for reform of the bureaucracy to allow trained economists to fill positions immemorially reserved for line generalists, all the way to fretful outbursts by a few conservative nationalists to the effect that Japan should rearm offensively and be prepared to settle its differences with other countries by traditional means. Tokyo is a hothouse of policy ideas of all sorts that have as yet come to little focus. Some foreign observers have called Japan a post-Marxist society, but this is surely premature: agreement on foreign policy continues to be impeded by ideological animosities. Some say it is post-nationalist, which comes nearer to the mark if it is applied to a wish rather than an accomplishment: there is a vague desire on the part of many people in Japan as in other countries of the industrial world to reject the conventional signs of nationalism—the power politics, weapons, force, "victories"—and to find some "moral equivalent" for them, some way of achieving national self-assertion through economic diplomacy or some other course of peaceful action. Yet at the same time many others regard such aspirations as naïve, utopian dreams, hardly applicable to the harsh environment of Asian politics since the last war.

There are those in the West who have seen the Japanese as lacking the will to accept major responsibilities in the world and who, perhaps influenced by Japan's persistent refusal to join sides in the Cold War in Asia in a military sense, have concluded that the country is destined to remain a secondary power, a trading nation but a nation whose opportunities for major power status, having failed once, have been rejected, perhaps beyond resurrection. Such people might agree with the Japanese official who recently asked: "What is wrong with being a well-fed second-rank nation?" But while Japan may not become one of the superpowers in the near future, I do not believe that this modest horoscope will continue to satisfy a people with such a strong conviction of their own abilities and skills and such an outstanding record of human performance, however lacking in consensus on anything political they may have been since World War II.

As far as China is concerned, the record since 1952 shows the dismaying sterility of Japanese efforts to form really significant economic relationships without conceding political points to Peking. Since such concessions were adjudged unacceptable, Japan's relations with the mainland have remained at an impasse, despite much rhetoric about cultural affinity. However, China is Asia's center and far too important to Japan's future national life for the Japanese to cease hoping and planning to re-establish more secure and profitable ties. The Japanese people have felt little or no physical threat to themselves from the Chinese revolution. Since 1964 there has been some uneasiness, but there is greater apprehension about the prolonged isolation from China, which is seen as a rival for commercial and political influence in the long run. Some anxiety is being expressed within the Liberal Democratic party that China may one day become a member of the United Nations Security Council, the permanent members of which would then be composed only of nuclear "haves." Some in the Japanese government have been urging that Japan should be made a permanent member of the Security Council and should participate in disarmament negotiations in Geneva as the representative of the "could have" nations. This interest in gaining status without becoming a nuclear power is not new, but a larger U.N. role, including a part in peacekeeping operations, might give the Japanese public a greater sense of its importance in the world without inflaming its "nuclear allergy."

To most Japanese the best possible solution of the China problem would be recognition of both Peking and Taipei, with diplomatic representation in both countries: "one Taiwan" and "one China." The difficulties in achieving this are of course obvious, but the perception of the Japanese of their role vis-à-vis China does not in any case include a permanent hiatus between the two; such a hiatus is regarded as unnatural, something to be amended no matter how long it may require. It may possibly be that here is the only situation in which the concept of Japan as a diplomatic and political "bridge" between Asia and the West, for so long talked about by Japanese commentators on foreign affairs, might have some force. Thus far Japan has complied without serious protest in the China policies of the United States. But the obvious Japanese fear of being isolated by some Chinese-American rapprochement in the future, however far-fetched that might seem now, suggests that the Japanese government wishes and may intend to recognize Peking before Washington does and, if so, might facilitate Chinese-American contacts. The timing of such a move is obscure; the Japanese are prepared to wait, and as long as China's posture is hostile and intransigent there is likely to be no change in Tokyo's attitude. The "bridge" concept itself is clouded by the strong tutelary instincts and the condescension of the Japanese toward China, as well as by ideas entertained by the Chinese of how Japan should serve their own interests. To become an effective bridge the Japanese would have to open themselves to a freight of ideas from both sides and facilitate their passage, not, as has often been the case, take refuge in a comforting insularity.

More normal ties with China could help to put economic relationships between the two countries in their proper public light for all Japanese to see and strip away some of the illusions many still have about the China trade. In a broader sense, more normal ties might test the strength and reality of Japanese confidence in their own political, economic, and social modernization more fully than these can be tested by relations with the smaller states of Southeast Asia. Normal relationships with China would also help to remove a troublesome psychological obstacle to more firmly based and realistic Japanese-American relations. Chinese propaganda would undoubtedly increase in Japan, and there might even be attempts at subversion. But Japan is not Southeast Asia; the Self-Defense Forces are well equipped to control such threats. Their danger would be outweighed by the removal of a sense of deprival, however based on vain expectations, where China is concerned, for which most Japanese hold the United States rather than China accountable. Dual recognition of Peking and Taipei, of course, would depend on a change in the foreign policy of Peking after Mao's death, as well as in the policy of the Nationalist regime in the post-Chiang era. Both would have to admit the existence of Taiwan as an autonomous state, neither "China" nor part of it.

Peking's acquisition of a nuclear capability raises the question whether the Japanese will have their own nuclear arms. Available evidence indicates that the government does not presently intend to build them. Some conservative nationalists, including some younger members of the Diet in the Liberal Democratic party and their defense intellectual associates, might like to "go nuclear," but the party's leaders have no wish to risk causing a domestic political crisis over this issue. Some moderate conservatives see a three-way nuclear stalemate approaching but fear a confrontation between America and China before it occurs. They would prefer not to abandon the Security Treaty, but on the other hand not to applaud everything the United States does in Asia, e.g., the bombing of North Vietnam. They would like to make government-level contact with China while remaining within an over-all pro-American orientation and to try to separate out those elements of foreign policy that might meet Japan's strategic demands at any given time and not to identify with those that do not. What is meant by this is not yet very clear, beyond a general distaste for the Vietnam war.

The Japanese will have nuclear weapons if they think their national security requires it. They may have them eventually for prestige purposes in spite of nonproliferation treaties, if, for example, Israel or India should get them. Or they may have them if they become convinced that only in that way can they acquire the technological and scientific information essential to continued economic growth. In spite of the professed aversion of the large majority of the Japanese people to such weapons, in spite of their considerable cost, it must be noted that there are today Japanese industrialists and financiers in some very important companies, some of them concerned with manufacture of the most advanced products, who are calling for full-scale rearmament, including the most sophisticated weapons, even nuclear weapons, by the mid-1970s, as the only way for Japan to maintain the desired pace of technological progress in the world.[2] These men, among whom are included the same individual who was head of the old Asia Association, also are insisting upon a much closer connection with the defense establishment based upon planning and ordering procedures adapted from the Pentagon model. Such points of view of Japan's "military-industrial complex" represent a minority of business and other opinion, but they ought not to go unrecorded. Orders for military defense purposes accounted for only about

0.5 per cent of total Japanese industrial output in 1966 or about 5 per cent of the total of three large firms: Mitsubishi Heavy Industries, Nihon Electric, and Kawasaki Heavy Industries.[3]

All Japanese recognize the Constitutional restraints upon the deployment of their military forces outside Japan. Most are glad of these restraints and do not want to remove them. However, some business interests now advocate not only an expansion of economic aid but an increase in arms sales, from which Japan has profited greatly in the Korean and Vietnam wars as well as on a smaller scale elsewhere in Southeast Asia, as a means of stabilizing other critical areas of the "southern countries." A few of these men even foresee the creation of a collective security organization in the Pacific, in which Japan would enroll alongside the United States and which could mean a greatly increased military role for the Self-Defense Forces in another decade or less. Some appear to think that a Japanese naval presence may be required at least as far as Singapore and perhaps into the Indian Ocean; some discussions are reported to have been conducted with the Australians on the subject. I repeat: this kind of thinking does not yet represent anything like a consensus, but the idea is being more casually expressed that Japan will in the future have to protect its growing economic interests in ventures like the Jurong complex or Malayawata and its lines of oil supply not just by relying on American power but through its own power as well.[4]

A number of Japanese in recent years have begun to compare their country's role in tropical Asia with the United States' role in Latin America. There are some parallels between the two: unscrupulous Japanese continue to want to exploit the region, more responsible ones foresee their country's leadership, tutelage, and repeated disappointment there. To the latter the Alliance for Progress is a dismal paradigm. But few Japanese of any persuasion would elect to undertake the job of helping the development of South and Southeast Asia alone, or would wish to try to enforce another Monroe Doctrine in the area. Some see Asian regionalism as a desirable long-term goal, but they do not think it is attainable without Western, meaning American, participation. Of course, should America withdraw from Asia entirely, it stands to reason that Japanese political as well as economic influence would flow into the resulting "vacuum." So would other influences adverse to the Japanese. Having chosen Southeast Asia as the principal focus of its aid activities, Japan's political interest in the area is bound to grow, but it is as yet under few illusions about the limitations of its influence. Moreover, Japanese know that analogies between Japan's role in Asia and ours in Latin America can serve to divert attention from the pressing need for more factual knowledge of the conditions of life and politics in the area. Talk of regional organization, while well-meaning, has often rested on inadequate appreciation of deep-seated differences between nations.

A more realistic line of thinking, one which I have found in some very hard-headed quarters in Japan, is along subregional lines. South Korea and Taiwan make one subregion, closer to Japan culturally and historically than the rest of the region. Without becoming part of another Japanese empire, these two states may well develop, or so some Japanese think, as an inner ring of Japanese influence quite unlike the states farther south. This may be understating the case: Japanese economic influence in Taiwan particularly is already impressive, and Japan's stake in the island's political stability seems bound to increase.

In the Philippines and even more in Indonesia the Japanese interest will be primarily in raw materials for some time to come, and Japanese influence is certain to grow. This will cause further charges of neocolonialism; but so long as the Indonesians lack the ability to get out the raw materials themselves they will have to rely on the help of others if they hope to develop. Their complaint of being exploited is understandable, but neither the Japanese nor anyone else will wish to invest in Indonesia until conditions there improve; meanwhile the Japanese hunger for raw materials is enormous and is going to increase. Singapore and its immediate vicinity will be a focus of Japanese strategic concern as long as most of the nation's oil transits the Malacca Strait. Other routes could be used, but the demand for naval protection of tankers in the area might possibly be heard in the future. At any rate, the Japanese stake in Singapore is large and rising.

With the mainland world between Singapore and Karachi the Japanese will have less intimate relations and exert less influence. I do not believe there is much force in the notion of a Japan-India axis against China or for any other reason. Indians are suspicious of Japan's rising influence in Southeast Asia, while Japanese regard India as chronically poised on the brink of national dissolution. What would the Japanese have to gain from such an alliance? Malaysia will continue to be linked in significant ways with Britain and the Commonwealth; the Japanese role there will be important but secondary. In Laos and Cambodia there is a desire for influence, perhaps more than anything else because of the weakness of American influence; witness Youth Volunteer Corps and other technical assistance activities, especially in Laos. In Vietnam Japan stands ready to go in with yen loans, machinery, and technicians, as it has not done with troops, once political conditions are stabilized. Yet I feel that Japanese interest in mainland Southeast Asia as a whole is less intense than in the island nations and grows weaker the farther one travels away from Japan itself. This could change if bauxite were discovered in commercial quantities in the Mekong basin.

I believe that the emphasis of American policy should not be upon the extension of Japan's military role overseas but upon closer cooperation with Japan in the economic development of the whole Asian area, including China if that becomes possible. In the 1950s America seemed insistent that the Japanese rearm their country not only for its own defense but also in order to contribute military forces to a collective security system of one sort or another in Asia. Since about 1960 we have said less about a Japanese military presence overseas, which neither most Japanese nor most other Asians desire. This is still a cherished dream of some Americans (as of some Japanese), most of whom have been very slow to move away from habits of thought formed in the Cold War. Recent American policy has made more of trying to encourage the Japanese to give more aid and take a more active part in regional organizations with developmental objectives. The policy of prodding and encouragement has been more intelligent than earlier efforts to press unwanted military roles on Japan. Japanese aid has increased, partly because of our prodding, more because of their desire for prestige and greater profits abroad. Meanwhile our own interest in foreign aid has diminished, and we have been too preoccupied with war in Vietnam and too congealed in our hostility toward China to look very far into more positive ways of cooperating with the Japanese or anyone else in Asia that might lead to fundamental economic and social change. We have reduced our expectations of what the Japanese would do to further our interests in a military sense, and this has been salutary; but we have apparently continued to hope that greater participation in regional aid would strengthen Japanese feelings of solidarity in anti-Communist causes with the countries of South and Southeast Asia. Our resentment has grown at Japanese unwillingness to "stand up and be counted."

The Japanese, however, were counted long ago. Forever in the midst of Asia and wishing above all else to avoid entanglement in ideological wars, they have shown a readiness to join in military arrangements with the United States that would protect their own security but none whatever to join in military pacts that would involve their going to the protection of others.[5] They see an Asia riven by big-power rivalries—most recently between China and the Soviet Union, in the future between whom? Their instincts for survival are high, but what they think will preserve them, and us as well, better than anything else is to go on exercising their genius for economic activity of all sorts in a free competition with communism or any other "ism" for the loyalty and respect of Asians. A link, however generalized, between economic development and the political status quo in Asia has gradually been established in some Japanese minds, as this study has shown. However, this has happened more because of demonstrated Chinese intransigence and the growth of Japanese prosperity and the need to protect and enlarge it than because of American prodding or feelings of common cause with the peoples of Asia. Markets and raw materials, joint ventures and plant exports are the common cause felt most powerfully by the Japanese in their relations with other states. Other feelings of commonalty are extremely weak and are going to remain so for a long time to come, regardless of cold wars. Japan is indeed a status quo power, but it has relied on the power of others to maintain the status quo. Although Americans may resent this, it will not change the fact. We may of course pull out of Asia entirely, leaving Japan to protect itself; and we should no doubt insist that it undertake a fuller share of its own defense as it has been doing for some years. But I am haunted by the thought that some day we may also look back on these years as a time when we were too preoccupied by Vietnam to take advantage of our opportunities to strengthen those elements in Japanese society which were most nearly internationalist and some of which came closest to being truly liberal.

Feelings of closer solidarity with South and Southeast Asia, if they are to come by the year 2000 or before, can only come in consequence of a much wider opening of Japan and the Japanese to the world in every sense, including the commercial, than has yet been the case. Much progress toward this openness has been made in the last 25 years, and the drift of Japanese life is in that general direction. However, the Japanese are still an extremely isolated human group. I do not believe that regional solidarity in Asia for productive, creative purposes is likely to be accomplished by a withdrawal of Western participation in the process, or that most Japanese want this. Prescriptions are still occasionally being written by Japanese for pan-Asian solidarity for the purpose of coping with the penetrations of the West; and there are some Americans who apparently would be glad to see the Japanese become our surrogates in Asia. But this is an illusion, and would be in the best interests of neither the Japanese nor ourselves. For regionalism to be fully productive for all concerned and for the hopes of the liberal Japanese projection quoted above to be realized, Westerners should join with Japanese and other Asians in a more realistic program for Asian development after Vietnam. This should of course be done out of a concern for U.S. security, but U.S. actions in Asia and attitudes toward Asia have for too long been too narrowly limited to security alone. Americans need to think positively and respectfully of the human future of all Asians, including the Japanese, not just of how they can serve America's immediate political or economic ends. The United States needs to join far more fully and meaningfully with Japan and other Asian nations not just to fend off ideological enemies but also to build a better life for the region as a whole.

New opportunities for more imaginative policies may be present after the war in Vietnam ends. But there are ways available at present for Japanese and Americans to work together, and the record to date has not been wholly reassuring. I have been struck by the discrepancy between our rather paternalistic prodding of the Japanese to "play a role" and our quite limited interest in and knowledge of what they are doing in specific countries and cases. In country after country in Southeast Asia it is noticeable how little contact exists or even seems to be sought between Americans and Japanese. Feelings of local Americans toward them are ambivalent at best. One hears a good deal about not wanting to sponsor them because they are not popular. Comments about their inability to speak English, or their social stiffness, are common: The Japanese are the most awkward people to play through on the golf course; at international conferences they distinguish themselves by the narrow commercialism of their arguments, when they talk at all; and so on.

Part of the reason for these attitudes lies in the fact of Japanese linguistic and other problems. But part of it lies in the inadequacy of American education. After 25 years of "Asian studies programs," one might reasonably expect that more Americans would have a sophisticated knowledge not just of Japan or India or Indonesia, but of all three and how they hang together as a whole. However, most Americans in Southeast Asia are woefully ignorant of and uninterested in Japan. It is striking how few American citizens, whether they be scholars, government officials, businessmen, journalists or whatever, have much competence or much interest in more than one Asian country.

It may be protested that an increase in those with a knowledge of anything Asian is an improvement over the past. But Americans familiar with Japan often are quite naïve about China; China specialists often carry a burden of hostility toward Japan, while those who know some part of Southeast Asia well are often rank amateurs where Japan and China are concerned. India specialists tend to inhabit a world to themselves. Such narrowness, encouraged by our universities, limits the capacity of so-called educated men to recommend policies, do business, or study foreign societies in a richer, possibly wiser frame of reference. Until U.S. schools and colleges interest themselves in education in breadth as well as depth in foreign affairs, and our other institutions provide more opportunities for such broadly trained individuals to be usefully employed, our perception of Asia and actions with respect to it will continue to be partial at best and often dangerously myopic. We will continue to be unable to respond wisely either to the creative occasions or the crises that are bound to arise.

Some private American organizations, with their large-scale, relatively expensive programs in India and elsewhere, sometimes dismiss Japanese efforts in agricultural or industrial assistance as too small, inept, politically uninfluential, or otherwise beneath notice. The notion that more cooperation in specific cases on the local level might possibly be worth trying elicits little or no response. We seem to fear competition with Japanese locally, both commercially and in our aid programs, even as we prod them to do more at the policy level. In Indonesia I was told that nobody wanted people of other nationalities telling American foundation executives how to spend their money. Yet it seems most unfortunate if budgetary nationalism restricts joint projects with Japanese where these might produce richer results than they would if conducted singly. Of course, the Japanese might complicate things. And it goes without saying that they are not simply waiting expectantly to be asked to cooperate with Americans in Southeast Asia. Efforts have been made on at least one occasion to recruit Japanese economists for an advisory team working with the Indonesian government, to no avail; the Japanese preferred to name their own economic adviser independently. My suggestion to American officials and others that Japanese agricultural assistance in Indonesia might be better coordinated with American programs there, and that there might be some virtue in joint efforts with exchanges of personnel was met by the response that Japanese know-how in tropical agriculture was not very outstanding and that the Japanese did not indeed have a very clear understanding of how their own processes of modernization can be applied overseas. An American official in Bangkok repeated the view heard elsewhere that Japanese seemed to think that all the rest of Asia had to do was to copy the experience of the Meiji Restoration, which, after all, occurred in another age, with leaders of different motives and training, and a people with very different values from those of tropical Asia in the 1960s. Private American advisers to foreign business in a number of Asian countries reacted with skepticism when I suggested that they might join forces with Japanese business consultants in specific cases.

There is some justice in all these criticisms of cooperation with the Japanese, as many Japanese themselves would admit. The advantages of bilateral implementation of public or private aid activities are obvious. Multilateral cooperation will not be easy and is not automatically desirable. Yet, Americans ought to have much closer knowledge of what Japanese are doing in the field and much closer personal relations with them, if all the talk in the chanceries about "partnership" and a "larger role" is not to be just hypocritical. It is only too easy to push off multilateral cooperation onto United Nations agencies and to argue that Japanese would get in the way of American operational procedures and processes. Americans complain about their poor English, and it is often poor, or condescend to their personal characteristics but seldom realize how keenly they feel such condescension, and how they hoard resentment at being made to feel isolated and unequal at international conferences and on other occasions. But if, as the record strongly suggests, Japanese influence is going to increase vastly in Asia and Japan is going to be a major power in the area, if not *the* major power, should America not, in its self-interest if for no other reason, be working harder to achieve a truly equal relationship with the Japanese, not just to issue paternalistic urgings and proddings? Surely there are areas of activity where more could be done. The Japanese Youth Volunteer Corps is very proud of its stress on technically proficient volunteers. It sends not teachers who might be unable to explain their subjects verbally, but welders, carpenters, nurses, and stockraisers, people with skills that can be demonstrated with a minimum of words to others. Our Peace Corps has its own policies, and its members vastly outnumber the Japanese; but both are in theory at least a road to help others to help themselves. This may be altogether naïve, but one would think that they could share experience and produce more mutual advantage; yet contact appears to be slight and often accidental at best. Similarly, Japanese consultants in the field of small industries or fishing are useful to United Nations agencies, but their activities and their very presence seem to be unknown to most AID offices in Asian capitals.

Few Japanese tears have been shed over other Asians. Yet Japanese ideas and people sometimes have a relevance and point that Americans could profit from. For example, a Cabinet Minister in Tokyo in 1968 thought that a practical goal of, say, $200 per capita income should be set up for Southeast Asia and all international efforts devoted to reaching that goal. To him, President Johnson would have been much wiser to mention such a figure instead of promising a billion dollars for development after Vietnam—a Texan gesture, perhaps, but one lacking in concreteness to most Asians. The Cabinet Minister echoed his fellow countrymen's emphasis on self-help, hard work, and long-range planning and thought that if per capita income in China and Southeast Asia could be raised, political moderation and modernization there might begin to become possible. (He did not suggest how long this might take or how much it might cost.)

I am merely suggesting that there are things Americans could learn from the Japanese that might increase their own flexibility. It should also be quite clear that I think there are things they could learn from America. The possibilities of self-righteousness in discussing this subject are very great. How, it may be asked, can Americans criticize Japanese for condescending to others or for having had a sense of their own peculiar mission? Indeed, in much of what I have written of Japan's attitudes toward Asians we can find mirrored American stereotyped views of Asia, including Japan. Americans have their share and more of cultural and racial prejudice, their own parochial nationalism; they live in their own glass house. But no one who has a respect for the human qualities of Japanese as individuals as well as for their technical skills can fail to believe that those qualities and skills should be brought to bear in a constructive way to help raise Asian living standards and strengthen national economies on a far wider scale than has been the case up to now, if the welfare world envisioned by the rational economists and political scientists in Tokyo, and which stems ultimately from Western examples, is ever to be realized.

This is not a matter of sponsoring the Japanese but of joining and remaining a part of their energy and ingenuity and possibly even channeling it in imaginative, constructive ways. A great potential for secular good is latent in Japanese experience, even if that experience cannot and should not be copied verbatim in other countries. For the United States to miss an opportunity to move forward with this potential merely because it fears Japanese competition, or thinks the Japanese are unpopular, or odd fellows, or because it continues to want aid recipients to become little democrats overnight, would be an egregious error of judgement.

What institutional forms cooperation may take, apart from closer coordination of aid programs in third countries and multilateral organizations like the Asian Development Bank, is not yet clear. For a number of years discussions have been going on among the so-called Pacific nations—the United States, Canada, Australia, New Zealand, and Japan—looking toward formation of some sort of Pacific Free Trade Zone or community of nations. Australian interest in these talks has been especially great, as has Australian interest in closer relations with Japan generally. Most Japanese who have watched these talks have felt that it was best for Japan to expand and make mutual trade more free with all parts of the world. However, there has been a good deal of apprehension about further compartmentalizaton of world trade, which the Japanese see EEC as representing, as well as the possibility of a turn away from a commitment to global free trade on the part of the United States. For a variety of reasons the Pacific Free Trade Zone idea is still premature; the United States still stands for free trade, and the five nations involved are at very different stages of industrial development and would benefit very unevenly from complete liberalization of trade. Japan might benefit most. These countries often find it hard enough to cooperate, let alone to integrate their economies. But whatever the future of such concepts, the meetings and writings that have come out of them already are helping to provide some machinery for the coordination of region-wide ideas for economic cooperation, especially as regards the future of foreign aid programs and their implementation. The need for such coordination of policies and programs after the Vietnam war ends is obvious.

As one Japanese economist reasons, again using the Latin American analogy:

> A joint aid programme . . . mapped out by a group of developed nations . . . could be more effectively carried out than one formulated by Japan alone. The GNP of North America is 15 times the aggregate GNP of all the countries of Latin America, and the GNP of Western Europe is 10 times that of Africa. However, Japan's GNP only equals the aggregate GNP of the nations of South and Southeast Asia. Thus aid to the developing countries of Asia is too gigantic a problem for Japan alone.[6]

Thus speaks the voice of reason and economic statistics. But whether reason will prevail is unclear. The possibility that Japan may abandon its attempts at openness to the world, may revert to a search for paramountcy within a smaller Asian portion of it, cannot be ruled out, just as it is conceivable that a massive threat of nuclear attack might result in Japan's caving in to the "other side," or "strategic surrender." A drastic withdrawal of access to Western markets and sources of raw materials would encourage such a backward movement, as would a return of menacing Soviet militancy and expansionism in Asia. Then one might hear demands for a new Asian bloc under Japanese leadership, implying conflict with Western interests. These trends do not seem probable at this writing, but they ought to be kept in the back of the mind as Americans do all that they can to keep lines of communication open and areas of common interest as broad as possible with as many kinds of Japanese as they can, encouraging those people and institutions that wish to keep moving toward the true rather than the specious liberation of all Asians, including the Japanese themselves.

Instead of turning away from the area in disgust after extricating ourselves from our errors of judgement in Vietnam, we should accept more realistically the limitations on our power and seek in a more selective, hard-headed way to help those regimes in Southeast Asia that show signs of helping themselves and wanting to promote genuine change. To do this at all meaningfully will require us to revise our simplistic view of aid recipients as friends or enemies and stop trying to use aid as a club to enforce anti-communism. As an Asian country surrounded by other Asian countries, Japan cannot afford to associate openly with such an approach. For Americans to persist in it is to risk further failures abroad and divisions at home, which may very well lead to more extreme forms of chauvinism and a vain attempt to shut our-selves away from Asian problems entirely.

These observations have been addressed primarily to Ameri-cans. In the final paragraphs of this book it may be proper to speak also to those Japanese who may possibly read it. In doing this I am again conscious of the danger of sounding self-righteous.

Many ironies surround the Japanese position in Asia. Their country is the country in-between. While some Westernized Japanese intellectuals wonder how accurately Japan understands the West, others elsewhere in Asia profess to believe that the Japanese as a people have lost their sense of identity as Asians in the mad rush to modernize. Thus the Burmese economist, U Thet Tun, regaled me in Rangoon in 1961 with the vulgarities of Tokyo's Westernized dress, entertainment, and other customs, and assured me that nothing of the sort would be permitted to penetrate Burma. Again, Japanese rightly resent the distorted ac-counts of their country that are still commonly given in Western school textbooks—pictures of Chinese people and scenes repre-sented as Japanese, and so on. Yet the education of Japanese from early childhood through the university about the rest of Asia is surely far from perfect; stereotypes persist in the Japanese mind as in the minds of all peoples.

It is sometimes stated, for instance, by Japanese writing on the subject that the Japanese as individuals are better adapted to Asian tropical living conditions than Americans, that they can somehow get closer to the people more rapidly and effectively, that they are less reluctant to leave the main cities and to live for extended periods under pioneer conditions in the hinterland.[7] However inaccurate this may have been in the past—one thinks of the hundreds of Americans in the Philippines who in the earlier part of this century spent their lives teaching in primitive schools in backwater provincial towns—today there may be something in this assertion. Japanese in some areas may, indeed, be readier than Americans to eat local food. It may be that the Japanese need for Western-style comforts in tropical environments is still relatively undemanding. I have received a good deal of inspiration from Japanese acquaintances who were ready to take off into the countryside in Burma or the Philippines to make some study or demonstrate some machine without much thought for their own comfort or safety. Certainly I shall never forget the young geographer studying at the University of the Philippines in the late 1950s who set out against the advice of his Filipino professor to make a field trip to southern Luzon. Traveling by public bus in a crowd of Filipino farmers and their chickens, piglets, and sacks of vegetables, he was soon spotted as a Japanese, and he had a sticky moment or two until he told them what he was doing and showed an interest in them. His English was good, and it got better as he asked his fellow travelers about their crops and their lives. By the time the bus reached its destination that evening, one Filipino passenger had invited him to spend the night at his home.

Perhaps all that this proves is that personal qualities are more important than any so-called national characteristics. And thus generalizations about which countrymen can adapt most readily to alien conditions are really not very useful. One could as easily argue that the Japanese as a people are far less adept at learning to speak foreign languages and less willing to leave their own country to live and serve abroad than some other people. The trouble with such national comparisons is that while they may have some academic interest, they often get in the way of the solution of practical problems. They are apt to lead in the Japanese case, as in others, to the notion that the Japanese are superior and that other peoples are inferior; this view may increase as the Japanese are disappointed in the performance of South and Southeast Asians, as they will surely continue to be; but this kind of thinking ought to be recognized and rejected as archaic.

When it comes to understanding other peoples, another point ought to be made. It has to be realized that there is often a discrepancy between the attitudes of the men on the scene and what they are doing practically and the attitudes of the national policymakers in Tokyo or New Delhi or Washington. Chapters IV and V of this study illustrate this point, which can be shown in other ways too. Nehru in his last years welcomed rice-growing experiments by Japanese farmers on a few pilot farms in India. He and his cabinet ministers were aware that Japan produces the largest yields of rice per unit of land of any country on earth and India one of the smallest (this was before "miracle rice" had been heard of), and that if Japanese methods of irrigation, seed selection, cultivation, and harvesting could be taught to Indian farmers there might be immeasurable dividends. (He also knew the difficulty of teaching these things.) At the same time Nehru himself was sick and tired of the phrase "Japanese method of rice cultivation." In much the same way Filipino politicians want Japanese know-how but don't want to be reminded of any presumed Japanese cultural superiority. In Tokyo there may be intellectual despair over Indian poverty and bureaucratic condescension toward Indian inefficiency and corruption. But all one has to do to grasp the possibilities of the Japanese contribution in the technical sphere is to go and talk with some of them on the scene in Southeast Asia, and, more important than talk, to watch them at their tasks.

How often, for instance, I recall a scene on the outskirts of Calcutta where Japanese mechanics were installing machine tools with which to train Indians wishing to set up small machine-powered industries. At one end of the unfinished cement building young Japanese mechanics were running around in baseball caps, T-shirts, khaki pants, and sneakers, bolting down lathes and power saws, organizing a modern machine shop, while at the other end of the building long files of Indian women in magenta-colored saris were slowly bearing away the refuse and debris of construction in baskets held delicately on their heads. The project director was a young Indian government official; the associate director was a middle-aged Japanese engineer who had spent many years in the Empire. They got along well together, and I left the construction site feeling that this was an example of really fruitful cooperation that gave the lie to all the palaver about national characteristics that one heard from Asians as well as Americans in the capital cities.[8]

There are other such examples. Japanese contributions in the techniques of economic planning, in taxation and agricultural credit, in collection and analysis of statistics, as well as in many industrial fields, all are of actual or potential importance to other Asian countries. Technical assistance can be a true bridge across which Japanese skills are transmitted to others. Where cross-cultural understanding and respect are weak, technical assistance, like other forms of economic assistance, can easily become an occasion for nationalistic pride or sentimental self-indulgence on the part of the giver, to be matched by resentment on the part of the receiver. Such cross-cultural understanding is weak where the Japanese as well as the Americans in South and Southeast Asia are concerned. Japan has much to receive from other Asian countries besides raw materials. Yet it is receiving very little. To give only one example: A great Japanese newspaper regularly sponsors elaborate festivals of Western music. But how much has been done to bring Asian music, art, or literature to Japan? How many Japanese read the vernacular literature or even the translated literature of other Asians and thus learn at first hand what they are thinking, what they are like? In such cultural priorities a nation reflects its own view of itself and its aims. It is perhaps natural that Japan should compare itself constantly with the West in the economic and cultural sphere, but this should not blind it to the cultural achievements of its neighbors to the south.

Japan can give to Asia more than it has given. But, to give fully, the Japanese like the Americans, will have to open themselves more fully to receive. One has the impression that some Japanese are disturbed by what they regard as a tendency for their country to take more from the world than it gives. One can hope that Professor Masamichi Inoki is correct when he writes: "Our experiences of the last quarter of a century have . . . drilled into the Japanese the one basic fact that the prime movers of Southeast Asian history are the peoples of Southeast Asia themselves." [9] Insularity, however, continues to breed Japanese indifference toward other Asian peoples except as their attention is teased by some political crisis or other. And, as I have suggested, what interest there is is usually expressed in terms of the quantitative results of national modernization. One is aware of the difficulties that face Japanese government and private organizations in exposing their people to the contemporary cultures of Asia on a far wider scale than has yet been undertaken; but this must be attempted if what the Japanese have to give is to register fully, and if they in their turn are to learn to receive from others in the deepest human sense and not just to react to the slogans of economic diplomacy.

Beyond Japanese technology and beneath Japanese nationalism lie qualities of self-respect, frugality, humor, appreciation for the discipline and dignity of work, and a sense of beauty that reflects and enhances a grace of the spirit. It may be true, as some intellectuals have suggested, that what Japan has to offer the world most importantly in the long run is estheticism—beauty rather than beliefs. One difficulty, in my view, is to get beyond a prideful belief in the beauty, beyond the "politics of flower arrangement," and to realize that other peoples have their own set of qualities that are no less human or admirable for being different; indeed they may amount to the same set of qualities manifest in a different way. Nobody has a greater relish for facts than the Japanese, and their opportunities in Asia are endless and open. I wish more Japanese would reflect on this relish for facts that some of them have about Asia, especially some who have been on the scene. Then they might see more clearly what it is that they, like the Americans, have to learn from the rest of Asia and how necessary it is to make the effort to understand.

Appendix Table

The Flow of Japanese Financial Resources to Less-developed Countries and Multilateral Agencies

	1961	1962	1963	1964	1965	1966	1967
	(net, in millions of dollars)						
Grants	67.8	74.6	76.7	68.7	82.2	104.7	138.4
of which							
Reparations and Others	65.4	71.0	72.2	62.9	76.2	97.2	127.4
Technical Cooperation	2.4	3.6	4.5	5.8	6.0	7.6	11.0
Direct Loans (Yen credits)	27.7	5.0	51.5	37.5	144.1	130.0	207.5
of which							
Refinancing and Consolidation Credits	0.9	−7.5	−8.8	−11.6	60.9	15.2	40.3
Subtotal, Bilateral Grants and Direct Loans	95.5	79.6	128.2	96.2	226.3	234.7	345.9
Contributions to Multilateral Agencies	11.4	7.2	12.1	9.7	17.5	50.6	44.7
Total, Official	106.9	86.8	140.3	105.9	243.8	285.3	390.6
Export Credits (Over one year)	176.0	141.4	103.1	205.2	269.6	287.0	380.2
Direct Investment	98.4	68.4	76.7	39.3	87.4	97.1	84.6
Multilateral Portfolio Investment	−4.6	0.7	..	0.3		−0.4	−0.1
Total, Private	269.8	210.5	179.8	244.8	357.0	383.7	464.7
Total, Official and Private	376.7	297.3	320.1	360.7	600.8	669.0	855.3
Less Ship Export Credits to Greece, Liberia, and Panama	−4.7	11.1	52.5	69.5	114.9	130.2	197.9
Net Total, Official and Private	381.4	286.2	267.6	291.2	485.9	538.8	657.4
Percentage of national income	0.92	0.61	0.51	0.48	0.71	0.69	0.71
Percentage of GNP	0.74	0.49	0.41	0.38	0.57	0.55	0.57

Left margin groupings: **Bilateral** and **Official** bracket the upper rows; **Private** brackets the Export Credits / Direct Investment / Multilateral Portfolio Investment rows.

SOURCE: Ministry of Foreign Affairs, Economic Cooperation Bureau, August 1968.

Bibliography

Asahi Shimbun.

Asahi Shimin Kyōshitsu [Asahi Citizens Classroom]. *Chūkoku no Kaku Senryoku* [China's Nuclear Strength]. Tokyo: Asahi Shimbun Sha, 1967.

Bangkok Post.

BENDA, HARRY J. *The Crescent and the Rising Sun.* The Hague: W. Van Hoeve, 1958.

BORTON, HUGH, et al. *Japan Between East and West.* New York: Harper, for the Council on Foreign Relations, 1957.

Christian Science Monitor.

CLARK, GREGORY. "Japanese Production-Sharing Projects, 1966–1968." *Bulletin of Indonesian Economic Statistics,* no. 10 (June 1968). Canberra: Australian National University.

Committee for the Coordination of Investigations of the Lower Mekong Basin. *Annual Reports.* Bangkok, 1962–67.

DENNEY, GEORGE C., Jr. "Japan's China Policy in October 1962; Steering Between Blocs." New York: Institute of Current World Affairs newsletter, n. d.

DICKS, ANTHONY R. "The Non-Agreement in Action: Sino-Japanese Trade." New York: Institute of Current World Affairs news–letter, ARD-21, May 29, 1968.

ELSBREE, WILLARD. *Japan's Role in Southeast Asian Nationalist Movements.* Cambridge Mass.: Harvard University Press, 1953.

FREE, LLOYD A. *International Attitudes of Four Asian Democracies.* Princeton, N.J.: Institute for International Social Research, 1969.

HALPERN, A. M., ed. *Policies Toward China*. New York: McGraw-Hill Book Co., for the Council on Foreign Relations, 1965.

HANNA, WILLARD A. "Bung Karno's Indonesia, Part XXI: The Japanese Pay Up." New York: American Universities Field Staff Report, WAH-32-59, December 1, 1959.

————. "Japan Begins to Pay Reparations." New York: American Universities Field Staff Report, WAH-4-55, November 29, 1955.

————. "Japan's Relations with Nationalist China." New York: American Universities Field Staff Report, WAH-3-56, February 1, 1956.

————. "Japan's Return to the Philippines." New York: American Universities Field Staff Report, WAH-2-55, November 1, 1955.

HOTTA, YOSHIE. *Indo de Kangaeta Koto* [Thoughts in India]. Tokyo: Iwanami Shoten, 1947.

Indian Investment Center. *Monthly Newsletter*. New Delhi: October 15, 1968.

IRIE, MASAMICHI, et al. *Kaku Jidai to Nihon no Kaku Seisaku* [The Nuclear Age and Japan's Nuclear Policies]. Tokyo: Hara Shobō, 1968.

ISHIDA, YASUAKI. *Indo de Kurasu* [Living in India]. Tokyo: Iwanami Shoten, 1963.

ISHIKAWA, TADAO. "Communist China's Policy Toward Japan." *Journal of Social and Political Ideas in Japan*, vol. 4, no. 3 (December 1966).

JANSEN, MARIUS B. *Japan and Communist China in the Next Decade*. Santa Barbara, Calif.: General Electric Company, 1962.

Japan, Cabinet Information Office. *Jiji Mondai ni Kansuru Seron Chōsa* [Public Opinion Poll on Current Affairs]. Tokyo, June 1968.

————, Cabinet Research Bureau. *Chūkyō wa Nihon no Kyōi to Naru ka?* [Will Communist China Become a Threat to Japan?]. Tokyo, n. d.

————, Ministry of Foreign Affairs. *Kankoku ni Okeru Shakkan Kigyō no Genjō* [Status of Yen Loan Enterprises in Korea]. Tokyo, 1968.

————, Ministry of Foreign Affairs. *Kongo no Keizai Kyōryoku no Arikata ni Tsuite* [Future Manner of Economic Cooperation]. Tokyo, August 1967.

————, Ministry of Foreign Affairs, Economic Affairs Bureau, East-West Commerce Section. *Shiberia: Kaihatsu Kyōryoku Mondai no Kihonteki Kenkyū* [Siberia: Basic Study of the Problems of Cooperation in Development]. Tokyo, 1967.

————, Ministry of Foreign Affairs, *Nihon no Baishō* [Japanese Reparations]. Tokyo: Sekai Janaru Sha, 1963.

————, Ministry of International Trade and Industry. *Keizai Kyōryoku no Genjō to Mondaiten* [Present Status and Problems of Economic Cooperation]. Tokyo, 1967 edition. Cited as *KKGM*.

————, Ministry of International Trade and Industry. *Tsūsan Hakusho* [White Paper on Commerce and Industry]. Tokyo, 1968 edition.

Japan Committee for Economic Development [Keizai Dōyūkai]. *Keizai Kyōryoku Taisei ni Kansuru Teigen* [Proposals for a Structure for Economic Cooperation]. Tokyo, February 1968.

Japan Economic Research Center. *The World in 2000, Report of a Japan Economic Research Center International Conference.* Tokyo, 1967.

Japan Times.

JSPIJ. Journal of Social and Political Ideas in Japan.

KKGM. See Japan, Ministry of International Trade and Industry, *Keizai Kyōryoku no Genjō to Mondaiten.*

KOJIMA, KIYOSHI, ed. *Pacific Trade and Development.* Tokyo: Japan Economic Research Center, 1968.

KŌSAKA, MASATAKA. "Nihon no Gaikōron ni Okeru Risōshugi to Genjitsushugi" [Idealism and Realism in Japan's Foreign Policy Debate], in Masataka Kōsaka, et al. *Anzen Hoshō to Nichibei Kankei* [Security and Japanese-American Relations]. Tokyo: Hara Shobō, 1968.

KUBOTA, YUTAKA. *Ajia Kaihatsu no Kiban wo Kizuku* [Building a Base for Asian Development]. Tokyo: Kokusai Mondai Kenkyūsho, 1967.

KUWABARA, SUETAKA. "Kōshinkoku ni Taisuru Nihon no Kyōryoku no Arikata" [Manner of Japanese Cooperation in Underdeveloped Countries]. *Ajia Keizai,* vol. 3 (March 1963).

Kyoto University, Center for Southeast Asian Studies. *Japan's Future in Southeast Asia.* Kyoto, 1966.

————. *Tōnan Ajia Kenkyū,* vol. 5, no. 4 (1967).

LENG SHAO-CHUAN. *Japan and Communist China.* Kyoto: Dōshisha University, n. d.

Mainichi Shimbun.

Manila Bulletin.

MATSUKATA, SABURŌ. "Nihon no Kongo Jūnen" [Japan Ten Years Hence]. *Chūō Kōron,* January 1955.

MINSHUSHUGI KENKYŪKAI [Democracy Research Association]. *Nihon Chūkyō Kōryū Nenshi* [Yearbook of Japan-China Interchange]. Tokyo, 1965 edition. Cited as *NCKN.*

MITCHELL, DONALD. *The Korean Minority in Japan.* Berkeley: University of California Press, 1967.

NAGAI, MICHIO. "The 'Take-Off' and 'Crash' in the Development of Japanese Education." Paper prepared for India-Japan Round

Table Conference, November, 1968. Mimeographed. Tokyo: Japan Committee for Studies on Economic Development in India and Japan, 1968.

NAGAI, YŌNOSUKE. "Japanese Foreign Policy Objectives in a Nuclear Milieu." *Journal of Social and Political Ideas in Japan*, vol. 5, no. 1 (April 1967).

NAOI, TAKEO, "Sino-Japanese Deadlock." *The New Leader*, September 29, 1958.

NCKN. See Minshushugi Kenkyūkai.

New York Times.

NIHON KEIZAI CHŌSA KYŌGIKAI [Japan Economic Research Council]. *Tōnan Ajia no Nihonkei Kigyō* [Japan-Connected Enterprises in Southeast Asia]. 2 vols. Tokyo, 1967.

NITCHŪ BŌEKI SOKUSHIN GIIN REMMEI [Dietmen's League for Promotion of Japan-China Trade]. *Nitchū Shiryō Shū* [Materials on Japan-China Relations]. Tokyo, 1967.

NITCHŪ YŪSHUTSUNYŪ KUMIAI [Japan-China Export-Import Guild]. *Nitchū Bōeki Hakusho* [White Paper on Japan-China Trade]. Tokyo: Daidō Shoin Shuppansha, August 1958.

ŌGATA, TAKETORA. *Nihon Naigai no Kyūmu* [Japan's Pressing Obligations at Home and Abroad]. Tokyo: Ajia Mondai Kenkyūkai, 1953.

ŌKITA, SABURŌ. *Ajia no Naka no Nihon Keizai* [Japan's Economy in the Midst of Asia]. Tokyo: Diamond Co., 1966.

———. "Japan in South and Southeast Asia: Trade and Aid." Paper prepared for India-Japan-Australia Conference, September 11–15, 1967. Mimeographed. Canberra: Australian National University, 1967.

———. "Japan's Dependence on Imported Resources." (Translation of article in *Chūō Kōron*, December 1967.) Tokyo: Japan Economic Research Center, n.d.

———. *Nihon Keizai no Bijiyon* [A Vision of the Japanese Economy]. Tokyo: Diamond Co., 1968.

OLSON, LAWRENCE. *Dimensions of Japan.* New York: American Universities Field Staff, 1963.

———. "Japan and Asia: An American Viewpoint," *Asia*, no. 8 (1967).

———. "Japanese Interest in India." New York: American Universities Field Staff Report, LO-4-58, March 31, 1958.

———. "Japan's Relations with China: Some Recent Developments." New York: American Universities Field Staff Report, LO-3-64, June, 1964.

———. "The 'Rhee Line': A Japanese View." New York: American Universities Field Staff Report, LAO-8-55, December 28, 1955.

————. "What Will the Government Do? Problems, Plans, and Progress in the North Kyūshū Area." New York: American Universities Field Staff Report, LAO-1-56, February 1, 1956.

Oriental Economist.

ŌSHIMA, TOSHIO. "Gaikō Seisaku no Kyokumen Kara Mita Keizai Kyōryoku" [Economic Cooperation from the Viewpoint of Diplomatic Policy]. Print of a paper delivered at a seminar on November 29, 1966. Tokyo: Japan Economic Research Center, n. d.

Philippine Reparations Commission. *Annual Report.* Manila, 1959.

Philippine Reparations Mission in Tokyo. *Annual Report, 1966.* Mimeographed.

SAEKI, KIICHI, *et al. Kyokutō no Anzen Hoshō* [Far Eastern Security]. Tokyo: Hara Shobō, 1968.

SAKAMOTO, YOSHIKAZU. "Sino-Japanese Relations in the Nuclear Age." *Journal of Social and Political Ideas in Japan,* vol. 4, no. 3 (December 1966).

SASE, ROKURŌ. "Tōnan Ajia no Keizai Kaihatsu to Nihon no Kyōryoku" [Economic Development of Southeast Asia and Japan's Cooperation]. *Nihon Oyobi Nihonjin,* February 1958.

SEKI, HIROHARU. "Systems of Power Balance and the Preservation of Peace." *Journal of Social and Political Ideas in Japan,* vol. 5, no. 1 (April 1967).

SHIBATA, MINORU. *Hōdō Sarenakatta Pekin* [Unreported Peking]. Tokyo: Sankei Shimbun Sha, 1967.

SHIMMYŌ, MASAHIDE. "Financial Collaboration." Mimeographed. Tokyo: Japan Committee for Studies on Economic Development in India and Japan, 1968.

SIMON, SHELDON W. "Maoism and Inter-Party Relations: Peking's Alienation of the Japan Communist Party." *China Quarterly,* no. 35 (July–September, 1968).

Singapore Eastern Sun.

STEINBERG, DAVID J. *Philippine Collaboration in World War II.* Ann Arbor: University of Michigan Press, 1967.

Taiwan Trade Monthly.

TAKAGI, RYŌICHI. *Nihon Kigyō no Kaigai Shinshutsu* [Movement of Japanese Enterprises Overseas]. Tokyo: Kokusai Mondai Kenkyūsho, 1967.

TAKASAKI, TATSUNOSUKE. "Ajia no Hanei to Nihon no Ummei" [Prosperity of Asia and Japan's Fate]. *Chūō Kōron,* January 1958.

TAKESHIMA, YASUHIRO. "Saiken no Naka no Shihon Sensō," [Capital Warfare in the Midst of Reconstruction]. *Purejidento,* August 1968.

Times, The (London).

266 / Bibliography

Tokunaga, Hisatsugu. "Industrial Collaboration." Mimeographed. Tokyo: Japan Committee for Studies on Economic Development in India and Japan, 1968.

Tokyo University, Tōyō Bunka Kenkyūsho [Institute of Oriental Culture]. *Tōyō Bunka*, no. 45 (March 1968).

Tōyō Keizai (weekly), May 10, 1969.

Wakaizumi, Kei. "Chinese Nuclear Armament and the Security of Japan." *Journal of Social and Political Ideas in Japan*, vol. 4, no. 3 (December 1966).

White, John. *Japanese Aid.* London: Overseas Development Institute, 1964.

Wightman, David. *Toward Economic Cooperation in Asia.* New Haven, Conn.: Yale University Press, 1963.

Notes

Chapter II. The First Steps: Relations with Southeast Asia and India

1. This term is variously defined. Japanese sources sometimes include within it the region from Pakistan, or even Afghanistan, to Taiwan, and occasionally Korea. In this book, Southeast Asia means the region from Burma to the Philippines inclusive, except as otherwise indicated, and excluding Australia and New Zealand. South Asia refers to India, Pakistan, and Ceylon.
2. W. A. Hanna, "Japan Begins to Pay Reparations." In this section I have drawn extensively upon Hanna's eye-witness reports of the progress of reparations negotiations.
3. *New York Times*, November 9, 1952.
4. Hanna, "Japan's Return to the Philippines."
5. *New York Times*, September 30, 1953.
6. *New York Times*, April 14, 1954.
7. D. J. Steinberg, *Philippine Collaboration in World War II.*
8. August 12, 1954.
9. Lawrence Olson, "The 'Rhee Line': A Japanese View."
10. *New York Times*, August 23, 1954.
11. Hanna, "Japan Begins to Pay Reparations."
12. *Christian Science Monitor*, March 28, 1955.
13. This term (*keizai kyōryoku* in Japanese) was the preferred euphemism for aid. The word for aid, *enjo*, was never much used.
14. Takasaki registered some sharp impressions of Japan's position in the mid-1950s. For instance, when he went to Manila to sign the reparations

agreement with the Philippines, President Magsaysay told him, "You are mistaken if you think the Filipinos will erase your cruel deeds from their minds simply because a reparations agreement is signed." Tatsunosuke Takasaki, "Ajia no Hanei to Nihon no Ummei," pp. 105–109.

15. Japan, Ministry of Foreign Affairs, *Nihon no Baishō*, p. 28.
16. *Ibid.*, p. 28.
17. *Ibid.*, p. 30.
18. *Ibid.*, p. 37.
19. *Ibid.*, pp. 38–39.
20. Japan's exports to non-Communist Asia rose from $868 million in 1956 to $2,630 million in 1966. However, the share of non-Communist Asia in Japan's total exports declined from 40 per cent in 1951 to 34.7 per cent in 1956, 32.6 per cent in 1961, and 26.7 per cent in 1964; imports from the non-Communist Asian area declined from 26.2 per cent in 1951, to 22.7 per cent in 1956, 16.8 per cent in 1961, and 16.3 per cent in 1964. By 1964 the share of Southeast Asia in Japanese trade had become stabilized at about 26 per cent of exports and 17 per cent of imports, or a smaller percentage of Japan's total trade than that with the United States in either category. See Saburō Ōkita, "Japan in South and Southeast Asia: Trade and Aid."
21. For the Japanese occupation record see Willard Elsbree, *Japan's Role in Southeast Asian Nationalist Movements;* Harry J. Benda, *The Crescent and the Rising Sun;* Steinberg, *op. cit.*
22. Personal interview, February 1, 1961.
23. Michio Nagai, "The 'Take-Off' and 'Crash' in the Development of Japanese Education."
24. Taketora Ōgata, "Tōnan Ajia no Tabi Yori Kaerite," in *Nihon Naigai no Kyūmu.*
25. Saburō Matsukata, "Nihon no Kongo Jūnen," pp. 20–27.
26. Quoted in Olson, "Japanese Interest in India," p. 3.
27. For a description of the state of Asian studies from this point of view, see Tokyo University, *Tōyō Bunka*, no. 45 (March, 1968), pp. 83–98.
28. Olson, *Dimensions of Japan*, Chap. 22.
29. Olson, "Japanese Interest in India," pp. 1–2. The quotations are from Yoshie Hotta, *Indo de Kangaeta Koto*, pp. 9–12.
30. *Ibid.*, p. 8.
31. By 1967 Japanese were involved in some 70 overseas ventures for exploitation of ferrous and nonferrous minerals, petroleum, timber or other resources. At least 44 of these were in Asia, and included tungsten and iron ore projects in Thailand; iron, bauxite, tin, timber and oil in Malaysia; oil, nickel, timber and sugar in Indonesia; copper, iron and timber in the Philippines; timber in Cambodia; iron and magnesia clinker in India. Japan, Ministry of International Trade and Industry, *Keizai Kyōryoku no Genjō to Mondaiten*, pp. 138–139. Hereafter cited as *KKGM.*

32. Olson, "Japanese Interest in India," p. 7.
33. *Ibid.*, p. 8.
34. Ryōichi Takagi, *Nihon Kigyō no Kaigai Shinshutsu*, p. 27. Statistics quoted from *KKGM*.
35. Japan, Ministry of International Trade and Industry, *Tsūsan Hakusho*.
36. Kishi was also active in promoting intraregional trade talks among the nations of ECAFE, to which Japan was admitted in 1956. These talks aimed at export promotion and solution of the already noticeable problem of finding products for some countries of Southeast Asia to sell in Japan to balance their trade with that country. Economic regionalism was debated from this time forward, but without much practical results. The political and economic obstacles to effective regional action were very great. Some Asians felt that given the economic disparity between Japan and the rest of the region, only the Japanese would profit much from a common market or other such regional arrangements. Others pointed to the fact that most of the trade of the area was with the old metropolitan powers and the United States. Still others feared a new co-prosperity sphere for Japan's benefit. Ideas of regionalism remained vague, but they persisted and were still being debated at the end of the 1960s. For an account of early discussions of economic regionalism in Asia by a Japanese who participated as his country's representative in ECAFE and took a realistic view of the problem, see Ōkita, *Ajia no Naka no Nihon Keizai*. For an English-language account of Asian regionalism, see David Wightman, *Toward Economic Cooperation in Asia*.
37. *KKGM*, pp. 62–67.
38. Olson, "Japanese Interest in India," p. 12.
39. Rokurō Sase, "Tōnan Ajia no Keizai Kaihatsu to Nihon no Kyōryoku," in *Nihon Oyobi Nihonjin*, February, 1958, pp. 40–58. The total of Japanese worldwide private investment in the same period was about $72 million. This included equity and loans connected with investment. See *KKGM*, 1967 ed., p. 77. Private investment in Southeast Asia rose to an estimated $197.6 million (517 cases) by 1965. But this represented only 21.1 per cent of total private Japanese overseas investment; see Takagi, *Nihon Kigyō no Kaigai Shinshutsu*, p. 18. Somewhat different figures can be found in Nihon Keizai Chōsa Kyōgikai, *Tōnan Ajia no Nihonkei Kigyō*, vol. 1, p. 3, where it is stated that the cumulative total of all overseas private investment from 1951 to March 1966 was $916 million in 2,150 cases. Of this, $190 million, or 20.7 per cent, was in Southeast Asia. The variation may be due to the writers' different definitions of Southeast Asia or their methods of defining investment. In any event, the figures match well enough to give some idea of the scale of Japanese investment, which did not reach a cumulative total of $1 billion worldwide until 1967, at which time it was growing at perhaps $80 million annually. Of the total, nearly 30 per cent, or the largest share,

was in Central and South America, about 21 per cent in the Middle East, about 28 per cent in North America, Europe and Oceania, and about 1 per cent in Africa.

40. *KKGM*, p. 77.
41. Nihon Keizai Chōsa Kyōgikai, *Tōnan Ajia no Nihonkei Kigyō*, vol. 1, pp. 1–9.
42. Takagi, *Nihon Kigyō no Kaigai Shinshutsu*, p. 71.
43. Olson, "Japanese Interest in India," pp. 10–11.
44. For the man and his ideas, see Yutaka Kubota, *Ajia Kaihatsu no Kiban wo Kizuku.*
45. For more detail on the Japanese in Burma in this period, see Olson, *Dimensions of Japan,* Chap. 24.
46. Japan, Ministry of Foreign Affairs, *Nihon no Baishō,* p. 55.
47. The 1959 official report of the Reparations Commission, established in 1958 to oversee the program in Manila, listed the following defects in the Reparations Law requiring urgent amendment. The Law, it stated:

1. Does not provide for strict priority rating of projects to be procured.
2. Does not contain any definite provision for the strict processing and screening of reparations projects as well as applicant end-users.
3. Does not specify any limit to the size of the tentative annual schedule being prepared by the Reparations Commission and used by the Mission in Tokyo as the basis for negotiating the agreed schedule with the Government of Japan.
4. Lacks adequate provisions to insure payment of reparations allocated to applicant end-users.
5. Contains no provision regarding dollar support that should be given to reparations projects.
6. Contains no provision which insures sufficient stability or permanency of the reparations schedule even after it is agreed upon with the Government of Japan.
7. Contains no specific provision governing the expeditious procurement of reparations.

The Commission report made the following additional criticisms and recommendations:

8. Provisions of the Law requiring the holding of a public bidding as prerequisite to the procurement of goods intended for government agencies should be made equally applicable to the procurement of goods intended for private parties as a deterrent against undue overpricing and/or in order to avoid suspicion of overpricing.
9. The Law contains no provision regarding the imposition of penalties for end-users who fail to take prompt delivery of reparations goods allocated to them.

10. The Law should incorporate additional provisions regarding publicity of reparations procurement and allocation.

See Philippines Reparations Commission, *Annual Report*.

48. Information derived from interviews with officials of the Bank of Tokyo, Djakarta, 1968. See also Hanna, "Bung Karno's Indonesia, Part XXI."
49. *Ibid.*
50. Japan, Ministry of Foreign Affairs, *Nihon no Baishō*, pp. 223–24.
51. Olson, "Japanese Interest in India," p. 13.
52. Ōkita, *Ajia no Naka no Nihon Keizai*, p. 60.
53. Translated and quoted in Olson, *Dimensions of Japan*, p. 294.
54. The Japanese share of the American market for imported cotton goods fell from 54.9 per cent in 1955 to 29.1 per cent in 1964; toys from 72.1 per cent in 1955, to 53.1 per cent in 1964; artificial flowers from 86.8 per cent in 1955 to 9.0 per cent in 1964. Ōkita, "Japan in South and Southeast Asia: Trade and Aid."
55. Several of the projects mentioned under Indonesian reparations, including the oil, timber, and nickel production-sharing schemes, were subsidized through the OECF, as were joint ventures in tin refining, fisheries, and steel in Malaysia; iron mining and sugar in Thailand; waterworks development in Laos; pearl culture in the Philippines and timber in Brunei. The OECF also administered important loans to Korea and Taiwan.
56. *Times* (London), December 1, 1961.
57. Ōkita, *Ajia no Naka no Nihon Keizai*, pp. 185 ff.
58. Japan, Cabinet Information Office, *Jiji Mondai ni Kansuru Seron Chōsa*, pp. 94–95.

Chapter III. The Long Wait: Relations with China and Korea

1. *New York Times*, May 7, 1952.
2. Besides these, many thousands of others were said by the Japanese to be unaccounted for in China. The Chinese replied that they preferred to remain there. Repatriation went on sporadically for years; it was still going on in 1965, when 298 persons returned. See *Nihon Chūkyō Kōryū Nenshi*, 1965 ed., p. 423. Hereafter cited as NCKN.
3. *New York Times*, March 23, 1953.
4. Some joined leftist unions in coal and other industries; in the great strike at Miike in 1959–60 the key leader of the striking union was a returnee from China.
5. NCKN, 1965 ed., p. 632.
6. *Ibid.*, pp. 625–26.

7. For a collection of these resolutions, see Nitchū Bōeki Sokushin Giin Remmei, *Nitchū Shiryō Shū, 1945–66*.
8. Leng Shao-chuan, *Japan and Communist China*, p. 20. In 1965 the number of Chinese visitors was still being carefully controlled by the Japanese authorities. A total of 399 came in that year, while 4,483 Japanese went to China. Nearly 50,000 Japanese went to the United States in 1965. See NCKN, 1965 ed., p. 423.
9. Leng, *Japan and Communist China*, pp. 28 ff. See also C. Martin Wilbur, "Japan and the Rise of Communist China," in Hugh Borton, *et al.*, *Japan Between East and West*.
10. Quoted in Olson, *Dimensions of Japan*, pp. 339–40.
11. Quoted in Olson, "Japan's Relations with China," p. 4.
12. For a fuller account of this period, see Hanna, "Japan's Relations with Nationalist China."
13. *Ibid.*, p. 13.
14. *Ibid.*
15. *Ibid.*, p. 2
16. Japan's trade missions were unofficial in the sense that no diplomatic relations existed; but more or less close liaison was maintained among such missions, members of the government party, and the various ministries in Tokyo.
17. See Takeo Naoi, "Sino-Japanese Deadlock," p. 9.
18. *Ibid.* The nationalistic tone of the Japanese press is noticeable throughout the period when compared with the soft voice of the government.
19. Marius Jansen, *Japan and Communist China in the Next Decade*, pp. 27 ff.
20. A. R. Dicks, "The Non-Agreement in Action: Sino-Japanese Trade." Cited by permission.
21. Olson, "Japan's Relations with China: Some Recent Developments."
22. *Ibid.*
23. For a full account of the rationale behind China's shifting policies during this period see Tadao Ishikawa, "Communist China's Policy Toward Japan," *Journal of Social and Political Ideas in Japan*, vol. 4, no. 3, (December 1966), pp. 20–29. Hereafter cited as *JSPIJ*.
24. While Japanese names are written with surname last, as is often done in Western books, I have adhered to universal usage and written Chinese surnames first.
25. Nitchū Yūshutsunyū Kumiai, *Nitchū Bōeki Hakusho*.
26. George C. Denney, Jr., "Japan's China Policy in October 1962; Steering Between Blocs." Cited by permission.
27. The so-called L-T offices opened in 1963.
28. Dicks, "The Non-Agreement in Action."
29. Olson, "Japan's Relations with China," p. 9.
30. Hotels were built in Fukuoka as early as 1955 in anticipation of more visitors and trade from China. See Olson, "What Will the Government Do?"

31. A. M. Halpern, ed., *Policies Toward China*, p. 123.
32. Yoshikazu Sakamoto, "Sino-Japanese Relations in the Nuclear Age," *JSPIJ*, vol. 4, no. 3 (December 1966).
33. Donald Mitchell, *The Korean Minority in Japan*, p. 122.
34. *Ibid.*, p. 136.
35. Olson, "The 'Rhee Line.' "
36. June 18, 1957.
37. Quoted in Olson, "The 'Rhee Line.' "
38. Mitchell, p. 144, note.
39. For a more detailed account of Japanese-Korean relations in this period see Olson, *Dimensions of Japan*, chap. 27.
40. Mitchell, p. 163. For provisions of the treaty, see *New York Times*, June 23, 1965.

CHAPTER IV. THE LEVEL OF RHETORIC: ASIA AS SEEN FROM TOKYO

1. For an exposition of the intellectual background of the security debate, see Masataka Kōsaka, "Nihon no Gaikōron ni Okeru Risōshugi to Genjitsushugi," pp. 1–32.
2. Hiroharu Seki, "Systems of Power Balance and the Preservation of Peace," *JSPIJ*, vol. 5, no. 1 (April 1967), p. 62.
3. *Ibid.*, p. 63.
4. *Ibid.*, p. 51.
5. Yoshikazu Sakamoto, "Sino-Japanese Relations in the Nuclear Age," *JSPIJ*, vol. 4, no. 3 (December 1966), p. 63.
6. Kei Wakaizumi, "Chinese Nuclear Armament and the Security of Japan," *JSPIJ*, vol. 4, no. 3 (December 1966), p. 78.
7. Their reverberations also spread widely among the people. Although popular reactions were more difficult than intellectual opinions to divine, government polls showed that a much greater percentage of citizens knew about Chinese nuclear activities than had ever heard about Japan's economic cooperation efforts in Southeast Asia. Japan, Cabinet Information Office, *Jiji Mondai ni Kansuru Seron Chōsa*, pp. 88, 159.
8. Sakamoto, "Sino-Japanese Relations in the Nuclear Age," *JSPIJ*, vol. 4, no. 3 (December 1966), p. 62.
9. *Ibid.* Italics in original.
10. Yōnosuke Nagai, "Japanese Foreign Policy Objectives in a Nuclear Milieu," *JSPIJ*, vol. 5, no. 1 (April 1967), p. 28.
11. *Ibid.*, p. 29.
12. Kiichi Saeki, et al., *Kyokutō no Anzen Hoshō*, pp. 199–202.
13. Sheldon W. Simon, "Maoism and Inter-Party Relations," p. 51.
14. NCKN, 1965 ed., pp. 5–6. According to the same source, sixty-three Chinese groups totalling 430 people visited Japan in 1965, of which thirty-nine groups with 263 people, or over 60 per cent of the total, were

in pursuit of technical know-how in electrical, mechanical, chemical or other fields. The Japanese report on this interchange concluded that the Chinese were suffering from the withdrawal of Soviet technical help and were in great need of Japanese expertise. For further comment on the Chinese effort to influence Japanese youth, see Fujii, "Chūkyō no Sekai Kakumei Senryaku" in Saeki, et al., *Kyokutō no Anzen Hoshō*, p. 203.

15. Minoru Shibata, *Hōdō Sarenakatta Pekin*, pp. 33, 59, 125 ff.
16. *Kyokutō no Anzen Hoshō*, p. 204.
17. *Ibid.*, p. 206.
18. A. R. Dicks, "The Non-Agreement in Action," p. 15.
19. Japan, Ministry of Foreign Affairs, Economic Affairs Bureau, *"Shiberia."*
20. Saburō Ōkita, *Nihon Keizai no Bijiyon*, p. 213.
21. *Japan Times*, August 15, 1968.
22. *Chūkyō wa Nihon no Kyōi to Naru ka?*
23. See Masamichie Irie, et al., *Kaku Jidai to Nihon no Kaku Seisaku*. This is vol. 5 of the "Hara Shobō" series on national security.
24. *Ibid.*, p. 20.
25. *Kyokutō no Anzen Hoshō*, p. 14.
26. *Ibid.* Italics added.
27. Asahi Shimin Kyōshitsu, *Chūkoku no Kaku Senryoku*, p. 211.
28. Irie, *Kaku Jidai to Nihon no Kaku Seisaku*, p. 118.
29. Masataka Kōsaka, et al., *Anzen Hoshō to Nichibei Kankei*, pp. 78–79.
30. Ōkita, *Ajia no Naka no Nihon Keizai*, p. 148.
31. Ōkita, "Japan's Dependence on Imported Resources."
32. Ōkita, *Ajia no Naka no Nihon Keizai*, pp. 130–32.
33. *Ibid.*, p. 132.
34. See, for example, Toshio Oshima, "Gaikō Seisaku no Kyokumen Kara Mita Keizai Kyōryoku."
35. For a description of talks leading up to the founding of the Asian Development Bank from a Japanese point of view, see Okita, *Ajia no Naka no Nihon Keizai*, pp. 76–78.
36. Japan, Ministry of Foreign Affairs, *Kongo no Keizai Kyōryoku no Arikata ni Tsuite*.
37. John White, *Japanese Aid*, pp. 14–15.
38. This is the yearbook cited as *KKGM* in chap. II, note 31.
39. *KKGM*, 1967, pp. 51–59.
40. Ōshima, "Gaikō Seisaku no Kyokumen Kara Mita Keizai Kyōryoku."
41. Japan Committee for Economic Development, *Keizai Kyōryoku Taisei ni Kansuru Teigen*. The chief drafter of the report was the President of the Industrial Bank of Japan, Sohei Nakayama.
42. Japan, Overseas Technical Cooperation Agency, *Gijutsu Kyōryoku Nempō*, pp. 233, 264.
43. Olson, "Japan and Asia, An American Viewpoint," *Asia*, no. 8 (1967), p. 91.
44. He then went on to the standard problems: language difficulties, not

only with English but with local languages which were often more vital to know than English in rural situations, and the problem of Southeast Asians wanting degrees to take home and Japanese universities reluctant to lower their standards to grant them. He revealed that not a single course in tropical agriculture was being given in Japanese government universities. Moreover, he reminded the symposium, one of the key reasons for the stagnation of so many agricultural programs in Southeast Asia was that those in charge of their administration often were amateurs without much political power. Kyoto University, Center for Southeast Asian Studies, *Tōnan Ajia Kenkyū*, vol. 5, no. 4, 1967, pp. 182–190.

CHAPTER V. THE LEVEL OF ACTION: JAPANESE ACTIVITIES IN NON-COMMUNIST ASIA

1. In textiles, Japan had made 15 loans totaling $58 million, other countries 22 loans worth $76.5 million; in cement, Japan had made 4 loans worth $45 million, others 7 loans worth $41 million; in fertilizer, Japan had made 2 loans worth $45 million, others 2 loans worth $68 million; in electric power, Japan had made 3 loans worth $35 million, others (including AID) 12 loans worth $185 million; in sea transport, Japan had made 2 loans worth $13 million, others 7 loans worth $97 million; in aluminum, Japan had made 1 loan worth $13.5 million, others 1 loan worth less than half a million dollars; in fisheries, Japan had made 8 loans worth $10 million, others had made 16 loans worth $55 million. Japanese Government, Ministry of Foreign Affairs, *Kankoku ni Okeru Shakkan Kigyō no Genjō*.
2. Data on licensing and investment provided by U.S. Embassy, Seoul.
3. In 1966, 137 Koreans were trained in Japan under government auspices, 115 by private Japanese organizations. See *KKGM*, 1967 ed., p. 171.
4. *KKGM*, 1967 ed., p. 175.
5. Chinese officials insisted that American interest in investing in the synthetics industry was so slight that they had no choice but to turn to the Japanese for know-how and capital.
6. Statistics on investment are from Japanese Embassy, U.S. Embassy, and First National City Bank, Taipei. See also *Taiwan Trade Monthly*, January 1967 and March 1968 issues; and *KKGM*, 1967 ed., pp. 177–78. Information on progress of the yen credit was provided by the Chinese government in Taipei.
7. *New York Times*, September 21, 1969.
8. Philippine Reparations Mission in Tokyo, *Annual Report, 1966*.
9. *Ibid.*, pp. 2–3.
10. This phrase is Douglas Paauw's.
11. *Manila Bulletin*, September 15, 1968.
12. Yasuhiro Takeshima, "Saiken no Naka no Shihon Sensō," *Purejidento*, August 1968, p. 43.

13. Gregory Clark, "Japanese Production-Sharing Projects, 1966–1968," *Bulletin of Indonesian Economic Statistics*, no. 10 (June 1968), pp. 68–77.
14. Takeshima, "Saiken no Naka no Shihon Sensō," p. 43.
15. This was a new creation and suggested the rising interest in Indonesia among businessmen. A Vietnam committee was also being formed in late 1968.
16. *Singapore Eastern Sun*, October 17, 1968.
17. *Oriental Economist*, April 1968, p. 11.
18. Japan, Ministry of International Trade and Industry, *Tsūsan Hakusho*.
19. *KKGM*, 1967 ed., p. 199.
20. Based on estimates by U.S. Embassy, Bangkok, and the Board of Investment of the Thai government. No suggestion is made that these figures are accurate in detail. The Board of Investment's statistics rested on information provided by the companies themselves.
21. Information from Thai Board of Foreign Investment, Bangkok.
22. For information about Japanese joint ventures in Thailand I am grateful to the Bank of Tokyo, Bangkok branch, and to Mr. Thurston F. Teele.
23. *Bangkok Post*, October 31, 1968.
24. Committee for the Coordination of Investigations of the Lower Mekong Basin, *Annual Report, 1967*, p. 13.
25. *New York Times*, February 15, 1969.
26. For more information on these projects, see Olson, *Dimensions of Japan*, chap. 23.
27. For further details of Japan's economic assistance to India, see *KKGM*, 1967 ed., pp. 231–35. See also Indian Investment Center, *Monthly Newsletter*, October 15, 1968. For information in this section I have also drawn upon a series of mimeographed papers prepared for an India-Japan Round Table Conference held in New Delhi under the sponsorship of the Japan-India Committee on Economic Development in November 1968, and especially the paper entitled "Financial Collaboration," by Masahide Shimmyō.
28. I have written more fully of these differences in *Dimensions of Japan*, chap. 23.
29. Hisatsugu Tokunaga, "Industrial Collaboration," a paper prepared for the November 1968 India-Japan Table Conference in New Delhi.
30. Olson, *Dimensions of Japan*, pp. 300–301.
31. Shimmyō, *op. cit.*, p. 18.
32. Yasuaki Ishida, *Indo de Kurasu*.

CHAPTER VI. CONCLUSION: A LOOK AT THE FUTURE

1. Japan Economic Research Center, *The World in 2000*, pp. 60–72.
2. *Tōyō Keizai*, May 10, 1969, p. 47. See also *Oriental Economist*, April 1968, pp. 11–15.

3. *Ibid.*
4. In October 1969 four Japanese Maritime Self-Defense Force destroyers visited Singapore, Manila, Bangkok, and other Southeast Asian ports. See *New York Times*, October 6, 1969.
5. Lloyd A. Free, *International Attitudes of Four Asian Democracies.*
6. Kiyoshi Kojima, ed., *Pacific Trade and Development*, p. 170.
7. See Suetaka Kuwabara, "Kōshinkoku ni Taisuru Nihon no Kyōryoku no Arikata," *Ajia Keizai*, vol. 3 (March 1963), pp. 94–101.
8. Olson, *Dimensions of Japan*, chap. 23.
9. Kyoto University, Center for Southeast Asian Studies, *Japan's Future in Southeast Asia*, pp. 172–73.

Index

Abdel Rahman, Tengku, 209
Afro-Asian Solidarity Conference, *see* Bandung Conference
Agency for International Development (AID), 250
Aid, *see* Foreign aid
"Ajiken," 67–69, 193
Aki, Kōichi, 219
Alliance for Progress, 182, 242
Asahi Shimbun, 141; on Indian iron ore agreement, 41; on nuclear weapons, 136; series on security matters, 133
Asanuma, Inejirō, 87
Asanuma Statement, 87
Asia: compared with Latin America, 182, 242–43; economic projections, 232–33; "green revolution," 153–54; Japanese-American competition, 183, 248–49, 252; Southeast, *see* Asia, Southeast; stability, 10; *see also individual country entries*

    Japan and: exports, 14, 15, 65; impressions of, 36–37; isolation from, 30–31, 34, 246; knowledge of, 3–4; renewed interest in, 34–36, 42; technological role, 5; World War II claims, 3; *see also* Asia, Southeast

Asia (*cont.*):

    United States and: aid to, 144–45, 251; Asian studies programs, 247–48; security interests in, 247
Asia, Southeast: British forces, withdrawal of, 159; communications difficulties, 172–73; Communist China's economic interest in, 33; "cultural distance" problem, 72; definition of, 267*n*; economic cooperation, 67, 159, 214; economic projections for, 232–33; investment environment, 47–48; Japanese-Chinese rivalry in, 67; Ministerial Conferences on economic development, 156–57, 182, 214; "new coprosperity sphere," 45; post–Vietnam War policies for, 158, *see also* United States, post–Vietnam War Asian policies; regional cooperation, 233, 243; reparations to, 228, *see also individual country entries*; as source of raw materials, 138; subregional cooperation, 243

    aid to, 138–58; Japanese, 43, 150–51; joint programs, 252–53; loans, 275*n*; U.S., 144–45; *see also individual country entries*

    Japan and: business activities in,

Council on Foreign Relations

Officers and Directors

John J. McCloy, *Chairman of the Board*
Henry M. Wriston, *Honorary President*
Grayson Kirk, *President*
Frank Altschul, *Vice-President & Secretary*
David Rockefeller, *Vice-President*
Gabriel Hauge, *Treasurer*
George S. Franklin, Jr., *Executive Director*

Hamilton Fish Armstrong
William P. Bundy
William A. M. Burden
Arthur H. Dean
Douglas Dillon
Hedley Donovan
William C. Foster
Caryl P. Haskins
Joseph E. Johnson
Henry R. Labouisse

Bill D. Moyers
Alfred C. Neal
James A. Perkins
Lucian W. Pye
Philip D. Reed
Robert V. Roosa
Charles M. Spofford
Cyrus Vance
Carroll L. Wilson

PUBLICATIONS

FOREIGN AFFAIRS (quarterly), edited by Hamilton Fish Armstrong.

THE UNITED STATES IN WORLD AFFAIRS (annual), by Richard P. Stebbins.

DOCUMENTS ON AMERICAN FOREIGN RELATIONS (annual), by Richard P. Stebbins with the assistance of Elaine P. Adam.

POLITICAL HANDBOOK AND ATLAS OF THE WORLD (annual), edited by Walter H. Mallory.

THE GREAT POWERS AND AFRICA, by Waldemar A. Nielsen (1969).

A NEW FOREIGN POLICY FOR THE UNITED STATES, by Hans J. Morgenthau (1969).

MIDDLE EAST POLITICS: THE MILITARY DIMENSION, by J. C. Hurewitz (1969).

THE ECONOMICS OF INTERDEPENDENCE: Economic Policy in the Atlantic Community, by Richard N. Cooper (1968).

HOW NATIONS BEHAVE: Law and Foreign Policy, by Louis Henkin (1968).

THE INSECURITY OF NATIONS, by Charles W. Yost (1968).

PROSPECTS FOR SOVIET SOCIETY, edited by Allen Kassof (1968).

THE AMERICAN APPROACH TO THE ARAB WORLD, by John S. Badeau (1968).

U.S. POLICY AND THE SECURITY OF ASIA, by Fred Greene (1968).

NEGOTIATING WITH THE CHINESE COMMUNISTS: The U.S. Experience, by Kenneth T. Young (1968).

FROM ATLANTIC TO PACIFIC: A New Interocean Canal, by Immanuel J. Klette (1967).

TITO'S SEPARATE ROAD: America and Yugloslavia in World Politics, by John C. Campbell (1967).

U.S. TRADE POLICY: New Legislation for the Next Round, by John W. Evans (1967).

TRADE LIBERALIZATION AMONG INDUSTRIAL COUNTRIES: Objectives and Alternatives, by Bela Balassa (1967).

THE CHINESE PEOPLE'S LIBERATION ARMY, by Brig. General Samuel B. Griffith II U.S.M.C. (ret.) (1967).

THE ARTILLERY OF THE PRESS: Its Influence on American Foreign Policy, by James Reston (1967).